THE BIG 50
PHILADELPHIA FLYERS

The Men and Moments That Made
the Philadelphia Flyers

Sam Carchidi and Wayne Fish

30 YEARS

TRIUMPH
BOOKS

Library of Congress Cataloging-in-Publication Data available upon request

This book is available in quantity at special discounts for your group or organization. For further information, contact:

Triumph Books LLC
814 North Franklin Street
Chicago, Illinois 60610
(312) 337-0747
www.triumphbooks.com

Printed in U.S.A.
ISBN: 978-1-62937-620-2

Design by Andy Hansen
All photos courtesy of AP Images unless otherwise indicated.

To my grandson, James. You make Poppy's
and Nonna's hearts sing, little man.
—Sam Carchidi

For MaryAnn: When your wife is a
hockey fan, the rest is easy.
—Wayne Fish

[Contents]

THE BIG 50
PHILADELPHIA FLYERS

1

A HUMBLING START

In an attempt to generate interest for their inaugural season, the Flyers planned a parade down Broad Street in 1967 after the team returned from training camp in Quebec City.

It seemed like a good idea at the time, but it turned into a dud. The players and club personnel sat in open convertibles, waving to the crowd.

Problem was, only about 25 people showed up. That wasn't shocking because Philadelphia had a checkered past in terms of supporting major and minor league hockey teams.

"There were more people *in* the parade than there were people watching it," defenseman Joe Watson, an original Flyer, said in a 2017 interview. "I said, 'Hell, we're not going to be here very long.' One fan gave me the finger and said, 'You'll be in Baltimore in six months!'"

Welcome to the City of Brotherly Love, guys.

"I thought it meant you're going to be No. 1," Watson said of the fan's gesture. "But obviously it didn't mean that," Watson laughed heartily.

"It wasn't a big welcome. And Mayor [James] Tate was supposed to welcome us to the city at the chamber of commerce hall downtown, and he doesn't even show up for the function," Watson said. "I never forgot that because seven years later when we won the Stanley Cup, [Frank] Rizzo was the mayor, and I got up and I said, 'Where the hell was the mayor seven years ago? He never showed up and now we're such a big deal.' And Rizzo said to me, 'I wasn't the mayor then, so don't blame me!'"

There would be growing pains as the team tried to find its place in the Philadelphia sports market.

For the first season, the team's payroll was around $130,000. Goalie Bernie Parent had the top deal—three years for a total of $57,000. Club officials predicted the team would meet its financial obligations if it drew 11,000 fans a game.

That was going to be difficult because only 2,132 season tickets were sold by opening night.

At first, fans were slow to accept the new team. Tickets were $2 to $5.50 per game during that first season, and just 7,812 showed up for the home opener. Gradually, as the Flyers sprinkled in wins against the Original Six teams, attendance picked up. By February, they had their first home sellout.

The Flyers would average 9,625 fans per game for that season. That number increased dramatically in the coming years. And the Flyers became the hottest ticket in town after winning consecutive Stanley Cups in 1974 and 1975.

In the early 1960s, however, the Flyers weren't even a thought when Ed Snider was in the record business. While in New York on business, a sales associate took Snider to a hockey game at Madison Square Garden to watch the New York Rangers face the Montreal Canadiens.

"It was the greatest spectator sport I had ever seen," said Snider, the Flyers' cofounder who died in 2016, years later.

Not many years after he watched that game, the Flyers were created.

"In our first season, *The Hockey News* thought we would be the team least likely to succeed, but were they ever wrong!" Snider said.

Six expansion teams were added in 1967. From among the dozen candidate cities, the league chose Los Angeles and Oakland to occupy the western flank and Minnesota and St. Louis for the middle. The last remaining question at the expansion meeting that February was who would join Pittsburgh in the East—Baltimore or Philadelphia?

Baltimore had success in the AHL and appeared to be the front-runner, but the NHL wanted 15,000-seat arenas, and Baltimore's building held only 12,000. When officials there killed plans for a new building, Philadelphia, with plans to build the Spectrum, got the sixth expansion franchise.

The franchise was purchased for $2 million, and Snider and Jerry Wolman got the Spectrum built for $12 million. A bogus contest was held to name the team. Bruisers, Quakers, Liberty Bells, and Croaking Crickets were among the hundreds of names submitted in a contest sponsored by Acme Markets, but Snider's sister, Phyllis, had actually chosen the name Flyers months earlier.

At a news conference to announce the team's name, three female models displayed the Flyers' new colors.

"It's comforting to know that the team's colors are orange sweatshirts and black mesh stockings," *Daily News* columnist Stan Hochman wrote, according to Jay Greenberg in *Full Spectrum*. "Let's hope the players can fight."

SIX-PACK MAKES HOME TEAM WOOZY

Little did Red Berenson know it, but he probably did the Flyers a favor by scoring an NHL record six goals on the road against them at the Spectrum on the night of November 7, 1968.

The six-pack of red lighters, leading to Philadelphia's humiliating 8–0 home-ice loss, helped show the Flyers they would have to make drastic changes and better draft picks (like taking Bobby Clarke in 1969) in order to compete with the big boys.

In the second period alone, Berenson took four shots on Flyers goaltender Doug Favell and scored on each one.

Ironically, Berenson didn't think his spectacular performance was particularly a big deal.

"I can tell you I probably had better games but just didn't have the numbers, the statistics, the goals to show for it," Berenson told NHL.com of his famous night. "You have good games, but sometimes they don't show up on the scoreboard. That game showed up on the scoreboard."

Yet Berenson did what Wayne Gretzky, Mario Lemieux, Mike Bossy, Brett Hull, and Jaromir Jagr couldn't—put the puck in the net six times in 60 minutes, and on the road no less.

"I'm surprised there haven't been more six-goal games," Berenson said, "especially in the '70s, when so many goals were being scored and you had guys scoring up to 100 goals a season and so many more gifted scorers—Lemieux and Gretzky and others who could have scored seven or eight goals in a game. [Ed. note: Actually, Gretzky holds the record with 92.]

"For one reason or another, it hasn't happened. All that means is I was lucky."

Lucky perhaps, but certainly unique.

Expanding from six to 12 teams was welcomed by players scuffling to reach the NHL.

"When you go back to that time, there were only six teams playing, and there were so many good players in the American League and all around Canada and the United States who never had the opportunity to reach the National Hockey League," said Lou Angotti, the Flyers' first captain. "When they went to 12 teams, it gave a lot of players a chance to extend their careers and get a chance to play in the National Hockey League. It was a wonderful opportunity for everybody."

General Manager Bud Poile, Coach Keith Allen, and the scouting staff did a great job in the expansion draft, selecting players such as goalies Parent and Doug Favell, defensemen Watson and Ed Van Impe, and right winger Gary Dornhoefer.

The Flyers were in the West Division with the five other expansion teams. The East Division was composed of teams from the NHL's Original Six.

"Our favorite saying when we played against the established teams was, 'Dump it out!'" Dornhoefer once told the *Philadelphia Inquirer.* "There was always a lot of pressure down our end of the ice."

In their first season, the Flyers "had a lot of small guys, and as the years went on, we got a little bigger, a little stronger, a little tougher," Dornhoefer said. "But we got beat up some nights, physically, in the early days."

The Flyers finished 31–32–11 in their first season, were outscored by 179–173, and won the title in the West. They won the championship despite playing seven home games away from the Spectrum because portions of the roof came crashing down late that season.

The Flyers clinched the West championship on the next-to-last day of the season when second-place Los Angeles, needing a victory to stay alive, was tied by Oakland. The Flyers were on the road in Pittsburgh, but when the Kings didn't win, the Orange and Black's final regular season game was meaningless.

When Snider heard the Kings' result, "he got most of us out of bed and we went to this after-hours place and celebrated 'til 5 in the morning," Watson said.

The Flyers lost to St. Louis in the opening round of the playoffs, falling in seven games.

"They beat the hell out of us, physically," Watson said. "Mr. Snider said it would never happen to a Flyers team again."

In the years that followed, they would add muscle by selecting wingers like Dave Schultz, Bob Kelly, and Don Saleski in the draft and by acquiring defenseman Andre "Moose" Dupont in a trade. More important, they drafted players like Bobby Clarke, Bill Barber, and Jimmy Watson, acquired Rick MacLeish, Bill Flett, and Ross Lonsberry, and reacquired Parent in 1973 after dealing him to Toronto two years earlier.

That set the stage for future success. The 1974 parade they held would be nothing like the one that welcomed the team seven years earlier.

Two million people showed up for this one.

2

ED SNIDER: THE SOUL AND SPIRIT OF THE FLYERS

Ed Snider, the son of a grocery-store-chain owner, became a billionaire entrepreneur and one of the most enthusiastic owners in Philadelphia sports history.

The Flyers, the team he cofounded, were his baby. He had more passion for his team than the people in the nosebleed seats, and nothing made him prouder than his Flyers. He was there for their birth, and he watched them grow into one of the National Hockey League's most respected franchises before his death on April 11, 2016, after a long battle with bladder cancer.

Club president Paul Holmgren called Snider "the face of the Flyers. He is, he was, he always will be. He took a risk. Who can take a bigger risk than what he had to do just to get the team here, get the Spectrum built? That story is incredible. . . . Look where we're at now. We're one of the most recognizable brands in the world of sport."

After his death, Snider's children issued a heartfelt statement: "Our Dad was loved and admired for his big heart, generosity of spirit, and dedication to his family. Despite his considerable business achievements and public profile, he was first and foremost a family man. He never missed a birthday, important family event, or the opportunity to offer encouragement. We turned first to him for advice in our personal and professional lives. We grew up tagging behind him in arenas, stadiums, and locker rooms; and his players, management, and team personnel were our extended family. He treated his employees with respect regardless of rank or position, and the man they called 'Mr. Snider' always would have preferred simply to be called 'Ed.'"

In 2017, 50 years from the day the Flyers played their first home game at the beloved Spectrum, they unveiled a nine-foot bronze statue of the late Snider outside the Wells Fargo Center, and his daughter, Lindy, asked everyone to start a tradition and rub the Stanley Cup ring he was depicted wearing because it would bring the team good luck.

"The greatest feeling was when I touched the ring," Hall of Fame goalie Bernie Parent said a few minutes after Lindy Snider's speech before about 700 onlookers. "I felt the power."

In the first year after his death, Lindy Snider said she and family members found it almost painful to be at the Wells Fargo Center and revealed she avoided going there for a while. "The Flyers and this building are so deeply a part of our lives and our families, and to come here still actually brought on a sense of grieving," she said. "But now, I think the time for grieving has passed, and perhaps the sculpture installation marks a new beginning."

At the ceremony, Dave Scott, the Comcast Spectacor president and CEO, and NHL Commissioner Gary Bettman talked about Snider's unbridled enthusiasm and work ethic.

"What a passion he had for winning, whether [it] was in sports or in business," Scott said.

"When I think about Ed, I think about the passion he had for Philadelphia, for the Flyers, for hockey, and for the vision he had," Bettman said. "Whatever he worked on, he was all in."

Bettman called Snider a "consummate ball of energy, a man who was constantly in motion, and it'll be a great tribute to him and all he accomplished that his imagery will stand here with us forever."

About 30 former players, representing every decade of Flyers hockey, attended the ceremony. "That speaks of the impact Mr. Snider has had on us as players," Holmgren said.

Snider also had an effect on the current players.

"He was awesome," right winger Jake Voracek said. "He made a decision to bring the team here and he never regretted it. He really enjoyed it like it was his child."

Just a few days before Snider's passing in 2016, the Flyers completed an improbable late-season surge to clinch a trip to the playoffs. Many players and team staff members cited Snider's failing health as an inspiration for doing so.

Snider, chairman of the Flyers' parent company, Comcast Spectacor, was named to the Hockey Hall of Fame in 1988 and over the years received numerous honors for his philanthropy and business

The Flyers unveiled a statue honoring founder Ed Snider outside the Wells Fargo Center on October 19, 2017.

success. Snider had a net worth that was reported at $2.5 billion by Celebritynetworth.com.

Most of all, though, he was identified with the Flyers.

Bettman called Snider "the soul and spirit of the Flyers, who have reflected his competitiveness, his passion for hockey, and his love for the fans from the moment he brought NHL hockey to Philadelphia in 1967.

"Ed created the Flyers' professional, no-nonsense culture, fostered their relentless will to win, and set the highest standard for every activity on and off the ice, including such initiatives as the Ed Snider Youth Hockey Foundation and the Flyers Wives Carnival," Bettman said. "While the loss of Ed Snider tears a hole in the heart of the Flyers and the city of Philadelphia, and leaves a massive void in the city's sports landscape, it also challenges all who knew him to carry forward the great works that are his legacy."

During the 2015–16 season, two days before the Flyers played the Kings in Los Angeles on January 2, the players, coaches, and support staff visited with the ailing Snider at his mansion in Montecito, California. They traveled on a bus after a practice at the recently opened Snider Rink, or Ice in Paradise in nearby Goleta, California. Snider was one of the rink's largest donors.

At Snider's residence, team captain Claude Giroux said one of the first things he noticed was the huge Flyers flag hanging in the driveway.

"The passion he has for hockey and Philadelphia hockey is really great to see," Giroux said at the time. "He's been a really good leader for us and to spend time with him today was really good."

Giroux said he didn't discuss much hockey with Snider that day. "We talked more about life," he said.

Earlier that season, there were signs that Snider's health was getting worse. He missed the home opener for the first time in recent memory. At the time, spokesman Ike Richman said Snider was "choosing to remain at his home in California, where he is resting and recharging after recent medical therapy." But he still kept close tabs on the team.

Snider was the treasurer and vice president of the Eagles when he and Eagles owner Jerry Wolman helped bring an expansion NHL team to Philadelphia for the 1967–68 season.

Snider and the late Wolman, who helped secure the financing, were also the driving forces behind the construction of the Spectrum, the Flyers' first home in 1967–68, and Snider assumed control of the building in 1971. However, Snider and Wolman later became bitter enemies. Wolman was part of the ownership group that founded the Flyers, but he sold his 22 percent to Snider before the team played a game.

Bobby Clarke, who was the heart and soul of the Flyers' Stanley Cup championships in 1974 and 1975, said it was "hard to put into words" what Snider meant to the players.

"He was a great owner, and it wasn't just because he wanted to win all the time," said Clarke, who after his Hall of Fame career ended did stints as the club's assistant coach, general manager, president, and senior vice president. "He treated us as players so much better than all the other teams when we first got started. We were the first team where the wives got Christmas presents, the first team to fly on the good airlines and stay in the good hotels."

Before the salary-cap era started in 2005, it wasn't unusual for Snider to spend more money on players than other NHL teams. That, combined with the way he treated players and their families, made Philadelphia a popular destination for free agents.

Clarke recalled when Flyers goalie Bruce Gamble suffered a heart attack during a 1972 game and how Snider stood by him and his family.

"Obviously [Gamble] had to retire, but Mr. Snider kept paying him after he was done and educated his children," Clarke said.

"Those types of things, they were human things. They weren't sports. Those weren't things that other owners were doing."

Snider had said that one of his proudest accomplishments was the creation of the Ed Snider Youth Foundation, which provides youngsters from urban neighborhoods in Philadelphia and Camden, New Jersey, with the opportunity to learn and play hockey. In a 2009 interview, Snider said that he had found something as rewarding as the consecutive Stanley Cups his Flyers won in 1974 and 1975. When asked to compare winning those titles to the joy he sees on the children's faces as they play hockey at the rinks, Snider smiled.

"I can't compare," he said. "It would be like trying to compare your children. It's all good stuff."

The foundation, which started in 2005, partnered with the city of Philadelphia and the commonwealth of Pennsylvania in 2010 to complete a $14.5 million construction project, completely refurbishing four public rinks for year-round use. The project included new

LAUREN HART'S EMOTIONAL FAREWELL SONG FOR ED SNIDER

Lauren Hart is the longtime Flyers national anthem singer whose father, the late Gene Hart, was the team's iconic broadcaster and is a member of the Hockey Hall of Fame.

Lauren Hart was close with Ed Snider, the Flyers chairman and cofounder, and when he was gravely ill in the spring of 2016, she emotionally sang "God Bless America" to him—3,000 miles away—before a playoff-clinching 3–1 win over Pittsburgh at the electric Wells Fargo Center. As she sang, and was joined by a video of Kate Smith to form a duet, she FaceTimed herself and the surroundings to Snider at his California home. Snider was surrounded by his family.

"If Ed Snider couldn't be in the building, I was bringing the building to him," she said.

After Hart was done singing, she blew kisses into the phone. Snider died two days later.

Hart said she asked Snider's daughter, her close friend Lindy, for permission to FaceTime with her father.

"It meant a lot to me because I was out there in February, and there was some hope he might be able to come home, and at some point, I realized that wasn't going to happen," Hart said. "I just couldn't imagine him never being there again. It broke my heart. I just wanted to bring that feeling to him. I wanted to give it to him one more time, what it felt like at the beginning of games."

Hart said she will always treasure singing to Snider one last time.

"I knew in my heart that that was his last game," she said. "I have that memory forever now, and I'll hold it dear."

classrooms, learning labs, and public meeting space. The young players get ice time, uniforms, instruction, skates, and sticks for free.

Snider was honored for his charity work by the Philadelphia Sports Writers Association in 2012, when the annual Ed Snider Humanitarian Award was created.

Before becoming involved with the Eagles and then the Flyers, Snider was in the record business in the 1960s. While in New York on business, a sales associate took him to a hockey game at Madison Square Garden, where they watched the New York Rangers face the Montreal Canadiens.

A few years later, the Flyers were born.

"It seems like yesterday," Snider said in February of 2016, when the Flyers celebrated the 50th anniversary of the franchise. The team started playing the following year. Before long, they became a Philly institution.

Respected for his shrewd business acumen, Snider created Spectacor in 1974 as a management company to oversee the Flyers and the Spectrum. In the next 20 years, Spectacor grew, as did its impact on the sports and entertainment business. The company developed and acquired nearly a dozen related companies.

In 1996, Mr. Snider merged Spectacor with the Comcast Corporation to form Comcast Spectacor, which initially consisted of the Flyers, 76ers, the American Hockey League Phantoms, the Wells Fargo Center, and the Spectrum. The company later joined with the Phillies to form Comcast SportsNet (now NBC Sports Philadelphia), one of the nation's highest-rated, regional sports cable networks.

About six months after his death, Snider's estate sold its 24 percent of the Flyers and other Comcast Spectacor properties to Comcast. The previous year, Forbes valued the Flyers at $660 million, seventh among the NHL's 30 teams.

"We look forward to building on Ed's vision," said Dave Scott, who was handpicked three years earlier by Snider and Brian Roberts, the CEO and chairman of Comcast Corp., to direct Comcast Spectacor.

Under Snider, the Flyers were one of the NHL's most successful teams during the regular season, but they have not won a Stanley Cup since 1975. Since winning their first Cup in 1974, the Flyers have reached the Final eight times, the most of any NHL franchise in that span. Since the Flyers' inception in 1967, only Montreal and Boston have a better winning percentage than Philadelphia.

Over the years, Snider remained close with his players, going into the locker room after each game, giving them hugs and handshakes and starting conversations to find out about their lives.

Clarke said Snider would regularly give $50,000 to the Flyers alumni association for former players who needed help.

"He had a big roar and a very soft heart," son Jay Snider said.

There was excitement in Jay Snider's voice when he recalled long-ago summer vacations the family took to a lake in Monmouth, Maine.

"For all of us growing up, we loved it," Jay said in 2016. "It was a very low-key lifestyle, and over time, we bought up some land there. The family now has five homes there, and he saw that it happened for the family because we all go there. All the kids can drive golf carts and the cousins visit each other. It's our favorite place, all of us.

"My dad saw into the future. He wanted to make sure he provided something for his whole family to stay together."

3

KEITH THE THIEF: THE FLYERS' UNSUNG HERO

Keith Allen was the first coach in the Flyers' history, but he became better known because of his shrewd moves as a general manager. He was Keith the Thief, the architect of the Flyers' Stanley Cup championships in 1974 and 1975. While he was the general manager, the Flyers won two Stanley Cups, reached the Stanley Cup Final four times, and compiled a 563–322–194 record for a .612 winning percentage.

"In my mind, he was and always will be one of the greatest general managers in the history of hockey," Flyers chairman Ed Snider said after Allen died in 2014 at the age of 90. "I never knew of a bad deal he made. This team would never have reached the level of success we have had over the past 48 years if it were not for Keith."

Allen added such players as Barry Ashbee, Rick MacLeish, Bill Flett, Ross Lonsberry, Andre Dupont, Reggie Leach, and Mark Howe, and he reacquired Bernie Parent. He was also responsible for drafting Bill Clement, Bob Kelly, Bill Barber, Tom Bladon, Jimmy Watson, Paul Holmgren, Pete Peeters, Dave Brown, Ron Sutter, Ron Hextall, Brian Propp, Ken Linseman, and Pelle Lindbergh.

In addition, he signed Tim Kerr, Orest Kindrachuk, Bob Froese, and Dave Poulin as free agents.

Keith the Thief.

"He more than anybody was responsible for us winning two Stanley Cups," said Bobby Clarke, the captain during the Flyers' best seasons. "Keith was one of those men you very rarely come across who was fatherly and grandfatherly to all us players and our families and yet was tough enough and strong enough to do the things that were necessary so we had the right players to win a Stanley Cup.

"Every player who ever played here under his leadership liked Keith. He was one of the few men in hockey, maybe one of the only men, who everybody liked. He didn't have a person who disliked him in the world."

Aside from his smart trades, Allen also convinced Snider to take a gamble on a very successful coach in the minor ranks named Fred Shero, an innovator who became a Hall of Famer.

Allen compiled a 51–67–33 coaching record over the team's first two years of existence. But he made his greatest impact as their general manager, and that is what earned him a spot in the Hockey Hall of Fame in 1992 in the "builders" category.

In the 1969 draft, Allen's first as general manager, the Flyers took a second-round chance on Clarke—a player with diabetes who would become their all-time leading scorer and their greatest player. He also got forwards Dave Schultz and Don Saleski in the fifth and sixth rounds, respectively. His first three picks in the 1972 draft were left winger Bill Barber and defensemen Tom Bladon and Jimmy Watson. All would play key roles during the Flyers' championship years.

In the Flyers' first season in 1967–68, Allen coached the team to the title in the old West Division, which was composed of the six expansion teams. He became the general manager in 1969 and held that position until 1983.

In a way, Allen was the godfather of the Flyers. He was there for their birth as their coach, and as the general manager he guided their stunningly quick rise to NHL kings in just their seventh season.

"Keith and I were awfully close in building the two Stanley Cup winners," Snider once said. "I was a lot more active on a day-to-day basis back then, and we worked very well together."

Allen built his reputation with numerous one-sided trades. In one of his best deals, he sent Mike Walton to Boston in a trade that netted MacLeish, who became a 50-goal scorer. He also got Reggie Leach, who would become one of the NHL's most prolific scorers, by dealing Larry Wright, Al MacAdam, and a first-round choice to California.

Keith the Thief.

But his best deal was probably the May 15, 1973, trade that sent a first-round pick (Bob Neely) and future considerations (Doug Favell) to Toronto for the rights to reacquire Parent and a second-round pick (Larry Goodenough). Parent blossomed into a Hall of Famer.

Allen spent 13 years as a pro player, mostly as an AHL defenseman. He played parts of two seasons with the Detroit Red Wings and was a member of their 1953–54 Stanley Cup championship team. Allen later coached in the Western Hockey League for nine years.

After he was hired by the Flyers to coach their first team, Allen and general manager Bud Poile did a masterful job in the expansion draft, selecting players such as goalies Parent and Favell, defensemen Joe Watson and Ed Van Impe, and right winger Gary Dornhoefer. Parent, Watson, Van Impe, and Dornhoefer would become fixtures when the Flyers won consecutive Stanley Cups in 1974 and 1975.

In the book *Keith the Thief*, lovingly written by Allen's son, Blake, Snider said because of the colorful and talented teams Allen built as a general manger, "the Flyers have fans everywhere, a fact reflected by how much orange you see in the stands when our team is on the road. I believe our profile in hockey is comparable to the Dallas Cowboys in football. And that started with Keith Allen. Keith didn't care about credit, only about Stanley Cups."

In the last four years of his life, Allen suffered from dementia and moved into an assisted living facility in Newtown Square, Pennsylvania, in 2012. He would spend his days playing bingo, watching movies, and participating in exercise and arts-and-crafts classes. He was also fond of participating in karaoke and belting out Frank Sinatra tunes.

Allen and his wife, Joyce, moved into the Sunrise Senior Living facility after their home in Beach Haven Park, New Jersey, was destroyed by Hurricane Sandy. After moving there, they were visited by a growing number of former Flyers and their wives, along with Snider, the team's cofounder.

"His spirits are up a bit, but he's going through a tough time, and it's tough on Joyce," Snider said at the time.

During his prime, Snider said, Allen "could evaluate players better than anybody. He would say that a certain guy would turn out like this, and he was always right. He had such a good feel for talent, and he could deal with any [general manager]. So likable. Not boisterous, but low-key and just a nice human being. Everyone trusted him."

That included the players. After the 1977–78 season, Joe Watson, who was about to turn 35, had his end-of-year meeting with Allen and Coach Shero. They told Watson they planned to go with younger players, but if he was agreeable to playing 35 or 40 games the next season, he was welcome to stay.

If not, they would trade him.

Watson, wanting to remain a full-time player, opted to be dealt.

ZEIDEL: NO LOVE FOR SHACK IN THIS STICK-Y MESS

There's lots of name-calling in hockey—that's been going on for a hundred years. But when things get personal, and involve religion, race, sexual orientation, and the like, trouble brews. Sometimes it gets physical and a fistfight breaks out.

Or, when things get really heated, sticks can get involved, like in a game between the Flyers and the Boston Bruins at Toronto's Maple Leaf Gardens on the night of March 7, 1968. (The roof had blown off Philadelphia's Spectrum, so the Flyers' home games moved to Toronto, Quebec, and New York.)

The Flyers' Larry "The Rock" Zeidel and Boston's Eddie Shack got into a nasty, stick-swinging duel in the first period that would end in bloody injuries, fines, and suspensions.

Cause of the brouhaha?

"Nearly the whole Boston team tried to intimidate me about being the only Jewish player in the league," Zeidel said. "They said they wouldn't be satisfied until they put me in a gas chamber."

An investigation by NHL president Clarence Campbell revealed, "It was not denied that Zeidel had been called 'Jew' or 'Jewish,' combined with a variety of abusive terms." However, Campbell stated there was no evidence to support Zeidel's claim of references to Nazi actions in World War II.

The stick-swinging feud actually began 10 years earlier on October 2, 1958, in an exhibition game between Zeidel's team, the AHL Hershey Bears, and the New York Rangers, Shack's team, at Niagara Falls. Both players were thrown out of the game but later resumed unpleasantries near the players' bench.

Zeidel, teammate Obie O'Brien, and Shack were all arrested when police got involved.

"They asked me where I'd like to go," Watson recalled during a visit with Allen in 2012. "I said, 'Well, I wouldn't mind going to Colorado. It's nice there, and I like to ski.'"

Watson laughed at the conversation.

"I got traded to Colorado, and I was there 16 games and broke my leg very badly and had to retire," he said.

Watson was injured in a 1978 game against St. Louis when he was checked into the boards and his thighbone was shattered.

"I'd tell Keith, 'You sent me out there to have fun, and I didn't have a lot of fun. I broke my leg, and I almost killed myself!' We used to laugh about it."

But Watson appreciated Allen's compassion as a GM. Snider agreed.

"He moved Joe where he wanted to go," Snider said. "He always tried to take care of our guys."

In other words, he was the quintessential general manager.

4

BOBBY CLARKE: FACE OF THE FRANCHISE

It was the game that changed everything.

No, not the day of the Flyers' first Stanley Cup title. Not the storied win over the Soviet Red Army. Not even the second Stanley Cup.

Many will tell you this extraordinary event happened the night of May 9, 1974, at Boston Garden.

In seven years, the Flyers had never won in that house of horrors, and the streak of futility continued in Game 1 of the Stanley Cup Final with a 3–2 loss to the Bruins.

Game 2 went into overtime, and the Flyers knew a second defeat would just about make the task of defeating mighty Boston impossible. In the second overtime, the Flyers' young captain Bobby Clarke flipped a rebound over goaltender Gilles Gilbert, and the curse was broken. Clarke leaped into the air for joy, perhaps realizing he had just changed the course of Flyers' history.

The 3–2 victory propelled the Flyers to a six-game series win over Boston.

It was one of just many special goals Clarke scored in his 15-year Hall of Fame career with the Flyers. But none were bigger than the one in Beantown because that success made the Flyers realize they had championship mettle.

Clarke holds a number of key team records, including career games (1,144), assists (862), points (1,210), as well as most assists in a season (89, twice).

He achieved all of this while playing with Type 1 diabetes, a condition he first learned of when he was only 13 years old.

As the years went by, it was clear that he could play through the medical issue. But as the NHL draft approached, some teams seemed reluctant to select him.

Not the Flyers. General Manager Keith Allen took Clarke with the 17th pick (second round) in the 1969 NHL Entry Draft and later refused two great offers to trade the 20-year-old rising star.

Flyers current president Paul Holmgren, Clarke's closest friend in hockey, continues to marvel at the way Clarke performed not only on the ice but off it as well.

"Well, he's diabetic and both my brothers were diabetic," Holmgren explained. "There was a connection there. Both my brothers died from complications from diabetes.

"We were both always talking about it, always discussing a possible cure, how close were they to finding a cure. It's easy to pick the guys who have had an impact on my life, because of all Clarke has done for me. We both live and die for the Flyers. That's a tough bond to break."

Perhaps the perception by scouts that Clarke's diabetes would compromise him as a player put a bit of a chip on the player's shoulder.

Although slight of stature, Clarke played the game with a great deal of edge, not afraid to swing a stick at someone's ankle (as he did in the 1972 Summit Series when he planted a two-hander on the ankle of the Soviet Union's Valeri Kharlamov) or trash talk the other team's bench.

At the end of the day, Clarke had the respect of his coach, Fred Shero, and his teammates in the locker room. That's all that mattered.

The approach Clarke took to the game could be summed up this way—he hated to lose more than he loved to win. Teammates like Bill Clement appreciated that.

"It came to me as an epiphany as I was driving in the car with Peter O'Malley, who was the president of the Washington Capitals after I got traded there [in 1975]," Clement said. "[O'Malley] said, 'We want to fill this team with guys who love to win, like you Flyer guys.'

"I was driving along and two minutes later I said, 'Hey, Peter, here's something. Fill your roster with guys who hate to lose [like Clarke]. Because everybody loves to win, but not everybody hates to lose.'

Bobby Clarke (right) left an indelible mark on the Flyers organization, leading his teams to the Stanley Cup Final three times and, as captain, winning it all twice.

"Bobby was absolutely that person. He had that disdain and a hatred for losing that he would do anything to win. That pushed him to do things like slashing Kharlamov in the Summit Series. Bobby Clarke was ruthless based on his hatred for losing. He would stop at nothing to win. But it was driven by that hatred for losing.

"That hatred of losing pushed him to do things as a leader that other guys who wore the 'C' had no concept of or no capabilities of performing, and that is the most difficult thing to do as a leader—I don't care if it's the corporate world or management—it's to have the tough conversations.

"If you weren't doing what the team needed to win, [Bobby] would come and tell you, [using] different styles with different players. He talked to Rick MacLeish way different than he talked to me most of the time. Bobby wanted everybody to hold themselves accountable, just like he did. He held himself accountable."

Clarke would serve briefly as a player–assistant coach for Pat Quinn in the early '80s, but he already was doing some of that in the Stanley Cup years.

"We were skating around the warm-ups before one of the Stanley Cup Final games in Buffalo in '75," Clement recalled. "There was a decision to make between two players. They chose me. I knew I was playing. Bobby said to me, 'You need to have a good game tonight. I'm the reason you're playing.' Now I knew the power that he had. But he also wanted me to be accountable for him being responsible for me being in the lineup. That showed me something."

Clarke grew up in a small mining town in Flin Flon, Manitoba, and his lack of knowledge about diabetes was, at first, a challenge. When he joined the Flyers in 1969, he was still finding his way and suffered two significant seizures during training camp.

Eventually Clarke realized he would have to keep his blood sugar count at a certain level, so he would drink soda and orange juice before and during games. On top of that, he gulped down chocolate bars and chewed glucose gum.

Out on the ice, Clarke, who won the Hart Trophy (NHL MVP) three times, gave as good as he got.

He didn't coin the phrase, "If you ain't cheatin', you ain't tryin'," but he certainly played by that credo.

The night-in, night-out intensity was there for all to see.

"I loved to get on the ice," Clarke said. "I loved to practice and I loved to play. The rest of the time, I wasn't that good at anything else, but playing and practicing, that's what I loved to do. So I could at least demand from other people that they work hard because I would always be able to do that."

Even his adversaries could respect Clarke's win-at-all-cost philosophy.

"He did a lot of things great by the book—his passing, his work in front of the net, the way he shifted play around the net, his faceoffs," said Islander great Bryan Trottier, who won four Stanley Cups in New York and two with the Pittsburgh Penguins. "And then there are the

ON THIS DATE

JANUARY 17, 1973

At 23 years old, Bobby Clarke is named the Flyers' third captain. At the time, he was the youngest captain in NHL history.

things he did that aren't in the book, that aren't hockey's bright spots, but that put another team off its stride—poking at you, slashing at your ankles, putting his stick up in your face just to put you off a little.

"Some players are just chippy and don't excel at the game, but he blended chippiness with skill. And he wasn't always chippy—he did it when his team needed it. I don't admire someone slashing ankles, but he didn't do it to end someone's career. He did it to help his team win. He did anything he had to do to help his team, and you become respected for that."

Clarke went on to become general manager of the team, and one of his first acts was to hire a coach. He found a diamond in the rough in Mike Keenan, a 34-year-old who had never coached in the NHL.

All Keenan did was take the Flyers to the Stanley Cup Final in two of the next three seasons.

After the 1989–90 season, Clarke was dismissed but wound up in Minnesota, where he also took the North Stars to the Final, although they lost to the powerhouse Pittsburgh Penguins.

Clarke returned to the Flyers as GM in 1995, and the Flyers were back in the Final again in 1997. Once again, another budding dynasty, the Detroit Red Wings, swept the Flyers, only the second time they've failed to win a Final game.

Today, Clarke serves as a senior vice president and continues to provide valuable talent evaluation. And why not? He set the standard by which all players in the organization aspire.

Clarke's sidekick, Bill Barber, probably sums it up best.

"He was a great leader in a sense of how you compete," Barber said. "Shift after shift, game after game, played through injuries, you name it. He was always there. It wasn't about Bob Clarke. It was about the team. He was very team-oriented. I think that spread through the dressing room. We all have to perform to our abilities to win, and he was a big part of that message."

Clarke didn't have to say much. He truly led by example.

"He wasn't really vocal, not a rah-rah kind of guy," Barber said. "He spoke through his play. When he spoke, the team listened. We were very fortunate to have him as a teammate because I think he made everybody better.

"It was a pleasure to play with him. You needed to be on top of your game at all times. It became part of your routine. You knew you're going to be at your best because that's the way you've been schooled."

Each year, the Flyers award the team's most valuable player with the Bobby Clarke Trophy, a bronze depiction/replica of a famous moment in Flyers' history.

What scene? Here's a hint—the hero is leaping for joy after scoring a dramatic goal.

5

BEST OF
ALL DRAFTS

How could a future three-time MVP, two-time Stanley Cup champion, and first-ballot Hall of Famer not be selected first overall in his draft year?

Or even in the first round?

Well, simple. When that player had a scary-sounding disease, one that could have an adverse effect on his performance, NHL scouts were sent running for the hills.

Bobby Clarke, an unheralded kid from Flin Flon, Manitoba, posted strong junior hockey numbers in the mid-'60s, but because he had Type 1 diabetes, all 12 teams passed on him in the first round of the 1969 NHL Entry Draft.

Fortunately for the Flyers, a scout by the name of Gerry Melnyk had been doing his homework in western Canada. He brought Clarke to team chairman Ed Snider's attention, and so the discussion took wing at the Flyers' draft table at the Queen Elizabeth Hotel in Montreal.

"I don't usually get involved [in the draft] to that degree," Snider would say later. "But we had Gerry Melnyk. We drafted another center [Bob Currier] in the first round that year, and [Melnyk] couldn't say it to the general manager at the time [Bud Poile], how distraught he was that we didn't draft Clarke. I said, 'Why?' And he said, 'He'd be our best player right away.' [Melnyk was] the one that checked with the Mayo Clinic about Bob's diabetes and found out that Bob could play, and that's the reason he was drafted so late. So I directed the general manager, who was very upset with me, to draft [Clarke] in the second round. And we did."

Good thing. Clarke would go on to play 15 seasons for the Flyers, leading them to the Stanley Cup Final four times and winning twice. Then he took over the team's GM post and steered the team to the Cup Final three more times.

Melnyk, who passed away in 2001, put hundreds of thousands of miles on his car as he tooled around western Canada, uncovering one jewel of a prospect after another.

He knew his stuff.

"In those days, the original teams didn't have a full-time western scout," Snider told NBCSports.com veteran hockey writer Tim Panaccio in a 2014 interview. "Don't ask me why. Yet we did have one in Melnyk, and the only reason we did was because Melnyk had a heart attack at training camp and when he recovered we made him a scout in the west."

Melnyk did his homework and, as previously mentioned, checked with the Mayo Clinic in Minnesota to see if Clarke could hold up under the rigors of the NHL.

"No one else did that," Snider said. "Everybody was afraid of [Clarke] because he was a diabetic."

Clarke was a hot item at the Flyers' table, so when Currier was selected in the first round, tension mounted.

"Everybody's eyebrows went up at the table," Snider said. "Everybody was going crazy. No one said anything. But I saw the atmosphere. No one could believe we took Currier. Gerry Melnyk looked like he was going to have another heart attack.

"[Coach] Keith [Allen] said to me, 'Gerry thinks this kid will step in and be our best player,'" Snider said. "And we took Currier. I said, 'Tell Bud about this and then I want you to check out this kid with your own sources.'"

Snider then instructed Poile to take Clarke in the second round, even if it meant taking two centers with the first two picks.

"Finally, I had to say, 'You will pick Bob Clarke,'" Snider said. "I didn't want to do that. I didn't know anything. I was still a novice. Poile didn't like me from that day on, but it worked out."

Clarke understood the concern about his health situation, but it had to hurt to sit there and hear less worthy players getting their names called.

"I was disappointed to be drafted that late," Clarke said, "but that's what happens when other people figure they are experts on something they really know nothing about. Like diabetes.

FOR FLYERS, A "GIFT" IN LUCKY DRAFT LOTTERY

The Flyers beat astronomical odds to move from 13th to second in the 2017 NHL draft lottery. In fact, it was the biggest jump in the history of the lottery, which started in 1995.

"It was an unexpected gift," said Paul Holmgren, the Flyers' president.

The Flyers had a 2.2 percent chance to get the No. 1 overall pick and a 2.4 percent chance to secure the No. 2 selection.

"I feel like we had a lot of bad luck this year and I'm hoping this is a turning point," General Manager Ron Hextall said after the lottery.

Some said it was karma and that the Flyers were "owed one" because they lost the draft lottery to Chicago in 2007. That year, the Flyers had the NHL's worst record and had a 25 percent chance to get the top pick. Chicago had the league's fifth-worst record and had just an 8.1 percent chance to land the No. 1 selection.

The Blackhawks ended up with Patrick Kane at No. 1, while the Flyers took James van Riemsdyk at No. 2.

In the 2017 draft, the Flyers ended up choosing center Nolan Patrick with the No. 2 overall pick. New Jersey, which advanced from No. 5 to No. 1 in the lottery, took center Nico Hischier with the first selection.

Patrick and Hischier, naturally, will be compared for many years to come.

"What really shocked me, though, was Philadelphia drafting me. I honestly had no idea where Philadelphia was. I didn't know whether it was on the West Coast, the East Coast, or in the middle somewhere. I actually got a little scared when I thought about going to a city I didn't know anything about."

Clarke stuck to himself for the first year or two in Philly, but by the time he was of legal age to drink, things got a lot more comfortable. Like all those liquid post-practice lunches at Rexy's.

Who were some of the other smart draft picks by the Flyers over the years?

Taking Bill Barber at No. 7 overall in 1972 wasn't a surprise pick. Barber's smooth skating and powerful shot were well known among NHL scouts.

But a sleeper pick that year was defenseman Jimmy Watson, who fell to the third round at 39th overall. Watson, younger brother of Flyer veteran defenseman Joe Watson, would go on to become an All-Star player.

A similar situation took place in 1975. The Flyers traded Bill Clement and Don McLean to Washington that June for the No. 1 overall pick. Philadelphia took Mel Bridgman, a strong center who went on to become captain of the team.

But down in the sixth round, the Flyers were able to select Paul Holmgren with the 108th pick. Holmgren would go on to enjoy a fine career with the Flyers, becoming the first American to score a hat trick in a Stanley Cup Final game (1980).

In 1979, Brian Propp went to the Flyers with the 14th overall pick. He finished with the third-most points in Flyers history.

The subplot that year was Pelle Lindbergh, a future Vezina Trophy winner, who had his life cut short by an auto crash. The Flyers got him with the 35th overall pick (second round).

How did Ron Hextall fall to No. 119 in 1982? Five years later, he became one of only two goaltenders to win a Conn Smythe Trophy while playing for a losing team in the Stanley Cup Final—and the only goalie to win the Vezina Trophy the same year.

The following year, Rick Tocchet landed in the Flyers' lap in the sixth round (125th overall). He became one of the franchise's top all-time right wings.

Another mystery: five teams passed on All-World Peter Forsberg in 1991. But not the Flyers. Unfortunately, Forsberg was traded away in the Eric Lindros megadeal.

In 1998 and 2000, the Flyers used first-round picks on Simon Gagne and Justin Williams, respectively. Both won Stanley Cup rings with other teams.

Perhaps the best one-two draft punch for the Flyers came in 2003, when they obtained Jeff Carter at No. 11 overall and Mike

Richards at No. 24. They were key players in the Flyers' run to the 2010 Stanley Cup Final, and each won a championship ring with Los Angeles.

There have been some notable names drafted by the Flyers in more recent years, including Claude Giroux on the 22nd pick in 2006, Sean Couturier (eighth) in 2011, Ivan Provorov (seventh) in 2015, and Nolan Patrick (second) in 2017. But none of these came close to causing the stir that took place in 1969. Players like Bobby Clarke only come along once in a lifetime.

6

FRED SHERO: THE "FOG"

"I have not failed. I've just found 10,000 ways that won't work."

Inventor, futurist, and pioneer Thomas Edison once spoke those words. He may have been alluding to all the trial-and-error attempts he made before he successfully created things like the electric lightbulb, the phonograph, and the motion picture camera.

Hockey coach Fred Shero never met Edison, but he sure must have admired his innovative thinking. The first and only coach to lead a Flyers team to a Stanley Cup championship was constantly thinking of ways to get a step up on the competition.

He's given credit for coming up with the concept of a morning skate, now a common practice for all NHL teams on game days.

He was the first to create the position of full-time assistant coach, installing Mike Nykoluk as his No. 2 man behind the bench.

He thought up the idea of using systems, studying film, and employing in-season weight/strength training on something called an Apollo machine, the precursor to Nautilus.

But perhaps what he is best remembered for are his little sayings, including the most famous of all, posted on May 19, 1974, just before Game 6 of the Stanley Cup Final against the Boston Bruins: "Win today and we walk together forever."

Legend has it that Shero was so out there that he eventually earned the nickname "Freddy The Fog," because so much of his thinking was so far outside of the box that it seemed almost wacky— although others credit the moniker to an incident that took place during a game in 1948. But more on that later.

Oddball, maybe, but most of the time it worked. Like the famous Flyers–Soviet Red Army game on January 11, 1976, at the Spectrum. Shero spent hours studying the Soviets on film and had his team primed when they hit the ice. To no one's surprise, he and his players beat the Soviets at their own game.

"I've always considered Fred a leadership pioneer," said Bill Clement, who played on Shero's 1974 and 1975 Stanley Cup teams and is now an analyst on Flyers' TV broadcasts.

"He was an innovator. Not in Xs and Os. Not in having the first assistant coach, not in dividing the ice in two so you could have much more going on—after he studied the Russians.

"[With other coaches], it was always top-down management. If you were inferior, it was always the coach with the whip. And never sugar. It was salt all the time. Players weren't allowed to feel good about themselves if they lost. God forbid they should laugh. Players were regularly berated in front of their teammates and in front of anybody. The coach didn't care. It was negative-based motivational tactics. Freddy was, to my knowledge, the first positive-based motivational tactician."

That particular psychological approach worked. It's safe to say players wanted to play for Shero. In fact, they weren't sure whether to laugh or cry after a win or loss. Shero would make his players practice hard when they won, much easier when they lost.

"He would have 8:00 AM practices," Hall of Famer Bob Clarke says. "If you lost a game, the next day practice was low-key, almost lackadaisical. But if you won, he would work the hell out of you. He always felt if you were winning, you could get more work out of a man.

"If you were losing, your energy was low, and let's get it back and not waste it in practice. But when we won, and we won a lot, we practiced. It's the exact opposite philosophy of coaches today where if a team plays bad, they skate the hell out of you. He never did that. His practices were always for the purpose to get better."

Shero believed he could get more out of his players when they were feeling good about themselves.

"So instead of a penalty if you did it wrong, Freddy always had a carrot or a reward to try to get players to do things right," Clement said.

Nearly to a man, Flyers alumni from those glory years remember Shero as a coach who treated them like adults—like professionals. He appealed to their sense of pride. During games and at practices, Shero hardly ever berated a player. But he did keep mental notes, and if a

FRED SHERO STANDS TALL AMONG FLYERS COACHES

Fred Shero is the most successful coach in Flyers history—and not just because he directed the franchise to its only two Stanley Cup championships. Shero has coached the most games (554) and has the highest points percentage (.642) among Flyers coaches. Terry Murray has the highest winning percentage in the playoffs (.609), while Shero is second (.578). Shero has the most regular season victories (308), well ahead of the No. 2 coach, Mike Keenan (190).

Fifteen of the Flyers' 20 coaches have had at least a .500 points percentage. Only seven of their coaches, however, have had a winning playoff record: Murray (28-18), Shero (48-35), Pat Quinn (22-17), Keenan (32-25), Paul Holmgren (10-9), Ken Hitchcock (19-18), and Peter Laviolette (23-22).

player wasn't pulling his weight for the team, Shero knew how to take care of the problem.

"Freddy was the first coach I ever had that led his players through respect and when I came to the Flyers, there were guys I knew who were going out after curfew," Clement said. "[Shero] had a disdain for checking up on guys—knocking on doors, hiding in the hotel lobby.

"The guys that abused Freddy's trust that he put in them, they all got traded, [including] four or five of the main guys within the first two years that I was there. I could tell these were the guys who weren't respecting Freddy back. They were playing for themselves. Freddy wanted to respect all of his athletes and I believe that he did. If he didn't, the Flyers got rid of them."

The ones who respected Shero—Clement, Clarke, Bill Barber, Rick MacLeish, Ed Van Impe, Reggie Leach, Bernie Parent—did stick around, and they made him proud.

If not for several major injuries in 1975-76 (including one to Parent), the Flyers might have won three straight titles.

Born the son of Russian immigrants on October 23, 1925, in Winnipeg, Shero was a quiet person even then. Because he was a first generation "foreigner," Shero was the target of bullying and took backroads home from school to avoid confrontations. By age 13, he took matters into his own hands and trained to be a boxer. Hockey, however, was still first and foremost on this mind.

By 17, he made up his mind to pursue hockey and signed a contract with the New York Rangers. A year of military service during World War II interrupted his journey to the NHL, but eventually he made it. On October 16, 1947, he made his NHL debut at the Montreal Forum against the defending Stanley Cup Champion Montreal Canadiens in the 1947–48 season opener. However, he only played 19 games with the Rangers that year while splitting time with the St. Paul Saints in the United States Hockey League.

That's when the real origin of his nickname "The Fog" may have come about. In a game at St. Paul, Minnesota, the high humidity resulted in a fog bank forming just above the ice surface. The fog was so thick that hardly anyone could see the puck. But one player claimed he could: Shero. And that supposedly is where the nickname was coined, and it stuck.

Following a nine-year playing career in the NHL and AHL, Shero coached 13 seasons in the minors until 1971, when Flyers general manager Keith Allen, frustrated by his team's inability to perform up to its potential, brought Shero aboard. Not only did Shero reward Allen's faith with two Stanley Cup titles, but he also put together four straight seasons with a .700 winning percentage.

Following the 1977–78 season, Shero expressed a desire to return to the Rangers, his original team, and attempted to get out of the last year of his contract with the Flyers. The Flyers balked and ended up getting a compensatory draft pick to allow Shero to leave to coach the Rangers, using the pick to draft Ken Linseman.

Shero would go on to coach the Rangers to the 1979 Stanley Cup Final, which resulted in a five-game loss to the defending champion Montreal Canadiens.

Three years later, Shero stepped down. He returned to the Flyers in 1989 to become a special assistant coach on Paul Holmgren's staff, but he passed away a year later.

Shero was inducted posthumously into the Hockey Hall of Fame in 2013.

There are a thousand stories about Shero's quirky personality, but one of the best is set after a game at the old Omni Coliseum in Atlanta. It seems Fred left the arena through a door with no reentry and was locked outside prior to the post-game press conference. At the press conference no one knew where Shero was, and reporters unsuccessfully searched the arena for him.

During the 1972–73 season, Shero wrote a quote on the team blackboard, and the Flyers won that night. Perhaps being superstitious, Shero continued to write inspirational sayings, and the habit stuck.

After the Flyers won their first Cup, Shero won the Jack Adams Award as the NHL's best coach. Shero had reached the top of the mountain.

"He did more things in the 10 years that he coached than some guys did in 30 years," said Joe Watson, one of Shero's favorite players. "People never talked about systems in the '70s, but when Fred came along he instituted systems. Teams never had assistant coaches; he brought that into the game."

Like the test model bulb in Edison's lab, Shero's light was always on. And for the Flyers it burned brightly.

7

HEARTBREAK HILL: DAYS THAT LIVE IN INFAMY

It takes only six letters to spell the two biggest words in sports: w-h-a-t-i-f?

Fans have been crying in their beer since the 1800s, often because of that old expression, "We was robbed!" Be it an official's perceived bad call, a horrible misplay, or just plain hard luck, a team's destiny can be decided by the fates.

For the Philadelphia Flyers, there has been a veritable book of crazy, infamous events during the past five-plus decades to argue about over a cold one at the corner bar. At the top of the list has to be the so-called "Leon Stickle Game," namely Game 6 of the 1980 Stanley Cup Final between the Flyers and the New York Islanders played in Uniondale, New York.

Trailing in the best-of-seven series 3–2, the Flyers gave an inspired effort on Saturday afternoon, May 24, before a sold-out Nassau Coliseum. With the score tied 1–1 in the first period, New York's Clark Gillies carried the puck up the left wing, across the blue line, and into the Flyers' zone.

Then the left wing passed the puck backward, clearly back out of the zone, before center Butch Goring picked up the puck and carried it back across the line a second time. Clearly offside.

But wait. Linesman Leon Stickle failed to blow his whistle. Play continued, and the Islanders' Duane Sutter scored at 14:08 to make it 2–1 New York.

While this was still early in the game, the Flyers felt like they had been wronged and let Stickle hear about it. Stickle realized his mistake and confessed as much after the game.

"I guess I blew it," he said. "Maybe there was tape on the stick and it confused me. Maybe I was too close to the play."

The Islanders would go on to win the game 5–4 on a Bob Nystrom goal in overtime to give the Islanders their first Stanley Cup title.

For the Flyers, it was a bitter defeat.

Coach Pat Quinn, not exactly a big fan of officials to begin with, did not want to take anything away from the Islanders' success, but he acknowledged the error might have been costly.

"[Officiating] is something I've complained about all year," Quinn said at the time. "I would clear away from talking about it now because the Islanders deserve all the glory they can get.

"What's done is done. It should be an embarrassment to that official, but it's not going to change the outcome. To argue now would be a waste of time."

The Flyers were only hoping to win that game and send the series back to the Spectrum in Philadelphia for a Game 7.

Defenseman Behn Wilson was one of several Flyers who were upset with the officiating.

"I'm sure you guys saw the replay," Wilson grumbled. "Was [Gillies] offside? Well, whether there was a bad call, it won't change the game. The whole team worked hard, but I guess we weren't destined to get the breaks."

Added Bill Barber, "We did our best. I just wish the officials had done theirs. I'm proud of every one of our guys, but I'm not proud of the officiating."

A decade before all this happened, the Flyers were victims of another inopportune play, and it cost them a whole season's worth of work. The Flyers appeared to be on their way to the 1969–70 season playoffs heading into the final few weeks of the season. But a late collapse saw them drop into a tie with Minnesota and Oakland, going into the final game of the campaign, an afternoon contest on April 4 against the North Stars at the Spectrum. The Flyers needed a win in the matinee to keep their playoff hopes alive.

It wasn't to be.

With time running down and the game scoreless, defenseman Barry Gibbs fired a long shot at the Flyers net. Goaltender Bernie Parent inexplicably missed the puck as it entered the cage.

Later, Bernie tried to explain the misplay away by saying he was

ON THIS DATE

JANUARY 16, 1968

Leon Rochefort becomes the first Flyer to participate in an NHL All-Star Game.

momentarily blinded by sunlight beaming through the long windows of the old building.

Either way, it was off to the golf course where, by all accounts, there was even more bright sunlight.

Similar misfortune reared its ugly head a couple years later. Approaching the final game of the 1971–72 season, the Flyers—who had missed the playoffs in 1970 and been unceremoniously swept out in the first round in 1971 (by a margin of 20–8) by the Chicago Blackhawks—needed a win or a tie to beat out the Pittsburgh Penguins for the final playoff spot in the East.

They were tied with the Buffalo Sabres 2–2. Time was running out. All the Flyers needed to do was keep the puck from going in their net. It didn't happen.

With four seconds to play, former Flyer Gerry Meehan launched an innocent-looking shot from the top of the left circle, about 45 feet away. Somehow, the puck eluded Flyers goaltender Doug Favell, and it was another visit to Heartbreak Hotel for the orange and black.

While there was short-term pain, there were some benefits to the comical tragedy. The Flyers vowed they would be better for this.

In fact, according to Bobby Clarke, team chairman Ed Snider went down to the Flyers' locker room after the game to tell his players that.

"That was [Coach] Fred Shero's first year," Snider told the *New York Times*. "Actually I took the whole team out to dinner afterward, too. I wanted to make sure we didn't get depressed because I saw a lot of good signs in that first year.

"We were on our way. It was the strangest game I ever attended, because we were in third place going into the game, then halfway into the game we were in fourth place, and with four seconds left we were in fifth place and out of the playoffs. You can't have a more difficult game than that."

Snider's words proved prophetic. The Flyers would not miss the playoffs again for the next 18 consecutive seasons.

As for other meetings with Lady Luck (or Lady Bad Luck), the headliner has to be losing the 2007 NHL Draft lottery and the chance to take Patrick Kane, who became a three-time Stanley Cup champion player.

The Flyers' 2006–07 season was arguably the worst in team history. They put together only 56 points in 82 games, eclipsing the dubious distinction of the 1969–70 team, which posted 58 points (and that was in a 76-game season). In years gone by, the Flyers would have been first in line to select any player they might want in the NHL Entry Draft.

And Kane appeared to be the obvious choice.

But the NHL had instituted a lottery system, and as fate would have it, the Chicago Blackhawks pulled the lucky number and moved up four places to take Kane.

The Flyers, relegated to second, were left to take one of the best of the rest, which happened to be New Jersey native James van Riemsdyk. The University of New Hampshire product debuted with the Flyers at the start of the 2009–10 season. While he played well for three seasons in Philadelphia, he was eventually traded to Toronto for defenseman Luke Schenn.

Schenn turned out to be a disappointment and later was shipped to Los Angeles along with Vinny Lecavalier for Jordan Weal and a draft pick.

Sometimes things come full circle and, six years later, van Riemsdyk (or JVR), who registered a career-high 36 goals in the 2017–18 season in Toronto, wound up back in Philadelphia after signing a five-year, $35 million, free-agent contract.

Paul Holmgren, the general manager who was left to draft van Riemsdyk, said at the time it was unfair to make comparisons between the two players.

"Patrick Kane is already a star, one of the elite players of the game," Holmgren said in 2010. "James is just a player trying to figure it out on most nights. Some nights he looks great, some games he just looks like a regular player."

JVR never plays the "what if" game, or so he says.

"Obviously this [going to the Flyers in the draft] was always a possibility, but things happen for a reason and I'm happy with how things turned out," he said.

8

BERNIE PARENT: "ONLY THE LORD SAVES MORE"

There have been some outstanding bumper stickers spotted on Philadelphia cars over the years.

Notables include, ORANGE AND BLACK: HATED BY THE NHL SINCE 1974, or IN PHILLY, WE BRAKE FOR ALL ANIMALS, EXCEPT PENGUINS!

And don't forget, IF THEY DON'T HAVE FLYERS TV IN HEAVEN, I'M NOT GOING.

But the only one that truly belongs in the bumper sticker Hall of Fame was created in the 1970s: ONLY THE LORD SAVES MORE THAN BERNIE PARENT.

This one has to be the all-time classic, alluding to the Flyers' remarkable goaltender who was voted MVP (Conn Smythe Trophy) both years they won the Stanley Cup (1974 and 1975).

Bernie embodied everything the Philadelphia sports fan likes in an athlete: passion, courage, big in the clutch, good with the public, funny, irreverent, and, especially in Parent's case, a debonair French accent (with a deep voice) to make his one-liners that much funnier.

All this combined to make Parent perhaps the most popular Flyer of all time.

Teammate Bill Clement still chuckles at the mention of the famous "Only the Lord… " sticker.

"That was great," said Clement, a TV analyst with the Flyers. "As sacrilegious as it might have been…every father of the priesthood, every sister, every nun, every Catholic, every Protestant loved the bumper sticker. If anyone was going to get special dispensation from a religious order, it was Bernie Parent for what he did in Philadelphia. Every diocese wanted to adopt him."

In 2018, *The Hockey News* rated Parent the 11th greatest goaltender of all time.

Some of the netminders listed behind him include five-time Stanley Cup champion Grant Fuhr of the Edmonton Oilers; Georges Vezina of the Montreal Canadiens (for whom the annual Vezina Trophy is named); Stanley Cup winner Tony Esposito of the Chicago

Blackhawks; Stanley Cup winner Ed Belfour of the Dallas Stars; and four-time Stanley Cup champion Billy Smith of the New York Islanders. At his peak, Parent was virtually a brick wall against enemy shooters.

The powerful Boston Bruins found this out one May day in 1974 when Parent turned back the likes of Bobby Orr, Phil Esposito and company for a 1–0 shutout, clinching the Flyers' first Stanley Cup title.

Only a neck injury kept Parent from possibly taking the Flyers to a third straight Stanley Cup after the 1975–76 campaign.

Just a few years later, an errant stick found its way through the eyehole in Parent's mask. In an instant, a brilliant career was over.

Growing up, Parent idolized Montreal goaltending great Jacques Plante, and the two actually played on the same Toronto Maple Leafs team in 1971 when Parent was 26 and Plante 43.

After a superb junior career, Parent joined the Boston Bruins for the 1965–66 season but was claimed by the Flyers in the 1967 expansion draft. In his initial tour with the Flyers, Parent split time with Doug Favell and eventually became the number one netminder. In his first year in Philadelphia, the Flyers won the NHL's West Division.

The goal-challenged Flyers then traded Parent to Toronto in a three-team trade with Boston that brought Rick MacLeish to Philadelphia.

With the Maple Leafs, Parent was united with his boyhood hero, Plante, who served as mentor and confidant.

Two years later, Parent found himself a free agent and decided to sign with the new World Hockey Association. Originally, Parent came to terms with the Miami Screaming Eagles, making him the first NHL player to jump to the fledgling circuit. But the Eagles never took off, so Parent then signed with the Philadelphia Blazers.

After one season of that, Parent had enough. He looked for a return to the NHL, so Toronto traded his rights to Philadelphia, ironically enough, for Favell. The rest, as they say, is history.

Over the next two campaigns, Parent was outstanding, winning the Vezina Trophy twice and recording a total of 30 shutouts. In the Flyers' first championship season, he played 73 of a possible 78 games with a 1.89 goals-against average and 12 shutouts.

IT'S OVER WHEN KATE SMITH SINGS

"From the mountains, to the prairies, to the Schuylkill, white with foam...."

With apologies and all due respect to songwriter great Irving Berlin and his masterpiece, "God Bless America," a Philadelphia version of the ode to the United States seems appropriate, given how many times the original rendition has been played before Philadelphia Flyers games.

And it's all because the legendary vocalist Kate Smith made it so popular, beginning innocently enough on the night of December 11, 1969. The Flyers chose that night to play a recording of the song she had previously made instead of the traditional national anthem. If the Flyers had lost to the Toronto Maple Leafs, who knows if "God Bless America" would have been played again. But the Flyers won 6-3, and that's where it all started.

Fast forward to October 11, 1973, and before the Flyers' home opener against the Leafs, out of a service tunnel pops Smith herself to sing "God Bless America." The Flyers win again.

The next time she appeared live, there was a lot more on the line, namely Game 6 of the 1974 Stanley Cup Final. Hall of Famers Bobby Orr and Phil Esposito of the Bruins tried to break the jinx by shaking her hand after the performance but to no avail. The Flyers won 1-0 to take their first Cup.

Smith, affectionately nicknamed "The Songbird of the South" for her Virginia roots, wasn't done yet. She sang live before Game 7 of the 1975 Stanley Cup semifinals against the New York Islanders. New York's Ed Westfall tried to break the hex by giving her a bouquet of flowers, but that didn't work either. Flyers 4, Islanders 1.

The Flyers' record with Smith's "God Bless America" is 101 wins, 31 losses, 5 ties.

In a controversial decision made after the 2018–19 season, the Flyers discontinued using Smith's recording, citing two problematic songs she performed in the 1930s.

Parent's quirky, disarming sense of humor had a way of breaking the tension in a pressure-filled situation.

"Listen, everybody is more intense [in the locker room or during game action], but in general, Bernie wasn't that much different than he is today," Clement said. "He loved everybody; he loved to laugh. He wanted to have fun. He seemed really straightforward. There was no agenda.

"He loved us all winning together. Very late in Game 6 [against the Bruins], I remember Bernie tried to do something to relieve his own tension and mine.

"The puck was just about to be dropped in our end and I was taking the faceoff. It was a defensive zone faceoff to his left. All of a sudden his arms go up and he starts saying, 'Wait, wait, wait, wait.' He said, 'Billy, get over here.'

"So I'm hunched over on my pads. I go over and go, 'Bernie, what is it?' He goes, 'How's she goin'?' I said, 'What?' He said, 'How's it goin'?' I had to smile. I skated back and won the faceoff. Bernie was larger than life because of how he played. He loves life and loves people. [He was] one of the most intense guys but I always found him relaxed and wanting to relax other guys."

Teammate Paul Holmgren, now president of the Flyers, had similar experiences.

"He would always disarm you with a comment," Holmgren recalled. "It would take you out of the funk you were in.

"I remember scoring on him once in practice and he chased after me. He was literally pissed when he got scored on. Especially a stiff like me."

Coach Fred Shero relied on Parent so much in those years that he tended to play him for a month or more without a game off. One time Shero played Parent in 37 straight games until he finally relented and let backup goalie Bobby Taylor start a game.

When asked by the media how he arrived at the decision to play Taylor, Shero simply shrugged and said, "Because it was his turn."

In the following season, 1974–75, Parent continued his streak of excellence. He capped it off with another shutout, this time 2–0, in a Game 6 clincher at Buffalo to win another Stanley Cup.

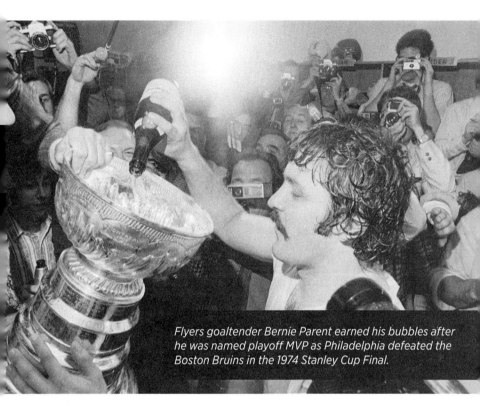

Flyers goaltender Bernie Parent earned his bubbles after he was named playoff MVP as Philadelphia defeated the Boston Bruins in the 1974 Stanley Cup Final.

Surgery to repair a neck injury kept Parent out for all but 11 games in 1975–76. The operation was not a complete success as the removal of a disk and section of bone to relieve nerve pain left him with side effects that continued to plague him the rest of his career.

Still, he remained an upbeat figure in the locker room.

"I remember my first year with the Flyers [1976–77]. I was seated next to [Parent] in the room," Holmgren said. "We beat the [New York] Islanders in the first game of the season.

"So I come in, sit down and then Bernie comes in and sits down. In this big French accent, he goes, 'Paul, just think. Only 79 more to go.'"

The end came in a game on February 17, 1979, when the aforementioned stick found its way into Parent's right eye. Some of his sight came back but not to the level required to play in the NHL, causing Bernie to retire at age 34.

Upon retirement, he worked as a goaltending coach for several years, tutoring such up-and-coming talents as Pelle Lindbergh and Ron Hextall.

The early forced retirement had an adverse effect on Parent's personal life. He turned to alcohol and eventually ended up in the Alcoholics Anonymous program. He has been sober ever since, nearly four decades.

To this day, Parent continues to serve as a Flyers goodwill ambassador to the faithful fans.

He could be spending more of his time on his 45-foot boat, the *French Connection*, down in Wildwood, New Jersey, but the lure of interacting with hockey people is just too strong.

"It's very simple: I love people," Parent told Randy Miller of NJ.com a few years back. "I love to socialize with people. It's never the same, and when you approach life that you care about people, then socializing with them becomes a beautiful thing. I've always said the Delaware Valley is part of my family and I love everybody here."

The feeling is certainly mutual. Whenever all the old Flyers get together for alumni games, like they did for the 2012 Winter Classic in Philadelphia, Parent is at the center of it all. Just like he was in the '70s.

"It just seemed like he blended in with everybody," said Hall of Famer Bill Barber, one of Parent's best friends on those championship teams. "He could be funny but he could be quiet, too, when the pressure was on.

"There were a lot of practical jokes in those days, like cutting the sleeve off someone's shirt just for laughs. His personality was just right for that time and place. It helped win us a lot of games."

9

RICK MACLEISH: UNDERRATED STAR LEFT US FAR TOO SOON

Bobby Clarke's words made your eyebrows rise when he talked about center Rick MacLeish.

"Ricky was the most talented player the Flyers had during the 1970s," Clarke said after MacLeish's death in 2016.

During that era, the Flyers won two Stanley Cups and had numerous star forwards, including Clarke, a three-time league MVP, and Bill Barber. Both of those players are in the Hockey Hall of Fame. So is goalie Bernie Parent. You could make a case for MacLeish being Hall-of-Fame-worthy, too.

Barber compared MacLeish to Hall of Famer Gilbert Perreault of Buffalo. "They had speed and the skill," he said. "Perreault was a little better stick handler, but Ricky was invaluable to our team."

"Although he played in the shadow of Clarkie, he was every bit as good as Clarkie," said Bob Kelly, another winger on those Flyers teams that won consecutive Stanley Cup championships in the 1970s.

The smooth-skating MacLeish had one of the league's most dynamic wrist shots, and he became the first 50-goal scorer in franchise history in 1972–73. MacLeish, the NHL's leading playoff scorer when the Flyers won Stanley Cups in 1974 and 1975, was a three-time All-Star who finished with 349 career goals.

According to Barber, a star left winger who later became a Flyers coach, "Ricky was like poetry in motion on the ice. He was so fluid with his skating style and his wrist shot. He was an exceptional skater, and you have to realize that in that era, the good skaters stood out."

MacLeish, nicknamed "Hawk," centered Ross Lonsberry and Gary Dornhoefer during his best days with the Flyers.

"I'll tell you what, he was probably the fastest player on the ice," Dornhoefer said. "As far as a wrist shot is concerned, there was no one better at getting that shot away and accurate. Ross and I would talk and say, 'Let's just give Ricky the puck and he'll put it in.' If you look at the amount of goals he scored, well, that's why we kept giving him the puck. Ross and I had cement hands, so we'd pass the puck to him."

The Flyers could have a mediocre game, but because of MacLeish's skills, "He could carry us," Dornhoefer said. "He was that gifted. I always felt that during the years he played he never got the recognition that he properly deserved."

MacLeish had been battling meningitis and kidney and liver problems late in his life, according to his daughter Brianna MacLeish. He was 66 when he died.

"Life after hockey wasn't fair to Ricky," Clarke said. "He left us far too soon."

Club president Paul Holmgren said the Flyers had lost "one of their legends," and he called MacLeish a "good father, grandfather, teammate, and friend. Rick will be missed by all who were fortunate to come and know him over the years. His happy and friendly demeanor was front and center everywhere Rick went."

MacLeish's daughters, Danielle and Brianna, put together a statement, calling their father "an amazing dad and grandfather. We are comforted in knowing he is with his grandson, Tyler, who he was very close to. We want to thank the Flyers family and fans for their outpouring of support." Tyler died in 2007 at age 4.

MacLeish was drafted fourth overall by Boston in 1970, and he played for the Flyers, Hartford, Pittsburgh, and Detroit in a career that ended in 1984.

He made an indelible mark with the Flyers.

"He was a great skater with a great shot," said Dave Schultz, one of MacLeish's teammates on the Flyers. "He scored a lot of big goals for us."

MacLeish created one of the most famous moments in Philadelphia sports history on May 19, 1974, at the percolating Spectrum, redirecting Andre "Moose" Dupont's power-play drive past Boston goalie Gilles Gilbert to give the Flyers a 1–0 first-period lead in Game 6 of the Stanley Cup Final.

It was perhaps the most important goal in franchise history, and it was the only tally in the epic, series-clinching game. In just the franchise's seventh season of existence, the Flyers were Stanley Cup champions.

In the early 2000s, MacLeish suffered a heart attack while playing in an alumni game and underwent surgery a few days later.

"I wasn't excited about having open-heart surgery, but the doctor reassured me that he could do the surgery with one arm tied behind his back," recalled MacLeish, known for his laid-back and quiet demeanor.

"I said, 'When you operate on me, you make sure you are using both arms!'"

MacLeish was a 21-year-old prospect when he was acquired by the Flyers for Mike Walton on January 31, 1971. The Flyers had acquired Walton and Bruce Gamble earlier in the day from Toronto as part of a trade that sent Bernie Parent to the Maple Leafs. The Flyers got Parent back two years later in another deal.

MacLeish struggled in limited duty during his first two seasons with the Flyers and was sent to the minors. He was moved from left wing to center in 1972–73, his first full season in Philadelphia.

It turned out to be his coming-out party.

MacLeish erupted for 50 goals, becoming the first player from an expansion team to reach the milestone and, at the time, the youngest player—he was 23—in NHL history to accomplish the feat.

MacLeish finished with 100 points that season. During the first part of the season, he centered Barber and Dornhoefer. Barber was later moved to the top line with Clarke and Bill Flett, while Lonsberry joined MacLeish's unit.

MacLeish was the NHL's top point producer in the Flyers' playoff runs that culminated with Stanley Cups in 1974 and 1975. In the 1974 playoffs he had 13 goals and 22 points in 17 games, and in the 1975 playoffs he had 11 goals and 20 points.

"He was probably one of the better pressure players the Flyers have ever had," Barber said.

In a 2005 interview with Flyers public relations director Zack Hill, MacLeish recalled being accidentally sliced in the neck by the skate of the Kings' Marcel Dionne during a 1978 game.

ON THIS DATE

APRIL 1, 1973

Rick MacLeish becomes the first Flyer to score 50 goals in a season—and, at the time, the youngest player (23) in NHL history to accomplish the feat.

"It really did not hurt. It just felt like a boot hit me," MacLeish said at the time. "When I skated to the bench, I put my hand up to my neck and my fingers went into my neck. The blood started spurting out, and that is when I realized it was serious. Thank goodness the carotid or jugular was not severed.

"Luckily our team doctor was there. He went out to the bus and got his kit and 180 stitches later I was all sewn up. He started stitching me in the first period and did not finish until the end of the game." [Ed. note: Other accounts say he received 88 stitches.]

After the game, MacLeish said, "We went out for a couple of beers and cigarettes. [Defenseman] Joe Watson said there was some smoke and beer coming out of my neck. I am not sure what it was, but it was definitely something. Around 4:00 AM that morning I woke up, and I was bleeding all over the place because the stitches had broken. We called the team trainer, and he took me to get new stitches."

MacLeish grew up in Cannington, Ontario. He was a racehorse enthusiast, and he owned several of them since purchasing one for $5,000 while a minor leaguer in the Boston Bruins system. After retiring from the NHL, he went into the insurance and financial business and kept involved in the harness racing world.

Watson, a Flyers defenseman during their glory years in the 1970s, said MacLeish was "one of the most naturally skilled players" in Flyers history. He said he'd put him up there with Claude Giroux, Eric Lindros, and Peter Forsberg "in terms of natural skill."

MacLeish was survived by his daughters, his former wife, Carolyn, and his second wife, Charlene. He was the fifth player from the 1974 or 1975 Stanley Cup champions who had died. Barry Ashbee, Wayne Stephenson, Flett, and Lonsberry were the others.

Heading into the 2018–19 season, MacLeish was fourth on the Flyers' all-time list with 697 points and fourth with 50 game-winning goals. He was tied for sixth in franchise history in assists with 369, tied for sixth in games played with 741, second in career hat tricks (12), and sixth in goals with 328.

In the team's playoff history, he was tied for first in goals (53), fourth in assists (52), and fourth in points (105).

When you consider the Flyers have been one of the most successful teams in NHL history in terms of winning percentage since they entered the NHL in 1967, those numbers should merit MacLeish consideration when the Hall of Fame committee meets. He has more goals and points than numerous Hall of Fame forwards, including Clark Gillies, Bobby Bauer, Bob Gainey, Bob Pulford, George Armstrong, and Dickie Moore.

10

BILL BARBER: THE COMPLETE PLAYER

Moments after the Flyers won their first Stanley Cup, an iconic photograph was taken of two grinning players lugging the cherished hardware around the Spectrum ice. There should have been a third.

While Bobby Clarke and Bernie Parent were worthy choices to make the first trip across the rink, an equally important piece of the puzzle was missing.

That was Bill Barber.

In a way, it typified the career-long plight of No. 7, who worked in the shadow of Clarke and Parent for so many years. Not that it seemed to bother him.

He finished his career with 420 goals, a franchise record that remains safely intact to this very day.

Clarke would be the first to tell you the value of Barber to the Flyers' two championships and four trips to the Stanley Cup Final in the space of seven years. According to Clarke, Barber had the tools to be the Flyers' most complete player.

"He had size, he could shoot, think...play the power play, kill penalties," Clarke said. "Also, a real physical player. He's a legitimate Hall of Fame player."

How good was Barber?

In a 1980 Stanley Cup semifinal series win against the Minnesota North Stars, Barber scored an incredible nine goals in just five games. Included in that burst was a four-goal performance in a 5–3 Game 3 Flyer win, meaning that Barber had scored half of the game's entire goal total. Coach Pat Quinn even put Barber on the point during Philadelphia's power play, and he connected for a goal more than once from long distance.

"He could do it all," said teammate Paul Holmgren. "If you needed a guy to play defense for a couple games, he could do that. He was that good."

When Clarke and Barber were united with Reggie Leach to form the LCB line for the 1974–75 season, things really fell into place.

"We had a line of three different kinds of players on it—the LCB line," Barber told James Bisson of *The Score*. "We scored a lot of goals. Reggie was a sniper and a shooter, Clarke did a lot of forechecking and grunt work, and I was the in-between guy where I needed to play some offense and also play defensively, too, which I took pride in. I always wanted to be someone that played both ends of the ice.

"We just seemed to complement one another. We knew where one another were on the ice at all times. We knew how to get open, and when to take a chance, and when not to take a chance. It was definitely a special year for us. In today's game, any line that could put our numbers up would be considered a very, very special line."

Knee problems had dogged Barber as his career advanced, and things finally came to a head in 1984. He needed a major knee construction, and when it was over, so was his career.

With two championships in his pocket and his ticket punched to the Hockey Hall of Fame, Barber had few regrets.

But he did have one. As Holmgren mentioned, coaches had no trouble putting Barber on the point on the power play because if the puck got turned over, he could skate backward well enough to play passable defense. Late in his career, Barber wondered if he might give the back line a shot before he had to call it quits. Maybe that would have prolonged his career.

He did get into a handful of games on defense in the early '80s until some injuries started to pile up.

"The only thing that I wanted to do was to change positions to play longer," Barber told *The Score*. "I grew up a defenseman, and at a young age they moved me up because I was always up ice and didn't get back half the time. I would have loved to have the opportunity to go back and play defense for a couple of years. I did that for Pat Quinn when he was coaching; we had a defense problem, so I ended up playing about seven or eight games as a defenseman.

"I loved it, because you're pretty much out there every second shift. And Quinn would say, 'I don't want you to change—I want you up the ice with the puck. If you get the chance to go, I want you going.' That's the only thing I wish I could have had a shot at; it would have been like being a young kid again, trying to make the team as a defenseman at an older age."

For Barber, it all began back in 1972 when he was drafted seventh overall by the Flyers. He was called up after 11 games in the AHL with the Richmond Robins. In his first season with the Flyers, Barber scored 30 goals and 34 assists and was a contender for the Calder Memorial Trophy for rookie of the year. Some believed Barber was a better choice than New York Rangers freshman Steve Vickers, but the voters didn't see it that way.

Barber scored at least 20 goals every season of his career. His best season was 50 goals and 62 assists in the 1975–76 season. In the Flyers' successful 1974 and 1975 Stanley Cup playoff campaigns, Barber contributed three and six goals, respectively. Barber also contributed another six goals in an unsuccessful 1976 playoff run.

One of his finest moments also came in 1976 at the Canada Cup. Trailing Czechoslovakia in the title game, Canada got a big lift when Barber scored late in the game to send it to overtime, where Canada won.

Clutch situations always seemed to bring out the best in Barber. He finished his career tied with teammate Rick MacLeish for the most playoff goals (53) in team history. Barber was voted into the Hockey Hall of Fame in June 1990 and had his No. 7 retired by the Flyers on October 7, 1990.

Once his playing career ended, Barber got into coaching. He did some coaching with the Hershey Bears in the mid-'80s. His greatest success came in 1998 when he led the Flyers' AHL affiliate, the Philadelphia Phantoms, to the American Hockey League's Calder Cup.

That payday led to Barber taking over as head coach of the Flyers from December 2000 until April 2002, winning the Jack Adams Award for the 2000–01 season.

Barber became director of player personnel with the Tampa Bay Lightning from 2002 to 2008, then he returned to his "home" team, the Flyers, to become a scouting consultant, a position he continues to hold.

SIGN MAN: THOSE SIGNS ARE WORTH A THOUSAND WORDS

There's the signpost up ahead—your next stop: the Dave Leonardi Zone.

For the better part of a half-century, Leonardi, aka "Sign Man," has been inspiring, entertaining, and mystifying Flyers fans with his clever placards. He even takes a bow for coming up with so many of the colorful nicknames that dot the franchise's history, from Bird (Don Saleski) to Rick the Quick (Rick MacLeish).

Sitting behind the opponent's net for the first and third periods of games—first at the Spectrum and later the Wells Fargo Center—Leonardi gets a kick out of making people laugh...often at an opponent's expense.

Signs aimed at Flyers' foes, like "START THE BUS," "NEXT GOALIE," and "INSERT PUCK HERE," (with a downward pointing arrow) are among his favorites.

Leonardi became so famous he's even listed on a Hockey Hall of Fame website called "Legends of Hockey Time Capsule—the '70s" featuring such colorful characters as Don Cherry, Tiger Williams, and former Flyer Cowboy Bill Flett.

Some of his best signs are stuff of legend: "SNAP, CRACKLE, PROPP!" (an homage to Flyer great Brian Propp), "TELL IT TO THE CZAR" (as the Flyers were beating the Soviet Red Army in 1976), and "KERR-PLUNK" (whenever Philadelphia great Tim Kerr notched a particularly pivotal goal).

Leonardi for the Hockey Hall of Fame "sign-makers wing" (if they ever build one)? Why not? Start a petition and sign right here.

"Bill's a charismatic guy," said Holmgren. "He's not at a lot of games live but still has a good handle on players.

"From his coaching days, he has a good eye for what's going on with a team's play. In most cases, you really have to take your coaching glasses off and see the game differently. But Billy seems aware of all of it.... He can wear both at the same time."

Clarke added, "Based on what he's produced on the ice, he's a good hockey personnel evaluator. Don't forget, he was Coach of the Year for the Flyers."

Always a team player, Barber showed his true personality with his comments about his induction into the Hockey Hall of Fame in Toronto, when he spread the credit for his honor.

"It's not so much about scoring goals and the numbers you put up as how you conduct yourself and how you play the game," he said.

"I think that's more important. You have to have a passion to play hockey, and you have to express that passion for the people who come to watch you when you're playing. It's character. It's about being willing to pay the price. I think that's what the Hockey Hall of Fame is all about.

"But I look at it as recognition for all the players on our team who didn't get the recognition—from Bob Kelly to Dave Schultz to Orest Kindrachuk to Gary Dornhoefer and Ross Lonsberry. Without those guys, there was no opportunity for me getting there."

Look around the Internet hard enough and you can find a photograph of Bill Barber holding the Stanley Cup high above his head. It might not be with Bobby and Bernie, but it's deserved nonetheless.

'74 STANLEY CUP CHAMPS: A DAY TO MAKE HISTORY

It was the parade of all parades.

More than two million people showed up to shower affection on a hockey team full of Canadian players, orchestrators of one of the greatest upsets in professional sports history. The Flyers, barely seven years old, had just played David to the Goliath known as the Boston Bruins, winners of two of the four previous Stanley Cups.

It wasn't easy, mind you. After all, the Boston team sported Bobby Orr, arguably the best player of his generation. Then there was high-scoring Phil Esposito and a cast of bruisers that would make any NHL team flinch.

Except maybe the Flyers, who didn't give an inch. Under the guidance of coach Fred Shero, the Flyers were instructed to dump the puck down the ice to the corner patrolled by Orr—a rather blatant attempt to tire out the superstar. And it worked.

The Flyers vanquished the Bruins with a 1–0 decision on the afternoon of Sunday, May 19, 1974, and a couple days later, the party could begin.

What a celebration it was. As the procession made its way down Broad Street, all the conquering heroes were on display—Bobby Clarke, Bill Barber, Bernie Parent, Rick MacLeish, Shero, general manager Keith Allen, and team founder and owner Ed Snider. Confetti flew, the beer flowed, and the whole shebang ended near the Spectrum, where history had been made.

"The parade was unbelievable," said Snider. "I don't think I've ever seen a parade like it since. If it had been in Los Angeles or New York, it would have been national news. In Philly, it was sort of local.

"I remember some reporters commenting that it was that sort of a celebration because nobody had won [anything] in a long time and everybody was so excited, but I saw Flyers T-shirts on everybody on a beautiful May day, and I didn't think in that regard."

If nothing else, the parade proved that there were more hockey fans in Philadelphia than just the 17,000 or so who filled the Spectrum every night.

This was gratifying to Snider, who bristled at the notion that hockey was some sort of niche sport in Philadelphia and other NHL cities.

"The next year we had a parade that was even bigger," Snider said. "Both times they estimated two million people, and they couldn't give that excuse the next time.

"A lot of people think hockey [fans are] a small group of people that are very loyal. But we have almost 20,000 seats, and in many instances four people hold those tickets [for one seat]. We have hundreds of thousands of fans. We know that we are much bigger than the press sometimes gives us credit for."

The successful journey over the hazardous road to the first Cup was an accomplishment worth shouting about.

In those days, there were only two rounds to get to the Final. The Flyers made quick work of the Atlanta Flames in the first round, but then came the New York Rangers. The home team won each of the first four games, with the Flyers winning a pivotal Game 5 in Philadelphia. The Rangers won Game 6 in overtime in New York, but then came Game 7 in Philadelphia.

This contest is remembered for the famous Dave Schultz–Dale Rolfe brawl. Schultz got the jump on the Rangers defenseman and pummeled him while Rolfe's teammates stood idly by.

The Flyers' bench (and the Spectrum crowd) got energized, and the Flyers went on to a 4–1 win.

The Boston Bruins were picked by just about everyone to win the Final.

But Bobby Clarke's famous overtime goal in old Boston Garden on May 9 turned the tide in the Flyers' favor. In the memorable Game 6, Rick MacLeish tipped in a point shot from Andre Dupont, Bernie Parent supplied the acrobatics in goal, and the Flyers had themselves a title.

"What I remember first about that Cup was being afraid of Bobby Orr right to the end," said former player Bill Clement, now a hockey analyst on Flyers' TV broadcasts. "Seeing him every time he was on the ice. Understanding that this could be the time our ship sinks because of Bobby Orr. I still get goosebumps when I think that we defeated a healthy Bobby Orr and the Boston Bruins."

As the game ended, fans rushed on to the ice, sort of preventing the measured "victory lap" celebration of current times.

"We didn't hoist the Cup out there. We didn't get a chance to," Clement said. "Because 300 fans poured onto the ice in Philadelphia.

"It was like a Bobby Orr movie with the curtain finally coming down and 'The End' being flashed across the screen when the final seconds ticked off.

"The last three or four minutes of that game were an eternity."

Barber didn't mind the Bruins having the home-ice advantage or the designation as favorites.

Clearly, the Flyers were on a mission to prove they were worthy of being the first NHL expansion team to win a title.

"We were underdogs," Barber said. "But I think everyone felt we had a chance to beat the Bruins. We didn't say we could beat them, but we felt like we could. From a standpoint of our team, we used everybody. We kept dumping the puck into Orr's corner and making him go back and get it. Maybe the wear and tear got to him a little bit."

Like Clement, Barber wishes the players could have each raised the Cup to the heavens moments after the final horn.

"The unfortunate thing is we didn't have a chance to do what they do today," Barber said. "I remember having the Cup at Mr. Snider's place."

While there was bedlam on the ice, there was relief off it. Snider had to blink once or twice to make sure he wasn't dreaming.

"I can tell you that the tension of a game 1–0 like that, it's pretty amazing," Snider said. "It was like constant tension throughout the game, and the relief when we finally won and when Bobby Orr was called for the penalty [in the last few minutes].... It was mind-boggling that this could really possibly happen.

"The reason it was so mind boggling—we had a good record during the regular season, but Boston, as you know, owned us up until then. The fact that we were able to beat them in six games to me is still the most amazing thing I can remember."

WATSONS: FARM BOYS LIGHT UP THE BIG CITY

It's really cool to win a Stanley Cup or two with teammates you call friends, but how much more special it must be when your brother is on the ice right by your side.

Joe and Jimmy Watson, the pride of Smithers, British Columbia, know the feeling. The two were lucky enough to play on both of the Flyers' Stanley Cup teams in 1973–74 and 1974–75.

Joe was a loud-laughing, rambunctious defenseman who started his career in Boston before joining the Flyers. Jimmy was a bit quieter and went on to become an NHL All-Star backliner.

This twosome was instrumental in Stanley Cup Final series wins over Boston and Buffalo. Later, Joe scored a momentum-changing goal in the Flyers' historic 4–1 win over the Soviet Red Army team in January 1976.

Joe was always looking out for his kid brother, but at some point Jimmy became a star in his own right.

"I know he's always idolized me," Joe once said. "Now I think it's the other way around."

Like Jimmy, Joe won his share of individual awards, too, including the first Barry Ashbee Trophy (1975) for the Flyers' best defenseman. But he said the privilege of playing with his brother through the glory years was a highlight.

"That was very special," Joe said. "Making the NHL, playing in an All-Star game, winning the Stanley Cup, and playing with my brother were all gravy to me. We were only the fourth brother combination in the history of the NHL to play in the NHL and win the Stanley Cup together."

It was after the exhausting series against the Rangers that Snider knew the Flyers had the right stuff.

"Beating the New York Rangers in seven games, which might have been the toughest series I've ever seen, led me to believe that we had a chance," Snider said. "I wasn't optimistic by any stretch of the imagination. I just felt that we were playing so well that we had a chance. With Boston having the home-ice advantage, I didn't think we were going to be able to do it."

Apparently there were other forces at work, like the psychology employed by Shero, who instilled belief in his players while in the back of his mind maybe even he had some doubts.

"That Boston team should've won in four or five games," Parent later admitted to Bill Fleischman of the *Philadelphia Daily News*. "But in life and sports, it doesn't matter what the odds are against you. What matters is what you believe."

Clarke looked at it through a more technical lens.

"We thought we were the better team," Clarke said. "We weren't being arrogant; we felt we were better coached and had better goaltending."

Whatever the case, the victory laid the groundwork for one of hockey's most storied franchises.

Anybody who attended that parade—four times the size of Woodstock—can attest to the recognition of such an accomplishment.

12

GENE HART: THE VOICE

"A man of the arts, a scholarly sort,
Conversant on Pavarotti,
But just as comfortable hanging out,
With guys like Lou Angotti."

Those were some lines from a limerick recited during a eulogy at the memorial service for the late Gene Hart in 1999. With all due respect to Hart, thousands in attendance at the Wells Fargo Center broke up in laughter at how true that description was.

For the Flyers' most famous announcer actually was a man for all seasons. He could be at a theater one night listening to an Italian opera and the next night rubbing elbows in the hockey team's locker room.

Because he started from Day One in 1967 at the now-long-gone Spectrum and because he brought enthusiasm and excitement to fans like no other, he's remembered as the "Voice of the Flyers."

Any doubt about that is erased when you enter the press box at the Wells Fargo Center. Step off the elevator in the Gene Hart Press Box and you are met with a memorial wall replete with photographs in which there might be star players but Hart is actually *the* star.

From his calls of "Score! For a case of Tastykake" (one of the team's long-time television sponsors) to "The Flyers win the Stanley Cup! The Flyers win the Stanley Cup!" Hart's boisterous presence lives on in the hearts, minds, and souls of Flyers fans everywhere.

"There will never be another like him," said veteran radio play-by-play announcer Tim Saunders.

Said former Flyer stalwart and current TV color commentator Bill Clement, "Gene performed. He didn't just do play by play. As a result of his desire to perform, and he seemed to be a born performer, his call was almost theatrical at times.

"And that's what separated him from everybody else. He was literally, and figuratively at times, larger than life because of his call.

"[It was] almost like seeing an actor stealing a show on the stage.... He not only loved what he did but he bled orange and black. Every broadcaster is dedicated to his team, but Gene was able to deliver such theater in his call. That to me is what separated him from most others."

A native of New York City, Hart and his journey to the Hockey Hall of Fame began in rather humble surroundings. In his youth, Hart and his family moved to South Jersey where Gene attended Pleasantville High School and later received a Bachelor of Arts degree in education from Trenton State College. After a stint in the military, he began officiating high school basketball, football, and baseball games.

Gene's big break came when Atlantic City High School radio broadcaster Ralph Glenn's partner failed to show up for work. Glenn enlisted Hart to help him out with a game in Trenton.

A booming voice and a hearty laugh quickly won over listeners, and Hart was on his way over the airwaves, at least as an avocation. That's because Hart had already started a teaching career, mainly high school history.

Then along came word of an expansion National Hockey League franchise possibly coming to Philadelphia. Gene thought, "What the heck," and submitted some recording tapes.

According to Flyers historians, the team couldn't afford a pricey Canadian broadcaster, so they brought Hart on board. He thought he would only stick it out for a year or two but ended up calling games for the next 29 years.

One of the game's broadcasting pioneers, Foster Hewitt, had a big influence on Hart, whose ability to raise the pitch of his voice a notch endeared him to hockey fans throughout the Delaware Valley.

Ron Hextall, widely considered the second-best goaltender in Flyers history behind only legendary Bernie Parent, said Hart made a connection not only with the fans but the players as well.

In fact, Hart was the one who really put the bully in Broad Street Bullies.

"Gene meant a lot," said Hextall, the Flyers former general manager. "He was essentially the link between us and our fans. I think Gene's passion for the Flyers and the game came through every night.

"There wasn't a night when you listened and didn't think he was excited about the game. I think that reverberates around to the fans and the hockey world. It was an exciting game when Gene was calling."

Hart was at the microphone for more than 2,000 games, and you would have been hard pressed to find a single clunker in the bunch.

"By being there at the start, Gene was there at the right time," Clement said. "The first 10 years, they were beleaguered at the start, getting pushed around. And then Keith [Allen, former GM who built the two Stanley Cup champions] fixed that and made them a more robust team, and Gene kind of played into that.

"It was almost as if his bravado as a play-by-play guy mirrored the bravado that the Broad Street Bullies lived with most of the time. I think he reveled in being part of Public Enemy No. 1, who also became champions twice.

"Just as none of the players felt less than a champion or guilty or inferior because people accused us of winning by how we played, Gene wasn't apologetic at all."

From a technical standpoint, Hart taught himself the game, and by the time the Flyers won their first Stanley Cup in 1974, he was proficient at analyzing the sport. Later, when former goaltender Bobby Taylor became his sidekick, the two developed a special chemistry filled with wit, sarcasm, and pinpoint observations.

"The thing that I think about when I think of Gene is he was such a great storyteller," Saunders said.

Being that "man of the arts" is what separated him from much of the hockey culture. And the teaching aspect came into play because, in a sense, he was teaching his listeners about the emotion of the game.

"He was a little different from the rest of us in that way better educated," Saunders said. "Perhaps better rounded in a lot of ways socially. When some of us would go sit in a bar, he would go sit at the opera."

At big events, like number retirement ceremonies, Hart came decked out in the finest tuxedo. And that's when he was at his very best.

"The words that came out of his mouth, they kind of resonated," recalled Mark Howe. "And they were right from his heart. Actually

FROM GENE HART TO JIM JACKSON, FLYERS BROADCASTERS KEEP FANS IN THE GAME

The beloved Gene Hart will always be known as the Voice of the Flyers.

Inducted into the Hockey Hall of Fame in 1997, he broadcast Flyers games on radio or TV—sometimes he did both in a simulcast—from 1967 to 1995. Not only did he bring unbridled excitement to his broadcasts (he shoots...he SCORES!!!!), but he was a teacher. When the expansion Flyers joined the league in 1967–68, he taught the nuances of the game to the fans in a friendly manner that was never condescending to the listener or viewer.

"Gene Hart was the Flyers' ambassador of hockey," club chairman Ed Snider said after Hart died in 1999. "He had the unique ability to explain and teach without offending those who already understood."

Hart broadcast Flyers games for 29 years. Jim Jackson joined the Flyers in 1993–94 and did two years of radio while Hart was doing TV. They traveled together, and Jackson said "[I] tried to sponge whatever I could from him because obviously he was one of the greats." Jim Jackson did his 25th year during the 2018–19 season.

Here are the Flyers' broadcasters over the years, according to the team:

TV play-by-play: Stu Nahan and Hart (1967–68); Nahan (1968–71); Bill White (1970–71, six games on WPVI Channel 6); Pat Shetler (1971–72); Hart and Don Earle (1971–77); Hugh Gannon on PRISM (1976–1980); Hart (1977–88); Don Tollefson (1982–84, six games on WPVI Channel 6); Mike "Doc" Emrick (1980–83 on PRISM and 1988–93); Hart (1992–95); and Jackson (1995–present).

Color commentary on TV: Larry Zeidel (1971–72); Bobby Taylor (1976–89); Bill Clement (1989–92); Gary Dornhoefer (1992–2006); Steve Coates (1999–2014, in-booth and rinkside analyst); Keith Jones (2006–present); Bill Clement (2007–present); and Chris Therien (2014–18, rinkside analyst).

The radio play-by-play announcers started with Nahan and Hart in 1967–68 and later included Hart and Earle (1971–77); Ralph Lawler (1976–77); Hart (1977–92); Emrick (1992–93); Jackson (1993–95); Steve Carroll (1995–96); John Wiedeman (1996–97); and Tim Saunders (1997–present).

Color commentary on radio: Taylor (1976–92); Coates (1992–99); Brian Propp (1999–2008); Therien (2008–14); and Coates (2014–present).

when I got into the Flyers' Hall of Fame and had my jersey retired, the only thing I wished would have been different on those nights was I wish Gene Hart would have been there. No disrespect to Lou [Nolan, longtime public address announcer], but that's how much I admired Gene and the way he spoke."

At speaking engagements, Hart could bring down the house.

"It's easy to find Bob Kelly's name on the Stanley Cup," Hart would crow. "It's the one written in crayon."

But in quieter times, Hart would keep his mind razor sharp.

"There was a lot more culture to his life than the typical hockey figure," Howe said. "My dad [Gordie, aka, Mr. Hockey] used to do crossword puzzles. I picked up doing crossword puzzles from him. Gene always did puzzles. So I either did the *USA Today*, the *Inquirer*, or the *Daily News*. Those were at least somewhat doable for me. Gene always did the *New York Times*.

"The amazing thing is, we would get on a bus and he would give it to me, and if I got 10, it was a good day. He would take it and in 10 minutes have it done."

The 1974–75 Flyers were the last All-Canadian player roster to win the Stanley Cup.

The "24th" player on that team was American Gene Hart.

"He was infectious in terms of how relaxed he was and how comfortable he was in front of the mike," Hextall said. "He made players feel more comfortable than they typically would be.

"If you do an interview with someone who's a little bit stiff or isn't real personable, it's kind of hard. You see guys come from different countries, they're not real comfortable with the language, and all of a sudden Gene made them feel comfortable.

"I think certainly Gene was one of the greatest hockey announcers of all time."

Play-by-play veterans like Saunders can only stand back and admire Hart's work.

"Maybe because I knew what he meant to this market, he had Hall of Fame written all over him," said Saunders.

"All of us, whether it's in play-by-play or color, know he's always going to be the voice of this team, no matter who follows him."

Hart may have had a bigger-than-life personality, but he always took time to help others.

"He was nothing but gracious to me," said Saunders, who arrived in Philadelphia in the early '90s. "And that meant a lot. I was nervous about starting my first NHL job, and he couldn't have been more helpful. So I think highly of him personally because of those exchanges."

Clement, like fans and players alike, loved Hart's style.

"While other play-by-play guys after him tried to emulate him, they had to contrive a lot of it," Clement said. "For Gene, it was just an extension of his everyday personality. [He was] loud, craved being the center of attention. If he didn't have an audience, he would create one and just by virtue of his personality."

Even the story about how Gene met his wife, Sarah, seems larger than life. It seems a much slimmer Gene was working at the Steel Pier in Atlantic City as part of a water show featuring the Binswanger Bathing Beauties back in the '50s. A fellow performer, Sarah Detwiler, had recently arrived from Florida to climb aboard the famous 40-foot horse dive into a large tank of water. As it turns out, her father had been a U.S. cavalryman so she was no stranger to horses.

Most of the performers knew each other, and Gene was taken by Sarah's beauty and bravado. Love was in the air at the ocean end of the Steel Pier, as well as great camaraderie among performers, who seized the crowd's attention with jaw-dropping stunts.

Little did Sarah know she was about to get involved with a future broadcasting legend. But if you're brave enough to jump off a 40-foot diving board on the back of a horse, then hitching up to a guy who would get to know Pavarotti and Lou Angotti down the road certainly wouldn't seem all that daunting.

13

DAVE SCHULTZ: GENTLE OFF THE ICE, A HAMMER ON IT

Dave Schultz has owned a limousine company, managed a skating rink, written a book, coached in the low minors, sold electricity, done some motivational public speaking, and dabbled as a stand-up comedian. But to millions of hockey fans, Schultz will always be "The Hammer," the one-time NHL bad boy who became one of the faces of the Broad Street Bullies, the dominating Flyers teams of the 1970s. Today, the most feared enforcer of his generation sells electricity to businesses.

"Ever since deregulation came in about 10 years ago, everybody can choose whether they want to be with their utility company," said Schultz, who lives near the Jersey Shore in Somers Point. "It's worked out well for me."

He is also an ambassador for the Flyers, doing public-relations work before and during home games along with former stars like Bernie Parent and Brian Propp.

"I love it," he said early in the 2018–19 season. "People will have groups at birthday parties and different events, and we do a lot of talking."

Schultz doesn't watch many road games. Today's game is about speed and finesse and doesn't have as much physicality or the checking that were a big part of the NHL when Schultz played. There also is not nearly as much fighting. In fact, the Flyers didn't have a fight until their 21st game in 2018–19, which was their longest stretch to start a season without a fight in franchise history.

"It's a different game," Schultz said.

Schultz enjoys the speed and skill of today's game, but he misses the body checking.

"Who doesn't like hitting?" he asked. "It's a physical sport, or at least it was, but they changed it. Everything is geared to the rules. Look at the rules from when I played to now; it's like night and day. I can see [reducing the] fighting.... But when the league changed some rules, they changed the whole game. The league controls the play; they do the suspensions. I don't even know what the referees do out there now."

* * *

When the soft-spoken Schultz went into the Flyers' Hall of Fame in 2009, he thanked the fans, the people in his life, and all those connected with the organization.

He had special words for his mom in Saskatoon, Saskatchewan.

"She would say to me, 'Dave, do you have to fight so much? I'm afraid you are going to get hurt.'"

The fans laughed.

Schultz, of course, was the one who inflicted most of the pain. He was the ringleader of the Broad Street Bullies, a brawling group. They also had players like Bernie Parent, Bobby Clarke, Bill Barber, Rick MacLeish, Reggie Leach, and others—highly skilled players who were among the game's elite.

Parent, Clarke, and Barber are in the Hockey Hall of Fame, as are the general manger (Keith Allen) and the coach (Fred Shero) of those powerhouse teams of the 1970s.

Shero was "the major reason I was able to do what I did," Schultz said in his acceptance speech. "He recognized something in me. He encouraged me, he guided me. He taught me the importance of the team, and to care about my team and my teammates."

Schultz was more than an enforcer. He scored 20 goals in the 1973–74 season, was a responsible defensive player, and had a knack for depositing key playoff tallies. In addition, he gave the Flyers courage on the road—and he packed opposing arenas because he made his team Public Enemy No. 1.

The Flyers seemed to thrive off that reputation.

When he was inducted into the Flyers' Hall of Fame, Schultz saluted his teammates, "particularly my linemates, Orest Kindrachuk and Don Saleski, and Bob Kelly, my partner in crime and great friend, who helped us become the toughest team in the National Hockey League. Together we proved toughness and hard work, complemented by great talent, was the key for success. So I thank all of my teammates for all of their great memories."

The Flyers won consecutive Stanley Cups in 1974 and 1975.

"I thank Mr. Ed Snider for his phenomenal leadership and allowing me to come back to the Flyers organization forever," Schultz said.

He later thanked executives Peter Luukko and John Page and the Flyers organization, with special thanks to Joe Kadlec, the team's public-relations director when Schultz played.

BLADON: EIGHT IS ENOUGH FOR "BOMBER"

Hall of Fame defenseman Paul Coffey once registered eight points in a game, but six of those were assists.

Bobby Orr, generally acknowledged as the greatest defenseman of all time, once compiled a seven-point game, but only three of those points came by way of goals.

So for many, the honor of the greatest one-game offensive display by an NHL defenseman goes to Flyers backliner Tom Bladon, who notched four goals on the way to an eight-point night against the long-forgotten Cleveland Barons on December 11, 1977.

Bladon, nicknamed "Bomber" because of his booming shot from the point, was a record-breaking plus-10 in an 11–1 victory over the Barons. At the time, he was only the fourth NHL player to achieve the milestone of eight points in one game.

Bladon played on both Flyers' Stanley Cup championship teams (1973–74 and 1974–75), often paired with Andre "Moose" Dupont.

Although he was considered the most offense-minded defenseman on the Flyers' title teams, Bladon often was cast as a defense specialist in certain situations.

It should be noted Bladon finished the 1977–78 season with 11 goals and 35 points, so he actually produced nearly a quarter of his season total in one night against the Barons.

Bladon's record performance came in his final year with the Flyers. He would go on to play for Pittsburgh, Edmonton, Winnipeg, and Detroit before heading into retirement. He was never able to come close to duplicating that one great night...but what a night it was.

Schultz thanked his three sisters—Barb, Janet, and Glenda—who traveled from western Canada to attend the event, and "my two wonderful sons, Chad and Brett, and their wonderful mother, Cathy, who all live in the Philadelphia area and love this place as much as I do.

"And to two special family members. My dad came here at the start of the '74 and '75 playoffs, and he never left until we carried the Stanley Cup down Broad Street. And to my brother, Ray, who loved Philadelphia as he was a member of the championship Philadelphia

One of hockey's greatest-ever enforcers, Dave Schultz still holds the NHL record for penalty minutes in a single season, with 472.

Firebirds. Although my Dad and Ray are no longer with us, I know they are looking down on us and smiling tonight."

Schultz, who averaged 13 goals per season in his four years with the Flyers, was showing an emotional, caring side of himself that seemed unimaginable when he was causing havoc on the ice and sitting in penalty boxes in the 1970s.

"But most of all, thank you to the fans," he said. "Philadelphia Flyers fans are the greatest! I love you all! I never had a bad day in Philadelphia. Flyers fans have always been absolutely wonderful and caring.

"Coach Fred Shero wrote on May 19, 1974, 'Win today and we'll walk together forever.' At the time, he was talking about my teammates and I. But I realize now that he was talking about all of us.

"Thank you for this great honor. For me, this is as good as it gets."

By today's NHL standards, Schultz wasn't gigantic. He was a solidly built, 6'1", 190-pound winger who was one of the most intimidating players in NHL history. He won most of his fights—and there were plenty of them—and led the league in penalty minutes in each of his first three seasons, including a record 472 minutes in 1974–75.

That's a record that may never be broken.

In a 2017 interview with the *Philadelphia Inquirer*, Schultz said he "never had a fight in my life off the ice. If anybody bothered me back in my hometown, I'd get my big brother to take care of the guy."

In junior hockey, he said, he was a "chicken" and that if he wasn't on the bench when a brawl started, "I went there. I was such a little pipsqueak chicken and intimidated."

Things changed after the Flyers selected him in the fifth round of the 1969 draft, shortly after the Flyers were physically intimidated by the St. Louis Blues in the playoffs and Snider vowed it would never happen again.

"I went to the Eastern Hockey League, the Salem [Virginia] Rebels. I got in a fight my first game and my second game, and my whole life changed," he said. "That wasn't my reason for doing it, just so I could make the NHL or stay there. I don't know that any player knows he can play in the NHL other than a star. It was a role that developed over a few years in the minors."

Schultz said he would go to sleep on the afternoon of a game thinking about getting into a fight several hours later, picturing it, and that night it would happen. "Some of those guys didn't know I'd beat the hell out of them that afternoon a number of times in my head," he said.

When he got to the NHL for good in 1972–73, it was a league where the rules made it easy for enforcers to go after a star player and take him to the penalty box. That was a win for the enforcer's team.

Schultz—who is hoping a screenplay about his life that was written by his son, Chad, is turned into a movie—had lots of wins for the Flyers during his 297 games in Philadelphia. He even had a hit song, "The Penalty Box," which he recorded in the mid-1970s during the height of Flyers mania.

"I listen to it every morning," a smiling Schultz cracked during the 2018–19 season. "No, I'm kidding. I can't believe I did it, really. I couldn't sing for s--t."

Singing didn't make him a Philly sports icon. Playing his role to perfection and helping deliver two Stanley Cups did.

14

BARRY ASHBEE: AN INSPIRATION FOR ALL

There is only one retired number hanging from the Wells Fargo Center rafters that does not belong to a Hall of Famer. Coincidentally, that player's photograph was the only one to ever adorn the walls of Flyers senior vice president Bob Clarke's office. In many ways, Barry Ashbee represents what all Flyers want to be, both on and off the ice.

The defenseman, who starred for the Flyers in the early '70s before losing his sight in one eye and later succumbing to leukemia at a tragically early age, was a pillar of strength in game action and an even braver man in everyday life.

His No. 4 floats proudly above the Wells Fargo Center ice surface, right alongside legends like Parent, Howe, Barber, Clarke, and Lindros.

Today, more than 40 years after Ashbee's passing, Clarke still speaks of him in a reverent tone. To a young Clarke, Ashbee provided inspiration.

Clarke would go on to win the Hart Trophy (NHL's most valuable player) three times and become a first-ballot Hall of Famer.

"Barry was extremely special," Clarke said. "A tough hockey player, but a really decent, honest man."

It seemed like Ashbee was destined to play for the Philadelphia Flyers as far back as his junior years when he played for the Barrie Flyers of the Ontario Hockey League. He spent nearly 10 years in the Boston Bruins organization—most of it in the minor leagues—getting a small taste of NHL action (14 games) in the 1965–66 season.

Ashbee experienced great success in the minors, playing for the Hershey Bears of the American Hockey League. He was named a co-captain, and the team won the Calder Cup for the 1968–69 season.

The one bit of bad luck came when he suffered a serious back injury, which caused him to miss the entire 1966–67 season. That problem still nagged him to the point where he was not selected in the 1967 NHL Expansion Draft.

This didn't deter Flyers general manager Keith Allen from adding him to Philadelphia's roster, which he did in a May 22, 1970, trade with the Bruins for Darryl Edestrand and Larry McKillop.

Upon Ashbee's arrival in Philadelphia, everything was not exactly rosy. Ashbee could not believe how uninspired some players were and he contemplated retirement.

All that changed when coach Fred Shero rode into town.

When Shero detected a player wasn't fully committed, he would call Allen and that player would soon be wearing a different color uniform.

Shero knew Ashbee wasn't one of those malingering types.

"I remember saying [in the locker room] my first season, 'We have nineteen chickens on one team.' I was just trying to get them ready for the game, but Ashbee took it personally. He wanted me to name names," Shero recalled.

Shero assured Ashbee that he was not among the "chickens."

At only 5'10" and 180 pounds, Ashbee couldn't barrel over opposing forwards, but he did neutralize their effectiveness by way of a good stick and outstanding positioning. And he was a consistent playmaker, just what the Flyers needed on a team with light-scoring defensemen like Andre Dupont, Joe Watson, and Ed Van Impe.

In fact, during the first round of the 1972–73 playoffs against Minnesota, Ashbee tied a record for NHL defensemen by recording three assists in one period.

But it wasn't until the following season that Ashbee showed some of his legendary courage. Playing with a chipped vertebrae in his neck, Ashbee led the entire team with a plus-52 rating. Opposing fans would make fun of the horse-collar neck brace Ashbee had to wear, but he usually got the last laugh.

The Flyers barreled into the playoffs on a high, and things looked promising as they reached the Eastern Conference Final.

Then something happened to Ashbee that even he couldn't battle through.

On April 28, 1974, a puck off the stick of Ranger defenseman Dale Rolfe struck Ashbee in his eye, eventually causing permanent blindness, which effectively ended his career.

ON THIS DATE

MAY 19, 1974

The Flyers become the first expansion team to win the Stanley Cup—in just their seventh season in the league. Rick MacLeish scores the lone goal and Bernie Parent is flawless as the Flyers defeat Boston in Game 6 1-0 to capture the Cup at the reverberating Spectrum.

The Flyers used Ashbee's misfortune for motivation and beat Boston for the Stanley Cup. That got Barry's name onto the Cup, but it was small consolation. He was forced to retire.

A year later, the Flyers offered Ashbee an assistant coaching job, which at first he was reluctant to take because he didn't want to be the object of sympathy. However, he finally acquiesced, and his former teammates were pleased. When the Flyers beat the Buffalo Sabres in the Cup Final in 1975, Ashebee got his name on the trophy a second time.

That, however, would be the only year Ashbee would coach. There were dark clouds on the horizon. Yet those who kept expressing sorrow were quickly admonished.

"Some people strive for sixty years and never make it," Ashbee told the press. "I got what I wanted [the Stanley Cup] when I was thirty-four."

In April 1977, Ashbee wasn't feeling well and went in for a physical examination. Doctors told him he had leukemia. He died the following month.

Ashbee's passing sent shockwaves through the Philadelphia hockey community. There was a visible outpouring of grief.

Clarke went so far as to tell team owner Ed Snider that after an early-round elimination from the playoffs at the hands of the Boston Bruins, the players had competed below par because they felt so badly for Ashbee's family. Snider refuted that and told Clarke in so many words that to blame Ashbee's plight as a distraction was disrespectful to the player.

That same year, the Flyers Wives' Fight for Lives Carnival was begun, with the spirit of Barry Ashbee as an inspirational force.

Also, the Barry Ashbee Trophy was created and awarded to the best Flyers defenseman at the end of each season. It's a tradition that carries on to this day.

Ashbee's bravery had a profound effect on all the players who competed on those 1970s teams.

The Carnival has evolved and now helps not only those in need of medical care but also people in need of housing and other things. More than $27 million has been raised for the cause.

Clarke was at the first carnival as a player and still stops in from time to time. When asked to provide a memory that would encapsulate Ashbee's character and personality, Clarke pauses for a moment.

"It was early in my career and I was playing quite a bit," Clarke said. "Freddy [Shero] was coaching, and we were just starting to become a good team.

"So Freddy lines everybody up on the goal line and we're skating up and back, up and back. He comes over and says, 'Clarke, off the ice, you played a lot the last game. And then so-and-so, you go off.

"He gets to Ashbee and tells him to get off. Ashbee says, 'I'm not leaving.' Freddy goes, 'You played 25 minutes the last game, get off the ice.'"

Here's where Ashbee's true colors came out.

Clarke recalled, "Ashbee said, 'No way, Freddy. As long as my teammates have to skate, I can skate!' I'm stayin'.

"I was 20 years old. It's something I will never forget.

"He was absolutely right. We're a team. I learned something that day. Just a special man."

Anyone who needs to be reminded of that just has to stand on the floor of the Wells Fargo Center and look up.

The proof is there for all to see.

15

PUBLIC-ADDRESS ANNOUNCER LOU NOLAN: A PHILLY SPORTS LEGEND

When you think of people with long associations to Philadelphia sports teams, you may think of Connie Mack, who managed the old Philadelphia Athletics for 50 years. Or perhaps you think of Rich Ashburn, Merrill Reese, Harvey Pollack, Dave Zinkoff, or maybe someone else.

But no one except Lou Nolan can say that he was with the Philadelphia Flyers when they started in 1967...and he's *still* there.

Nolan has been with the Flyers from the beginning, first working alongside public-relations director Joe Kadlec, and then becoming the Flyers' public-address announcer in 1972.

A consummate professional who doesn't take himself too seriously—the Groucho Marx "costumes" he gave to coworkers on Halloween were so popular that a player once wore one in the penalty box while the game was being played—Nolan was given a special achievement award by the Philadelphia Sports Writers Association in 2018 for becoming a true Philadelphia sports icon.

For a lot of years, selling securities to banks has been Nolan's primary job, but not his most rewarding one. That distinction belongs to his work at a rinkside seat near the sometimes-chaotic penalty boxes, first at the Spectrum and then at the Wells Fargo Center.

"It's been fulfilling, exhilarating, and unpredictable," Nolan said.

In 1972, during his first game as public-address announcer, Nolan was sitting between two players who went to the Spectrum penalty box during a preseason contest. The players were yapping at each other when, suddenly, the visiting player picked up a bucket of ice and heaved it at Flyers winger Bob Kelly. The ice never reached the player they called "Hound." Instead, it bounced off the side of Nolan's head and drenched his sport coat as the fans sitting behind him let out a collective roar.

Welcome to the NHL, Lou.

ON THIS DATE
──────────────────
JUNE 5, 1967

The NHL announces that the Flyers are one of six expansion franchises awarded, doubling the size of the league.

"In a way, it was my baptism to the NHL. Instead of holy water, I got christened with ice water," Nolan cracked. "Hey, just part of the job—and part of what has been an incredible journey."

"A lot of crazy stuff has happened down there. The first several years I did it, there was no glass around the box and you would get hit with pucks and sticks all the time. I was getting dinked. I remember Bob Kelly saying to me once, 'Louie, I'm gonna put somebody in your lap today.'"

Sure enough, Kelly checked a player over the boards and into Nolan's lap. "All the scoreboard buttons went off, and the scoreboard went crazy."

Nolan has been there for all the great moments in Flyers history: eight trips to the Stanley Cup Final, consecutive championships in 1974 and 1975, an epic win over the Soviet Red Army team, and key games in the remarkable 35-game unbeaten streak in 1979–80.

"I've been fortunate. Very, very fortunate," Nolan said.

Actually, it's the fans who have been fortunate—fortunate to have Nolan's classy, distinctive voice for parts of five decades.

Nolan's signature call—"The Flyers are going on the PECOOOOOOOOOOOOO power play!"—has been repeated by announcing wannabes from Cape May to Conshohocken...and everywhere in between. (PECO is an energy company.) Fans love imitating Nolan, which, of course, is the greatest form of flattery.

Even on the rare times when Nolan had to scold fans, they understood.

One scolding occurred during a 2016 playoff game against Washington at the Wells Fargo Center. It was the Flyers' first game after owner Ed Snider had died, and there was an emotional pregame

Public-address announcer Lou Nolan, who has worked for the Flyers since their inception in 1967–68, was in the Christmas spirit during a game around the holidays.

tribute. Fans were given light-up bracelets, which were used as part of the celebration of Snider's remarkable life.

The Flyers lost the game 6–1 and fell into a 3–0 series hole. Five of the Capitals' six goals were scored on the power play.

Late in the game, with the Flyers facing a 4–1 deficit and the fans unhappy with penalties that were assessed after a brawl, there were perhaps 100 bracelets that were thrown onto the ice.

"Show class," Nolan said over the public-address system. "The next one who does it will cause us a minor penalty. Do not do it!"

Less than three minutes later, the Capitals' Alex Ovechkin scored a power-play goal with 5:02 left in the game. More bracelets were thrown. A delay-of-game penalty was assessed on the fans.

"Way to go!" Nolan sarcastically announced.

The Flyers won the next two games, getting to within 3–2 in the series. For Game 6 at the Wells Fargo Center, fans were given orange T-shirts with a caricature of Nolan on the front and the words, "Stay Classy, Philly!"

"At first I was a little embarrassed when I heard about the shirts, but I was honored they did it," he said.

The night the bracelets were thrown, Nolan said he was "especially aggravated because it came on a night that Ed Snider was honored.... But again, it was less than one half of one percent who threw them."

* * *

Nolan is a true Philadelphian. He grew up in a row home in southwest Philly and attended West Catholic. He and his family spend a good part of the summers at their home at the Jersey Shore in Ocean City, New Jersey.

It was down the shore, in Margate, that Nolan met Joe Kadlec, who had been working in the *Daily News* sports department before being hired as the Flyers' first public-relations director in 1967. Kadlec and Nolan were introduced by some mutual friends in Margate.

In *If These Walls Could Talk: Philadelphia Flyers*, Nolan said, "It's strange how your life can take a turn by fate." Nolan said he and Kadlec "were young, single, and carefree, and we partied and chased women together."

After Kadlec got the Flyers job, Nolan told him he was a big hockey fan and had followed the old Philadelphia Ramblers and the NHL's Original Six teams. Nolan ended up getting hired by the Flyers and assisting Kadlec in the public-relations department.

During the team's first five seasons, men like Gene Hart, Marv Bachrad, Eddie Ferenz, and Kevin Johnson did some public-address announcing. When Johnson left the Flyers to become the public-relations director of the Philadelphia Blazers in the World Hockey Association, Nolan got the public-address announcer's job. The rest, as they say, is history.

Entering the 2018–19 season, Nolan was the last person left who was with the club continuously from its inception in 1967.

"I've never tried to be a cheerleader," Nolan said. "The players are the show."

Nolan is to the Flyers what Bob Sheppard was to the Yankees—a man with a booming, no-frills voice that echoes in your mind.

The venerable Nolan isn't always recognized by his face. But once he starts talking....

"They usually give me an eye and tell them I remind them of somebody," he said. "Or they'll say, 'I know that voice from somewhere.'"

There is a rhythmic cadence to his dignified scoring announcements—and they are done in an enthusiastic but professional manner. His most famous scoring summary was in Game 6 of the 1974 Stanley Cup Final at the Spectrum: "Flyers goal scored by No. 19, Rick MacLeish. Assist, No. 6, Andre Dupont."

It was the only goal scored as the Flyers defeated the heavily favored Boston Bruins 1–0 and won their first Stanley Cup.

"It was the biggest goal in Flyers history at that point," Nolan said. And it probably still is.

16

'75 STANLEY CUP CHAMPS: RETURN TO GLORY

If people have only foggy recollections of Game 3 of the 1975 Stanley Cup Final, there's a good reason.

It's because much of the game was played in exactly that: fog. With the temperature outside of Buffalo's Memorial Auditorium over 80 and the thermometer close to the ice surface approaching 90, the 35-year-old building's air conditioning never had a chance.

During the game, a scene unfolded that resembled something out of Jack the Ripper prowling the streets of London at night.

Officials instructed the Flyers and Sabres to skate around in circles with hopes of getting the fog to dissipate. It was a losing battle. Play had to be stopped on five different occasions in regulation time and seven more instances in overtime before the Sabres finally prevailed 5–4 on a Rene Robert goal past goaltender Bernie Parent at 18:29.

Bernie said it was so foggy he never saw the shot.

That cut the Flyers' lead in the series to 2–1. But Philadelphia eventually would prevail in the series, winning in six games for their second consecutive Stanley Cup.

In the clinching Game 6 at Buffalo, Bob Kelly scored the first goal of the game, and Bill Clement added an empty-net tally in the closing seconds for a 2–0 victory.

Parent thus recorded shutout wins in both Cup-clinching games, having blanked Boston the previous year in Game 6 at 1–0.

Unlike the previous year, when the Bruins were heavy favorites to win the Cup, this time the Flyers were the odds-on pick. So it was just a matter of sticking to the game plan and not letting the Sabres cast any doubt on what the outcome should be.

Bill Barber said the Flyers were supremely confident that season, right from the start of training camp.

"I don't think there was a question from the time the puck was dropped on opening night at the beginning of the year," Barber said. "No question. We had the experience of getting into the big game."

They once made a movie called *Kelly's Heroes*, and they could have made a sequel called *Kelly the Hero* because that's what he was in Game 6.

Kelly recalls that the deciding goal was the result of the hard work he put in during Coach Fred Shero's practices. First, he was inspired by all the people who doubted the Flyers could win a second straight championship.

"Everyone kept saying the first Cup was a fluke and we still had to prove ourselves. But we believed in ourselves," said Kelly.

Kelly and his teammates kept their eyes on the prize throughout the campaign and, once again, had a lot of fun along the way.

One of Shero's offbeat practice drills was to have his players take the puck behind the net, swing out quickly in front, and try to score. The winner received a $5 prize.

That particular exercise would pay off in Game 6. The game was scoreless going into the third period when Kelly struck.

Kelly stole the puck from towering defenseman Jerry Korab behind the Sabres' net and jammed the puck free. Swooping out in front of the net, he sent a shot past a startled Roger Crozier, the Buffalo goalie, for the most memorable goal of his career.

Grinning ear to ear and accepting hugs from his teammates, Kelly skated over to the bench and yelled, "Hey, Freddy, that's five bucks you owe me."

Then it was Clement's turn to score the goal of his career.

"It's just such an incredible feeling to be able to think back about it and say I helped," Clement said. "I think that's the reason we were so great because as a team, no one thought that they were responsible for any of the wins. I think every single player just wanted to help.

"It was sort of validation or confirmation, at least in that series, in that game, in that moment, I helped. That's all I wanted to do—help, not hurt. I wanted to leave more positive out there than negative."

Clement would be traded to Washington after that season and never really came close to that big of a stage again. But he has memories from that one game that will last forever.

"For me, it was when it happened and thinking back... I was just lucky enough to be in the right place at the right time," Clement said.

ON THIS DATE

MAY 27, 1975

The Flyers win their second straight Stanley Cup as Bernie Parent blanks the Sabres 2–0 in Game 6 in Buffalo. Parent becomes the first player in NHL history to win the Conn Smythe Trophy (playoff MVP) in back-to-back years. Bob Kelly's goal, scored 11 seconds into the third period, snapped a scoreless tie and proved to be the Cup winner.

"Nobody ever knows when their number is going to be called or when it's going to be their turn that they can get something done. There are as many guys who don't succeed as do succeed. I've often wondered, Why was it my turn? Why did I get that opportunity and why did it work out as opposed to shooting wide and having them go down and tie the game? I don't have the answer for that, but I just feel extremely lucky."

As difficult as it was to put the Sabres away, just getting past the New York Islanders in the conference finals may have been even tougher.

The Flyers made quick work of Toronto in the opening round of the playoffs, sweeping the Maple Leafs in four straight, outscoring them by a 15–6 margin.

Then came the Islanders, who had become just the second team in NHL history to overcome a 3–0 deficit to win a best-of-seven series when they rallied to stun the Pittsburgh Penguins with four straight victories.

Who could have guessed the Islanders would nearly repeat the feat in the conference finals?

The Flyers dashed to a 3–0 lead in the series, only to watch the Islanders win three straight games of their own, forcing a Game 7 back at the Spectrum.

However, the Flyers dominated in that deciding game, eventually winning by a 4–1 margin.

Those Broad Street Bullies were a fun-loving bunch, and they still have a few chuckles over that infamous Fog Game.

Before the fog formed, the Flyers and Sabres had to deal with a stray bat flying around the rink. That's right—one of those scary-looking winged mammals that are usually associated with Halloween more than hockey games.

It seems this particular bat resided in the Memorial Auditorium's rafters. It apparently decided to fly down and circle just above the ice in an attempt to cool off from the steamy air near the ceiling of the building.

Only one problem: Buffalo's Jim Lorenz got tired of this funny business and, using his hockey stick, swatted the pesky varmint out of the air, bringing a halt to the proceedings. The Flyers' Rick MacLeish then took off his glove, plucked the dead animal from the ice, skated over, and deposited it in the penalty box. Several players cautioned him that he probably shouldn't have touched the bat because they often are afflicted with rabies.

"What are rabies?" MacLeish asked.

As for the end of the game, the play became almost comical. It was difficult to see from one end of the ice to the other, and this obviously influenced Robert's winning shot in overtime.

"I saw Robert's shot too late for me to come out and stop it," Parent said. "I'm surprised the overtime took so long. It was hard to see the puck from the red line. If three men came down and one made a good pass from the red line, you couldn't see the puck. A good shot from the red line could have won it."

Robert said he wasn't even trying to score when he took the shot.

"It's almost impossible to score from that angle," Robert said. "But I shot at the net, hoping somebody could get the rebound. It seemed to me [Parent] wasn't ready for the shot. It went between his legs."

But for the Flyers, who eventually came home to Philadelphia to another parade with some two million well-wishers, all's well that ends well.

17

SOVIET RED ARMY GAME: FREE-WORLD HEROES

Everyone is familiar with the Cold War, the intercontinental ballistic missile crisis, and the threat of thermonuclear war between the country formerly known as the Soviet Union and the United States. But the "Ice-Cold War" was another conflict that took place in the winter of 1975–76, causing sweaty palms and sleepless nights on hockey rinks around North America. The Soviet Red Army team, one which had dominated world international play for decades, invaded Canada and the United States for a series of "our lifestyle is superior to your lifestyle" games.

It was called Super Series '76, and it truly was an ice-cold war.

As fate would have it, the red tide submerged nearly all NHL teams and was still unbeaten (it had settled for a 3–3 tie in Montreal on New Year's Eve) when it arrived in Philadelphia on January 11 to face the two-time Stanley Cup champion Flyers.

Talk about pressure.

And ironically, the Flyers fielded an All-Canadian roster to win that second Cup in 1975—the last time an All-Canadian team would hold that distinction. So one country was, in a sense, playing for the pride of another.

Leading into the game, there were all sorts of subplots. For instance, Flyers chairman Ed Snider hardly disguised the fact that he hated the communist-run Soviet government and its history of human rights violations.

Meanwhile, Flyers fans just wanted their team—seemingly on its way to a third straight Stanley Cup—to prove that it truly was the best team in the world.

So when the two teams squared off in a nationally televised game, there was a feeling that most of America was pulling for the Flyers, even though some of their recent Broad Street Bullies tactics had, in certain quarters, upset fans who didn't like their roughhouse style of play.

There wasn't a seat to be had at the famous Spectrum, and those among the 17,007 who were able to get in would not be disappointed.

Flyers coach Fred Shero had done his homework, just as he had three years earlier when he studied videotape and devised a plan to stop Boston superstar Bobby Orr in the 1974 Stanley Cup Final.

Now he was charged with a slightly different mission: figure out a way to stifle the Soviets' brilliant passing attack, featuring a lot of back passes to confuse forecheckers and throw off opposing defensemen. The Flyers, briefed by Shero on these tactics, skated out onto the ice a confident bunch.

It started out like a normal hockey game, but just about everyone knew something untoward was about to happen.

Keep in mind, this was less than four years after Flyers captain Bobby Clarke had swung his stick at the leg of Soviet star Valeri Kharlamov.

So what happened in this game?

The same player, Kharlamov, got leveled by a freight train named Ed Van Impe. Kharlamov was motionless as the Spectrum crowd showed its sympathy by booing louder than they did at Richie Allen in the old Connie Mack Stadium. Of course, no penalty was called on the play.

Indignant, Red Army coach Konstantin Loktev pulled his team off the ice in protest.

Snider told the Russians to return to the ice and finish the game, which was being broadcast to an international audience, or the Soviet Hockey Federation would not get paid the fee to which it was entitled. So the game resumed.

The Flyers dominated the game. Even light-scoring defenseman Joe Watson notched a goal. When the ice chips had settled, the Flyers had a 4–1 win.

Remember, this was four years before the Miracle on Ice at Lake Placid, and there was still a mystique surrounding the HC CSKA Moscow team. It had been one of the most dominant sports teams in history, winning 13 consecutive Soviet titles between 1977 and 1989. So there were bragging rights on the line for this Flyers-Soviet game.

By all accounts, the Soviet team knew what it was getting into when it arrived in Philadelphia. The players were aware of the reputation of the Broad Street Bullies.

Before the game, a *Pravda* (Soviet newspaper) cartoon had portrayed the Flyers as Neanderthal thugs wielding clubs instead of sticks.

The Soviets also knew the crowd would be particularly hostile, perhaps taking its vibe off its favorite team's owner, Snider.

Some thought the series might not even take place. Tough and often contentious negotiations took place with Soviet officials before the series became a reality. Snider was actively involved.

Also, Snider was criticized by some as being hypocritical for allowing his hockey team to participate in a series that would pump money into Soviet coffers.

But ultimately, it came down to the Soviets' finesse versus the Flyers' aggressive, we're-coming-through technique.

No doubt Snider wanted to prove to the Soviets that the Flyers were much more than just a goon squad, but rather a talented club featuring Clarke, Bill Barber, Rick MacLeish, Reggie Leach, and goaltender Bernie Parent.

Even a pregame party for the two teams had failed to ease the tension.

Announcer Gene Hart, who spoke Russian, taught Snider how to wish both teams good luck. When Snider got to the podium, however, he skipped right over that phrase.

Later, Snider said, "When I looked at all those cold faces, I just couldn't do it."

Clarke was no fan of the Soviets either. His side had prevailed, barely, in the 1972 Summit Series and, as he noted, "It was pretty nasty hockey. I think I was pretty good at that style of game, but because of the level of competition from both sides, it created a hatred."

Barber added, "They didn't like us and we didn't like them. So we were ready for a war."

Shero's scouting work paid off.

Philadelphia dictated the tempo and, using body checks, prevented the Soviets from getting their transition game going.

ON THIS DATE

DECEMBER 11, 1977

Tom Bladon sets an NHL record for points by a defenseman (eight) in a game, recording four goals and four assists as the Flyers whip the Cleveland Barons 11-1 at the Spectrum.

"I never gave into the thought that the Russians were as good as us," Clarke said. "They came into Philly when we were Stanley Cup champs and just got their asses kicked all over the world."

To this day, there are some Flyers who insist the feeling of winning that game was as good as beating the Buffalo Sabres for their second Stanley Cup in 1975.

The Flyers came back from the game stoppage more resolute than ever and wound up outshooting their opponents 49-13.

After the game Shero kidded Watson, telling him his shorthanded goal had set the Soviet program back 25 years.

For the Soviets, the bitterness didn't end there.

Even now, All-World goalie Vladislav Tretiak, who views the tie game in the Montreal Forum as the highpoint of the series, says that the Flyers won by playing "rude hockey."

Also, Coach Loktev called the Flyers "a bunch of animals." The Flyers, meanwhile, left with the belief that the Soviet team had confirmed their feelings that Russian players were skilled but soft.

Clarke said there were game-changing ramifications for the Soviets after that game.

"What happened as a result of that was the Russians had to change their system," he said. "Now they weren't going backward with the puck all the time. Now they had to go forward with the puck, throw it in and play the style that was played in the NHL."

Was there ever any doubt in Clarke's mind that the game would go on after the infamous stoppage? Clarke said he and his teammates had faith in Snider.

"The Flyers trusted him," Clarke said. "He was brilliant, he was tough, and he loved hockey. He wanted to play that game but he wasn't going to be disadvantaged or have people walk away from it."

The team captain said the Flyers never really thought of the political implications.

"We were young," he said, "and our knowledge of politics was pretty limited. We had a game, it was a game against the hated Soviet Union, and we were going to beat them."

And those are the ice-cold facts.

18

THE SPECTRUM: AN UNPRETENTIOUS BUILDING INTIMIDATED FOES

Just before they demolished the venerable Spectrum in 2010, Flyers cofounder Ed Snider spoke emotionally about an arena that hosted the franchise's first Stanley Cup championship.

"The great thing about the building is the memories—and not necessarily the bricks and mortar," Snider said. "And the memories will never go away."

Still, Snider couldn't bear to watch, and as the wrecking ball tore into "The House That Bernie and Clarkie Built," he drove away.

As the 43-year-old building came down and Bruce Springsteen's "Wrecking Ball" blared through the speakers, it stirred memories from the Flyers' players and coaches who competed there.

Defenseman Chris Pronger said the Spectrum had an aura to it, and teammate Sean O'Donnell said there are many graying and balding former players—those who didn't wear the Flyers' crest—who probably celebrated the news that a wrecking ball was tearing down the arena.

"It's a special building; it's not just a regular building," said O'Donnell, the Flyers' 39-year-old defenseman, in 2010. "It's the Broad Street Bullies. It's a synonymous nickname. It's a place where not a lot of people wanted to play."

He was talking about the Flyers' opponents.

"There are probably a lot of players from back in the '70s that are exorcising some of the demons, finally getting that building knocked down," he said.

Growing up in Ottawa as a youngster, O'Donnell said, "I remember my dad talking about it and the teams they had. They've always had tough teams. They were good and tough, and [you heard about the] Spectrum and the Broad Street Bullies and Dave Schultz and all those guys."

O'Donnell said there were probably a lot of former players in their late fifties and sixties "who are smiling and saying, 'Goodbye! I hated that place and never liked going there!'"

Craig "Chief" Berube, who was a Flyers assistant coach when the building was demolished, played his first NHL season there in 1986–87.

"It seemed like the fans were right on top of you," said Berube, who spent his first five NHL seasons with the Flyers. "It was loud and they were banging on the glass. I thought it was a real tough place for other teams to come in and play. It was like going into Boston Garden—a smaller rink, compact, lots of life and action. It seemed like a real blue-collar crowd in there."

As a rookie with Hartford in 1993–94, Pronger remembered "the aura of the Spectrum and the Flyers and their style and their fans. Obviously, there are a lot of fond memories for a lot of fans here and a lot of former players. I'm sure [the demolition will] be tough to take for some guys."

Before the 2008–09 season, the final NHL exhibition game was played at the Spectrum, with the Flyers beating Carolina 4–2. Prior to the game, many of the Flyers' former captains walked on the carpet, one at a time, toward center ice and received thundering applause.

Lou Angotti, who was the first captain in the Flyers' history, plus Ed Van Impe and Bobby Clarke were there. So were Mel Bridgman, Bill Barber, Dave Poulin, Ron Sutter, Kevin Dineen, Eric Desjardins, Keith Primeau, and Derian Hatcher.

Some were graying, some were stocky, some looked as if they were still in playing shape. All were caught up in the electric atmosphere that engulfed the Spectrum, the beloved building that was the site of the franchise's greatest achievements.

"This building is home for a lot of players and will always feel like home," Barber said.

The Spectrum, known as America's Showplace when it opened it 1967, was torn down to make room for an entertainment-dining complex.

The Flyers' 1–0 Stanley Cup–clinching win over the Boston Bruins in 1974 was the Spectrum's shining moment.

"The most important thing in my career," Clarke said.

There were many other memorable moments: the roof blowing off in 1968; Kate Smith, the team's good-luck charm, walking on the ice to sing "God Bless America" in the 1973 home opener; the epic win over the Russians in 1976; and the almost incomprehensible 35-game unbeaten streak in 1979–80.

Those who played at the Spectrum regard it as a cathedral of sorts. Poulin compared it to the Boston Garden and Chicago Stadium, two former arenas that were revered.

"At the time, the Spectrum was a new building, but it was [regarded as] an old building," Poulin said. "Somehow, it didn't become a new facility. It was very unique in many ways. The Flyers were an expansion franchise and they established an identity. And the building was part of that identity."

Other NHL arenas have "big infrastructures around them with big lobbies. The focus here is on the ice," Poulin said. "It's a tiny building, and somehow that made the fans closer to you physically, so they were closer to you emotionally."

Added Poulin, "The best thing about a building is when everybody else asks you what it was like to play in it, and guys from the other teams talked about how much they hated to come here. It intimidated teams."

Poulin smiled as he talked about the Flyers' 4–1 win over the Soviet Red Army in 1976.

"When the whole Russian thing went on here, the Philadelphia Flyers and the Spectrum managed to chase a whole political system out of the building, not just a team," he said. "They chased communism out of the building."

When they started to demolish the building in 2010, several thousand fans showed up. They came for the memories of the building's occupants, the Flyers and 76ers, and for the bands and singers they had watched perform there. Several athletes, including Sixers great Julius Erving and Flyers icons Bobby Clarke and Bernie Parent, spoke to the crowd.

The wrecking ball struck the building about two dozen times, ripping a relatively small hole in the brick facade and smashing through a bank of smoked-glass windows.

"In 1967 a man had a great vision, Ed Snider," Parent said. "He didn't let criticism or setbacks stop him.... If it wasn't for this man's

Erected in 1967 and razed in 2010, the Spectrum bore witness to the Flyers' 1974 Stanley Cup Final win and the team's emotional win against the Soviet Red Army hockey team during the Cold War, among other cherished moments.

vision and fortitude, there would have been no games. There would have been no shows."

Next, Snider spoke of his mixed emotions and shifted the focus to the "Wells Fargo Center or whatever it's called." [Ed. Note. It's had many names.] "Hopefully, we'll win a Cup in this building."

The Spectrum used to be Lou Nolan's second home.

"I was 17 or 18 when I started working there," said Nolan, who has been employed by the Flyers since their inception in 1967 and has been their public-address announcer since 1972, "so I grew up at the place. There were a lot of memorable times," he said.

Nolan handled the public-address duties for some of the most famous games in the Spectrum's history. "I was right in the middle of everything when the Russians walked off—the refs, the interpreters, and everything else," he said, referring to the brief walkout in the epic 1976 game.

Former Flyers goalie Marty Biron said he was a Quebec fan as a youngster and remembered watching NHL games at the Spectrum on TV and sensing the atmosphere. Then he found out firsthand.

BRIND'AMOUR: FITNESS FREAK LEAVES OTHERS WEAK

Rod Brind'Amour holds the Flyers' ironman record for consecutive games played at 484.

During a 1999 preseason game, Brind'Amour blocked a point shot off the stick of New Jersey defenseman Bruce Rafalski and suffered a broken bone in his foot.

When the regular season began, Brind'Amour tried to keep his streak alive, but there was just one problem—his foot was so swollen that he couldn't get his skate on.

Besides that, his foot actually had two fractures in it, with one from a previous injury.

The man they called "Rod the Bod" just couldn't contain his frustration.

"I've just got to get it fixed," Brind'Amour said at the time. "It's the type of thing that gets worse with every game that you watch in terms of being frustrated, but there's nothing I can do about it."

During his 20-year NHL career, Brind'Amour's diligent workout regimen reached legendary status.

"It's definitely a year-round job," Brind'Amour said. "I think the guys that approach it that way are the ones that last the longest. Especially with the amount of money guys make now, if you don't treat it year-round you're foolish."

Except for the season of the broken foot and later, a torn ACL in his knee in 2007–08, Brind'Amour missed only 29 of a possible 1,513 career games.

Call him a fitness freak and he laughs. For him, working out is just a true labor of love.

"When you walk in the building, you see all the banners hanging, and it feels like this historical building," he said. "There's nothing fancy about the building, but everything is well-done. The first time I was there, I couldn't believe the top level was so little and hardly had any seats," he said.

An unpretentious building, the Spectrum hosted six Stanley Cup Finals, four NBA Finals, and two NCAA Final Fours, including the famous 1992 game when Duke's Christian Laettner sank a last-second shot that defeated Kentucky in the national semifinals.

Bob Ford, a *Philadelphia Inquirer* columnist, said the Spectrum was usually "crowded and loud and hot and smelled of burned popcorn. There was gum under the seats and the concrete stuck to your soles sometimes. One narrow concourse served all three seating levels, and there weren't ever enough bathrooms. But great things happened there. All the time. Maybe they would have happened somewhere else, but maybe not. Maybe the Spectrum just knew how to open the doors and then get out of the way."

Clarke spoke for the fans and players at a pre-demolition ceremony.

"We will always remember the Spectrum," he said.

19

BROAD STREET BULLIES: RULING THE NHL

They didn't call them the Broad Street Bullies for nothin'. And they still don't.

The history books will show that sometime back in the early 1970s, the Flyers got tired of getting beat up by some of the NHL's more physical teams—most prominently the St. Louis Blues. So General Manager Keith Allen, at the behest of team chairman Ed Snider, began to stock his pantry with, shall we say, gentlemen who knew how to use their fists as well as their sticks.

The original cast included Andre "Moose" Dupont, Don "Big Bird" Saleski, Dave "The Hammer" Schultz, and Bob "The Hound" Kelly.

Later came such celebrated heavyweights as Dave Brown, Behn Wilson, Daryl Stanley, Dave Hoyda, Glen Cochrane, Rick Tocchet, Paul Holmgren, Donald Brashear, and Craig Berube.

That original crew, which was first called the "Broad Street Bullies" by *Philadelphia Bulletin* sportswriter Jack Chevalier, gained worldwide notoriety in the mid-'70s as the Flyers won a pair of Stanley Cups.

No one messed with the Flyers' skill players, such as Bobby Clarke, who was no angel himself when it came to initiating trouble. An early example of this came in a game between the Flyers and the Oakland Seals on the night of December 2, 1973. Clarke allegedly stirred up the trouble by jabbing his stick at Oakland rookie Barry Cummins' face.

Cummins responded by taking his stick with a level, two-handed grip and clobbering Clarke over the head right in front of the Flyers' bench, opening up a gash that would require a reported 24 stitches to close.

In the blink of an eye, about six Flyers came to Clarke's defense.

Kelly led the charge from the bench, and Bill Flett led the charge from the ice as Cummins tried to run, but there was no place to hide. The Seals also emptied their bench, but not before Cummins was buried under Flyers punches.

Later, after Cummins received a three-game suspension and a $300 fine, he called Clarke to apologize for the incident. It was one of the first shots fired in what would be a long list of incidents involving the Flyers over the years ahead.

"I wasn't an innocent player on that one [the Cummins incident]," admitted Clarke, who never wore a protective helmet for any of the 1,144 NHL games he played. "But you never hit somebody on the head with your stick."

If nothing else, skirmishes like this sent a warning message to the rest of the NHL that the Flyers were not going to get pushed around anymore.

"In those days, you stood up for your teammate," Clarke explained. "[Kelly and the other Flyers] did the right thing because you stood up for your teammate. You were supposed to protect each other."

Before this incident, there was another in Vancouver that bears mentioning. In a December 1972 game at Pacific Coliseum in Hastings Park, Don Saleski—he of the permed hairdo popular at the time—got into a skirmish with Barry Wilcox. Somehow, a fan reached over the glass and grabbed Saleski's hair.

This led to a half-dozen Flyers, led by backup goalie Bobby Taylor, rushing into the stands to find the perpetrator. A Vancouver policeman tried to intervene but was shoved aside by Taylor. The whole thing looked like a scene right out of the movie *Slap Shot*. Eventually, the players received $500 fines but no jail time.

"I was one of the only players who didn't go into the stands, but I was guilty by association," a sheepish Saleski said. "All I did was have someone pull my hair, and I ended up being arrested. I was a victim."

The Bullies, it seems, were just getting started.

One of the highest-profile fights came in the 1974 Eastern Conference Final. The New York Rangers had rallied to force a Game 7 at the Spectrum, and the Flyers felt like they needed a spark.

Or at least Schultz did. He proceeded to instigate a fight with New York defenseman Dale Rolfe—someone who rarely fought. In hindsight, this was viewed as a turning point in the game because Rolfe's teammates just stood there and watched him get beat up in a one-sided affair.

ON THIS DATE

DECEMBER 11, 1969

Kate Smith's recording of "God Bless America" is first played at a Flyers game, a 6–3 win over Toronto at the Spectrum. It becomes a good-luck song for the team, and Smith even performs live before four home games from 1973 to 1976. The Flyers had a 101–31–5 record when the song was played or performed live.

The Flyers, sensing a loss of energy on the Rangers bench, went on to an easy win and advanced to the Stanley Cup Final, where they defeated the Boston Bruins for their first Stanley Cup championship.

"There was no way we were going to lose the game after seeing how dominant Davy was in the fight," Flyers forward Bill Clement told *Philadelphia Inquirer* sports columnist Mike Sielski.

"Whether it won the game or not, it was reinforcing why we were so dominant at home. The crowd was insane. The Rangers were a proud franchise, but it reinforced the idea that there were a lot of guys who came to play the Broad Street Bullies who didn't want to play there. We had a feeling of invincibility."

Another iconic Flyers fight took place a few years later when Holmgren got into it with Boston tough guy Wayne Cashman at the Spectrum. Holmgren, who suffered a career-threatening eye injury less than a year before this fracas, nearly sustained a reinjury to the eye at the bottom of the scrum.

After some initial exchanges on the ice, Holmgren and Cashman were banished to their respective locker rooms for the remainder of the periods.

The only problem was that the Flyers and Bruins rooms were just about 75 feet apart, well within yelling distance, which is exactly what transpired.

Curse words led to more fighting in the hallway. Later a steel gate was erected in the hallway and remained there for the next 20 years of NHL action.

"Cash went after Jimmy Watson," Holmgren explained. "I jumped in to help Jimmy and somebody was pulling on my face [near the eye]. So we go down and things get going again in the hallway. All of a sudden we're surrounded by Bruins, so our guys came running down to help out."

There have been some other classic donnybrooks, as well.

How about April 22, 1976, when Toronto's Tiger Williams slashed Clarke, and Schultz came charging off the Flyers' bench to the rescue? The two men flailed away at each other for the better part of a minute before dropping their weary arms in exhaustion.

On March 5, 2004, ex-Flyer fighting machine Brashear apparently wasn't satisfied with the two-game suspension Ottawa's Martin Havlat had received for hitting Mark Recchi in the face with his stick a week before.

So Brashear sought some revenge of his own.

That revenge resulted in a 419-penalty-minute riot, which still holds a high spot in NHL record books.

Instead of going after Havlat, Brashear did the honorable thing and dropped the gloves against Senators enforcer Rob Ray. Benches emptied. It took over an hour to restore order. Even Clarke, then GM of the team and all of 55 years old, tried to run down to the Ottawa locker room to mix it up with Senators coach Jacques Martin. Fortunately, cooler heads prevailed.

The memorable fight on November 19, 1986, between Tocchet and Toronto's Wendel Clark at the old Toronto Maple Leaf Gardens is still viewed over and over again on YouTube with two men, holding their ground, swinging at each other with wild abandon. Not a person in the building could stay in his or her seat.

Ultimately, Flyers fans always debate who was the best fighter. Wilson? Brown? Schultz?

Holmgren says that, without a doubt, it's Behn Wilson. Who can argue? He once took on Clark Gillies, the Islander bad boy who was virtually unbeaten in the NHL, and scored a clear-cut decision.

"His rookie year, Behn fought everyone, and I mean everyone, in the league," Holmgren said. "He provoked all of them, and he won all of them—[Boston's Terry] O'Reilly, Gillies, [Boston's Stan] Jonathan, even nutjobs like Archie Henderson. Behn was hitting him so hard he was lifting him off the ground and the guy weighed 230 pounds."

By Wilson's third year, no one wanted to go near him. And for good reason.

"Behn had a screw loose," Holmgren said with a smile. "One time we're warming up for a game in Buffalo. It was the last game of our 35-game unbeaten streak [in 1980].

"In warm-up, Behn goes in, shoots, and [goalie Pete] Peeters doesn't even try to stop it. Pretended not to see it. So Behn goes after Pete and starts beating him up. Anything you did around Behn, you had to be a little careful."

Any of the original Broad Street Bullies reading that would have to smile. Just a chip off the old block.

20

PAUL HOLMGREN: MR. EVERYTHING

Second chances usually only come along once in a lifetime. For Paul "Homer" Holmgren, they happened twice and served as a reminder that such life-changing opportunities don't simply materialize by, well, chance.

Generally they come through the assistance of others.

It's why all of the Flyers—players, assistant coaches, head coaches, assistant general managers, general managers, presidents—feel the need to give back to those who might require a helping hand.

During a game way back in his first year with the Flyers, Holmgren found himself at the bottom of a scrum on the ice when an errant skate blade swung by and caught his eye.

The Minnesota native was rushed to a Boston hospital where he was administered a common type of anesthesia. There was only one problem—Holmgren was extremely allergic to this type of knockout drug and went into severe anaphylactic shock. Doctors had to roll in a cart with electric paddles and turn on the current four times to get the player's heart restarted. It was touch-and-go for a while. Things were serious enough that Holmgren's parents were flown in from Minnesota.

This was a harrowing night to say the least.

Only some quick, timely work by those doctors gave Holmgren a second chance at life. Somehow, Holmgren pulled through and would go on to enjoy an outstanding 10 years with the Flyers, including a 1980 trip to the Stanley Cup Final, where he became the first American-born player to record a hat trick in a Stanley Cup Final game.

The journey was not without its other injuries. One of the most physical players in Flyers history not only dished out and took body checks on every shift, but he was also willing to take on any and every heavyweight enforcer cruising around NHL ice surfaces.

Upon his retirement in 1984, Holmgren got into coaching as an assistant under head coach Mike Keenan as the Flyers found their way to the Stanley Cup Final again.

ON THIS DATE

FEBRUARY 14, 1977

Al Hill sets an NHL record for points (five) by a player in his first game, collecting two goals and three assists in a 6–4 win over St. Louis at the Spectrum.

When Keenan was relieved of command at the end of the 1987–88 season, Holmgren was promoted to head coach.

That tenure would last three seasons. After leaving the Flyers, Holmgren was named head coach of the Hartford Whalers. While all this was going on, the stress of coaching and the residual pain of those aforementioned injuries were catching up with him.

After a serious DUI incident in Connecticut, Holmgren lost his driver's license and had to be driven to work. Whalers owner Richard Gordon had grounds to fire Holmgren but didn't, resulting in second chance number 2.

When Holmgren returned to Philadelphia in 1994 to serve as assistant general manager under his friend and Hall of Famer Bob Clarke, Holmgren had already started on the road to rehab by going through the Betty Ford program. He's been on the straight and narrow ever since.

The story, however, doesn't end there.

Since taking a position of authority, first as Clarke's assistant GM and then as the head GM job in 2006, Holmgren has made it a point to help others who were in the same position as he once was.

Among those he's helped include ex-Flyer Todd "Fridge" Fedoruk, who said he was so entangled in substance abuse that without Holmgren's help, he would be "pushing daisies." There are countless others who shall remain nameless. The bottom line is this: Holmgren has been a guardian angel to many a player with a problem.

Clarke actually takes some of the responsibility for Holmgren's questionable habits as a young player.

"He was as hard a hockey player as the Flyers have had," Clarke said. "He would fight anybody and his reckless, hard play led to injuries.

And the injuries led to taking medication. It followed the path of him starting to drink beer.... He was about 23 and he never drank until he got to the Flyers.

"But the rest of the players [from the early Broad Street Bullies days] did. He and I were close. I drank, so obviously he felt it was the right thing to do."

At his peak, playing on the famed "Rat Patrol" line with Kenny "The Rat" Linseman and Brian Propp, Holmgren was at his best.

But the constant pounding took its toll.

"That's when he got into back problems and serious injuries from the way he played," Clarke said. "It ended up putting him in Betty Ford. That life was over. If he continued the way he was going, it was going to cost him his family, his life, everything."

Holmgren served as team president from 2014 until he stepped down in the summer of 2019. In late November 2018, he was faced with the unenviable task of relieving Flyers general manager Ron Hextall of his duties. Dismissing a friend was not easy but it was something that he believed had to be done in the best interests of the Flyers, a franchise he has remained loyal to for nearly his entire adult life.

Holmgren's former teammate, Mark Howe, admires both the player and the man off the ice.

"Quiet, tough, loyal," are the words Howe uses to describe Holmgren. "I had an awful lot of respect for Homer...for his commitment to the game, for his dedication to a team."

If you needed someone to watch your back against some of the NHL's nastier teams, Holmgren was your man.

"One thing you had to watch out for—every once in a while his eyes would get a little squirrely in practice," Howe said. "It didn't matter what team you were on. You had to have your head on your shoulders because Homer was coming."

A story from the 1982 season typifies Holmgren's dry wit.

"I still laugh," Howe said. "The very first shift I had as a Flyer, I brought the puck up, rushed up the ice, gave it to Homer, and I jumped through the middle. I'm maybe 30 feet from the net, he tries to return the pass to me, and it hits me right under the eye. Split me open for about 10 or 12 stitches.

STATUES MARK THE LEGENDARY MOMENTS, INDIVIDUALS

The area around the Flyers' home arena, the Wells Fargo Center, and adjacent eateries at Xfinity Live! have become Statue City. Numerous statues of people connected to the Flyers have been erected in this space.

In October 2017, 50 years from the day the Flyers played their first home game at the beloved Spectrum, they unveiled a nine-foot bronze statue of the late Ed Snider, the team's co-founder, outside the Wells Fargo Center. Snider's daughter, Lindy, asked everyone to start a tradition and rub the Stanley Cup ring he was depicted wearing because it would bring the team good luck.

"The greatest feeling was when I touched the ring," Hall of Fame goalie Bernie Parent said a few minutes after Lindy Snider's speech before about 700 onlookers. "I felt the power."

In 2014, a statue of Fred Shero, the coach who directed the Flyers to Stanley Cup championships in 1974 and 1975, was unveiled. At the ceremony, Shero's son, Ray, who was then the general manager of the Flyers' most bitter rival, the Pittsburgh Penguins, talked about his dad's remarkable stint in Philadelphia.

"In those seven years," Shero said, "not only did the Flyers win two Stanley Cups, but they beat the crap out of the Soviet Red Army."

"And the Penguins!" interjected a voice from one of the folding chairs filled with club executives and former players from the Broad Street Bullies days. The voice belonged to Snider, the Flyers' chairman.

Shero paused to allow the laughter to subside. It took a while.

Here are the other statues surrounding the Flyers' arena and the adjacent eateries: Legends Bobby Clarke and Bernie Parent hoisting the Stanley Cup; and Gary Dornhoefer leaping into the air after scoring an overtime goal to beat Minnesota in 1973, paving the way for the franchise's first playoff series win.

"So I'm being stitched up in between periods and he comes into the training room and says, 'Are you doin' all right?' I said, 'yeah.' He says, 'You know, you gotta learn how to take a pass.'"

The year Holmgren took over as Howe's coach, things didn't change much.

"When he became a coach, everyone respected him," Howe said. "He was a player's coach. He knew how to be tough, and you knew when he was mad. He kept you on your toes. He's one of the very few guys I ever played for that was a pleasure to play for."

Holmgren was a player's coach not only at the rink but away from it, as well. In a way, Holmgren feels almost an obligation to provide help to others because he received so much himself.

"When I was dealing with my own demons, people actually reached out to me and got me the help I needed," he said. "I don't know if I was looking for it, but I must have because I accepted it."

More than once, Holmgren brought a player to the Flyers who, in some people's eyes, was beyond hope. No matter. Holmgren saw the good in everyone.

Why?

It goes back to Hartford, when Holmgren's world was crumbling all around him. People like Brian Burke called to lend a hand.

"As I started to heal, the people who had reached out to me, they had given me a second chance," Holmgren said. "My wife, for sure. Some people in the game, like Brian, [commissioner] Gary Bettman.

"Mr. Gordon, I talked to him about what I was going through. He didn't fire me. He probably could have."

For that, Holmgren is grateful. He learned a valuable lesson during that brief period of time, and he uses it as a guiding light to this day.

"Today, I believe it's important when someone reaches out to you to give back because I believe in second chances," he said. "Had I not been given one, I don't know what would have happened. And I don't need to know."

21

PAT QUINN:
LAW AND ORDER ON THE BENCH

Pat Quinn was too intelligent to be a hockey coach. He could have been a lawyer, a college professor, or maybe even the prime minister of Canada. Instead he chose to follow his childhood dream—not only to play in the National Hockey League but one day coach and manage a team of his own.

It could have been different. Just three years into his NHL playing career with the Toronto Maple Leafs, Quinn had already earned a Bachelor of Arts degree in economics from York University in Toronto. After his playing career ended, he went on to get his law degree from Widener University School of Law in Delaware. Suffice it to say, Quinn's brain power served him well in a career behind hockey benches that lasted more than 30 years.

It started in 1977, right after Quinn hung up his skates.

Flyers head coach Fred Shero had pioneered the concept of an assistant coach just a few years before when he made Mike Nykoluk the first No. 2 man on an NHL bench. For the 1977–78 season, Shero expanded his staff by adding former Flyer player Terry Crisp and an ex-hard-hitting defenseman by the name of Quinn.

When Shero left the following year to coach the New York Rangers, Bob McCammon was brought in to run the show, and Quinn was appointed to coach the Flyers' American Hockey League affiliate in Portland, Maine.

In a rather bizarre turn of events, the Flyers—struggling in the standings—decided to change coaches midstream, with Quinn taking over in Philadelphia and McCammon going to Maine.

One year later, history was made. Quinn led the Flyers on a storybook run that lasted from October until January. The Flyers went an incredible 35 games without a loss (25–0–10), steamrolling one team after another.

The core of this team was a carryover from the team that won two Stanley Cup championships (1974, 1975) and reached the Cup

Final in 1976. Bobby Clarke, Bill Barber, Reggie Leach, and Rick MacLeish were still patrolling the boards at the old Spectrum, and now they were joined by up-and-coming stars like Paul Holmgren, Ken Linseman, Brian Propp, Mel Bridgman, and goalie Pete Peeters. It was the perfect blend of experience and youth, plus it had Quinn at the control board.

FLOCKHART: RAPID-FIRE GOALS HAVE THEM SINGING THE BLUES

They called it "Flocky Hockey," and while there was a bit of show-off to it, the individual exploits of Ron Flockhart never failed to entertain. For instance, there was that night against the St. Louis Blues when the 21-year-old rookie scored two goals in a team-record eight seconds. For some players, it takes longer than that just to skate twice from the red line to the offensive zone faceoff dots.

In an 8–2 rout of the Blues on December 6, 1981, Flockhart's speed and skill were on full display. With the Flyers leading 4–2, Flockhart stole a clearing pass and blasted home a 50-footer past goalie Gary Edwards at 5:10. Following the ensuing faceoff, Brad Marsh fed Flockhart, and the center beat Edwards with a 45-foot rocket high to the glove side at 5:18. Flockhart broke the mark set by Reggie Leach, who scored two goals in 20 seconds against the Los Angeles Kings exactly three years before.

Playing between proven scorers Brian Propp and Paul Holmgren that freshman season certainly didn't hurt Flockhart's transition to the NHL.

In his final season of junior hockey, Flockhart's flashy skills were in the spotlight as he registered 54 goals and 76 assists in 1979–80.

"The guys rib me a lot," Flockhart said after his record performance. "But I always thought to myself to use the wingers when I think it's the right time. A lot of times, though, it turned out to be the wrong time and that was my downfall.

"I'm working on utilizing my wingers more. With the unbalanced talent in juniors, I never had to pass the puck. But up in the pros, it's more even and I have to learn how to utilize the wingers."

For that night in 1981, no one seemed to care how Flockhart got it done. They were content to see history made in the blink of an eye.

Quinn's analytical mind, sharpened by his college education at York, was the perfect fit, according to Holmgren, who is now the team's president.

"You know how players today always ask why?" Holmgren said. "Pat was way ahead of the game. He'd say, 'This is what I want you to do and this is why.' I thought that was really groundbreaking."

When Quinn walked into a locker room, he commanded instant respect. A lantern jaw sitting atop a bar-bouncer's physique could make even the most rough-and-tumble player stay at attention in his presence.

"I remember Pat saying at one of his first meetings, 'You know, the average attention span of a human being is like four minutes!' He knew how long of an envelope he had," Holmgren said. "In any room, guys are drifting. Linseman would drift after about 10 seconds, but not when Pat was in the room."

After Quinn reached the Stanley Cup Final at the end of the 1979–80 campaign, winning him the Jack Adams Award for best coach in the NHL, his coaching tenure with the Flyers would only last another couple of seasons. Those aforementioned veterans were now in their mid–30s, and some of the incoming talent wasn't quite up to par.

Quinn was let go with just a handful of games remaining in the 1981–82 campaign, replaced by, of all people, McCammon.

Quinn—or "The Big Irishman," as he was nicknamed—didn't stay unemployed long. He would go on to coach the Los Angeles Kings, the Vancouver Canucks, the Toronto Maple Leafs, and the Edmonton Oilers. Along the way, he brought the Canucks to the Stanley Cup Final in 1994.

In addition, Quinn coached Team Canada to gold medals at the 2002 Winter Olympics, the 2008 International Ice Hockey Federation World U18 Championships (for players under age 18), and the 2009 World Junior Championship, as well as the World Cup championship in 2004.

During his playing career, Quinn was known for his take-no-prisoners style. He is perhaps best known for an infamous body check he laid on Boston superstar Bobby Orr in the 1969 Stanley

Cup playoffs, which left the young Bruin unconscious on the ice and provoked a bench-clearing brawl.

A chronic ankle injury forced an end to Quinn's playing career in 1977.

After his dismissal from the Flyers in 1982, Quinn briefly left hockey but remained in the Philadelphia area to attend law school at Widener. In 1984, he was named head coach of the Los Angeles Kings and went on to finish his degree at the University of San Diego.

Clarke kept a close eye on his friend. It was Quinn who had made Clarke, still an active player, an assistant coach prior to the 1979–80 season. The move was a bit controversial at the time because Clarke had to give up his captaincy in order to become part of the coaching staff. But it actually seemed like a natural appointment because the two had been close, going back to their playing days.

"Yeah, when Pat and I played against each other, there were some words against each other," Clarke recalled with a chuckle. "He'd say, 'You little bastard.' And I'd come up and stick him in the crotch and then get away because he couldn't catch me. He'd yell, 'You have to come to the front of the net sometime. I'll get you!' Those are fun things."

By becoming Quinn's assistant, Clarke got an up-close-and-personal sense of Quinn's coaching genius.

"I thought Pat, like Freddy Shero, was way ahead of his time," Clarke said. "We were okay at the start of the 1979–80 season, but he brought a style of game, a system of game that was somewhat similar to what [U.S. Olympic coach] Herbie Brooks beat the Russians with.

"Pat's system was attack. Everybody knows defense is important. He didn't like the defensive game where you lay back and let the other guy take it to you, like Jacques Lemaire did. He taught us how to play on the attack. We were a hard team to play against because we were coming and we were coming fast. And we were trying to score.

"Against the Islanders [in the '80 Final], he did as good a coaching job as any. Maybe the best of his career. And he was still young."

Perhaps some of Quinn's best work took place away from the NHL arena. At the 2002 Olympic Winter Games in Salt Lake City, Utah,

Quinn coached Team Canada to its first Olympic gold medal since 1952, with a 5-2 victory over Team USA in the gold medal game.

He returned to a hero's welcome in Canada. In fact, he received a standing ovation from the fans in Montreal for his efforts in his first NHL game back from the Olympics.

Then came the 2004 World Cup, and Quinn was at the top of his game again. He coached Team Canada to a gold medal with a perfect 6-0 record, capped off by a 3-2 victory over Finland in the final.

Quinn died in 2014 and was elected posthumously to the Hockey Hall of Fame in 2016.

Like Holmgren, Clarke believes Quinn was an innovator, a coach who cared for his players and one who knew not only how to break down a player's weaknesses but show how to fix them, as well.

"Pat was an extremely bright man," Clarke said. "When he came to talk to the team, it wasn't to give the team criticism. So many coaches over the years I've seen—and I still do—they give the team a hard time so the coach feels better. The players don't feel any better. Players feel worse.

"Your job as coach is to try to get the players on the ice and get them to play better. Give them a chance to win. You still see it constantly in all sports. If a player is playing bad, you take him somewhere, sit him down, and tell him he's playing bad. That's great. But the player wants to know how to play well. Your job is to teach them how to play well. Quinn was really good at that."

22

A STREAK FOR THE AGES

When the 1979–80 season started, the Flyers were a team in transition, a team with a patchwork defense and lots of young players, including rookie goaltender Pete Peeters.

There were going to be lots of growing pains, it seemed, after the Flyers were embarrassed by the Atlanta Flames 9–2 in the season's second game. Years later, Pat Quinn told the *Philadelphia Inquirer* he started questioning his decisions following that lopsided loss.

"It was my first full season and I was doubting myself," he said. "Was I using the right goalie? Was I using the right lines? You get to thinking like that, and soon you start wondering if you're ever going to win another game."

But Quinn didn't panic, and neither did his players. The Flyers rebounded from their thrashing in Atlanta, and the wins started piling up. No longer was Quinn questioning himself. Around the NHL, fans *did* have one question—will the Flyers ever lose again?

The Flyers would go two months, three weeks, and five days without a defeat, compiling a 35-game unbeaten streak—the longest in the history of major professional sports. They would win 25 games, tie 10, and finish nearly half a season with just that one loss in Atlanta.

Before the Flyers' run, the longest unbeaten streak in North American pro sports was 33 games by the NBA's Los Angeles Lakers in 1971–72. The Flyers crushed the NHL record of 28 straight unbeaten games held by Montreal in 1977–78.

The streak came out of nowhere. The Flyers' previous season had ended with a quarterfinal-round, five-game playoff loss to a New York Rangers team that was coached by Fred Shero, the man who had guided Philadelphia to two Cups. The Flyers lost those games by a combined 25–6, so yes, a lot of improvements were needed.

Outside of Bobby Clarke, Bill Barber, Reggie Leach, and Rick MacLeish, "we had a lot of no-name guys, up and coming [guys]," said Paul Holmgren, who was a winger on that team. "Kenny Linseman was a young guy, [Brian] Propp was a young guy, I was still pretty young in the game. Basically, outside of Jimmy Watson, Bob Dailey, [and] Moose Dupont, we had a lot of guys who were no-name guys on defense like Mike Busniuk, Norm Barnes, and Frank Bathe."

The Flyers had a blend of rookies and veterans who would need time to get accustomed to playing together—or so the theory went.

After scoring a 5–2 win over the Islanders in the opener, the Flyers suffered a seven-goal defeat at the Omni in Atlanta. Quinn said the manner in which the Flyers rebounded from that defeat would tell "the kind of team we have."

The Flyers didn't lose again for 86 days.

"We didn't think much about the streak early on because, to be honest with you, we had so many questions about that team," Quinn said years later. "But after about 15 games we all started to realize that this was something special. On the bench, the guys were starting to stand up for the entire third periods of close games. They were beginning to get excited. They just didn't want to see it end."

During the streak, Peeters compiled a 14–0–4 record, and Phil Myre went 11–0–6. Incredibly, Peeters didn't lose a game that season until February. He was 22–0–5 before suffering a defeat.

While a handful of stars from the '74 and '75 Cup teams remained, big, physical wingers like Dave Schultz, Don Saleski, and Gary Dornhoefer had been replaced by smaller, quicker players, such as Tom Gorence, Linseman, and rookie Propp.

"We had lots of new faces," Quinn said in 1990. "We were just trying to compete."

Early in their streak, the Flyers scored four third-period goals to rally past the four-time defending Stanley Cup champion Canadiens at the fabled Forum in Montreal, winning 5–3.

The team's confidence was growing.

As the streak increased, people around the league couldn't believe a team with a no-name defense was clicking so well.

"They'd look and see defensemen with names like Norm Barnes, Mike Busniuk, and Frank Bathe and a winger like Al Hill, and they just couldn't understand how we were able to play so well," Quinn told the *Inquirer* in 1990.

ON THIS DATE

JANUARY 6, 1980

The Flyers defeat the host Buffalo Sabres 4–2 for their 35th straight game without a loss—the longest streak in professional sports history. (The streak ends on January 7 as the Flyers lose in Minnesota 7–1.)

Quinn said the young players came in and "saw the Barbers and Clarkes working their tails off at practice and on every shift, and they knew right then and there what was expected of them. If someone didn't live up to Flyers' standards, those veteran players let them know about it."

But as the streak grew and the Flyers got closer to Montreal's record, Philadelphia's opponents wanted to play the role of spoiler.

"Everybody was primed for us," Clarke said.

This was years before shootouts, so ties were still part of the game. And there were six times in a nine-game stretch that the Flyers could only produce a stalemate before needing to avoid a loss in Boston on December 22 to set the NHL record for consecutive games without a defeat.

The driven, hardworking Flyers understood the magnitude of that game before taking the ice on that Saturday afternoon. They brushed it aside and, led by the 30-year-old Clarke, whipped the Bruins 5–2. Clarke scored early in the first period, and Barber added another goal less than three minutes later. The Flyers were on their way to a history-setting victory.

After the final buzzer sounded, the appreciative Boston fans stood and applauded the Flyers' achievement.

"A masterpiece of a game," Quinn said. "It was maybe as good as the team ever played during all my time in Philadelphia. As I said at the time, you could measure our desire that day in the number of stitches we took."

Behn Wilson, Holmgren, and Dennis Ververgaert were among the Flyers who required post-game facial repairs.

"Right now none of us feels a thing," Ververgaert said at the time. "This record just soothes it all."

For six more games, the Flyers extended their record, taking their streak into the new year, which earned Philadelphia the label "City of Winners" because of the remarkable success of the city's sports teams. Before 1980 ended, the Phillies had won their first World Series, the Eagles were completing a season that would conclude with their first Super Bowl appearance, and the Flyers and 76ers had reached their leagues' championship series.

The 35-game unbeaten streak ended in Minnesota on January 7, 1980, before a frenzied crowd of 15,962, the largest ever at the time at the Metropolitan Sports Center. The North Stars crushed the Flyers 7–1.

"It was a once-in-a-lifetime thing," Quinn said after the team's first loss in nearly three months. "I don't know, maybe I was part of something that will stand forever in history. Maybe it's not even important. I don't know."

Clarke had points in 26 of the 35 games during the streak, and Propp had points in 25 of the contests. MacLeish, Leach, and Barber combined for 19 game-winning or game-tying goals during the run.

"Just about everybody chipped in," said Lou Nolan, the Flyers' longtime public-address announcer. "I know it's a cliché, but it really was a total team effort."

For the rest of the season, the Flyers were far from dominating. They finished with a 48–12–20 record, compiling a 22–11–10 mark from the streak's end to the season's conclusion.

They reached the Stanley Cup Final, but linesman Leon Stickle's infamous missed offside call in Game 6 contributed to the Flyers' overtime loss, which gave the New York Islanders the championship.

Holmgren said Quinn, who died in 2014, was the biggest reason for the Flyers' streak.

"We went on that incredible run where we kind of snuck up on everybody," Holmgren said. "Most of the credit for that goes to Pat because of the way he got the team to believe in themselves and to come together as a group."

Holmgren said Quinn, who was affectionately known as the Big Irishman, always stressed puck possession, a staple of today's game, and being part of a team. "He'd say, '[It's] not about the individuals; it's about the group.' He brought those principles [every game]."

In 2016, when Quinn posthumously went into the Hockey Hall of Fame, Clarke talked about Quinn's impact during the streak.

"We had four defensemen up from Maine [the minor-league team] the year before," said Clarke. "[The streak] was all because of Pat. He got the best out of every player he had and a lot of us played above our heads that year because of him."

23

BRIAN PROPP: CHALLENGE OF A LIFETIME

There were many career-defining moments for the Flyers' all-time, third-leading scorer as a player, but none of those came close to the life-changing event that took place on September 3, 2015, long after his NHL days were over.

For Brian Propp, it was like a car skidding out of control on an icy road, a white-knuckle airplane flight through a thunderstorm, and a canoe approaching an unexpected waterfall all rolled into one.

Propp was vacationing with his family in Annapolis, Maryland, when he began to feel out of sorts. He went to bed suffering from a headache but didn't think much of it. And then the world turned upside down.

At approximately 1:30 AM, Propp awoke and realized something was terribly wrong. He had suffered a massive stroke. When he tried to get up, he fell out of bed, striking his head and losing two teeth in the process.

"My right arm and fingers didn't work, and I couldn't speak," Propp said.

"It was a scary time. I wondered: Could I ever speak again? Would I ever think clearly? Will I ever get better?"

It turns out things eventually got better, but the progress was painfully slow.

Doctors confirmed that Propp was heading to this crisis for quite some time. He had experienced an ablation of the heart in 2011 and was dealing with atrial fibrillation. He had been taking medication but had stopped, not totally understanding the risk. Eventually, that caused a clot near his heart, which traveled to his brain, thus causing the stroke. Fortunately, medical assistance arrived quickly, or things could have been much worse. As it stood, he was hospitalized for five weeks, and for three months, his ability to talk was practically gone.

"All I could say were the words 'and' or 'Bernie Parent.' I had to relearn things I already knew," Propp recalled.

"Rehab was a struggle. I wanted it to happen quickly, but it took a long time to get better. I was impatient, stubborn, moody. I learned that I need to take my time and be more positive about the time it takes to get better."

Words of encouragement came flooding in from former teammates, friends, and family members, all expressing concern for the Flyers' legendary player and a member of the Flyers' Hall of Fame.

"My family was always with me and they tried to help," Propp said. "I learned that I needed to be patient, be positive, work harder, be content, accepting, and be at peace with my brain injury," he said.

Now nearly three years later, Propp, a 59-year-old native of Saskatchewan, is in a much better place, although he continues to work through the long-term effects of the stroke. He still has to deal with aphasia.

"The words don't always come to me," he said, "so I have to slow down and take my time.

"My physical therapy went the fastest because I was in great shape. My occupational therapy took longer because my fingers and hand didn't work that well. I learned to sign my autograph with my left hand. My fingers still don't work well, so I can't tie a tie, shoelaces, or button my shirt.

"Today I have realized that it takes time for the brain to heal."

Medical experts have Propp going through a number of treatments, including sessions in a hyperbaric chamber (40 sessions of 90 minutes each, which helps with the oxygen flow to the brain), stem cell therapy (which helped improve his speech), and Bemer machine sessions (to improve circulation). In addition, he had something called Watchman surgery, which helps the left side of the heart to prevent future strokes.

"I don't get sick now, I am thinking clearer, have lots of energy, and feel relaxed all day," Propp said.

So much so that he's playing hockey twice a week with his morning league at the Pennsauken (New Jersey) Skate Zone and getting back on the golf links for the past two years.

Propp's rehabilitation and recovery from this health crisis have been an inspiration, not only to former teammates but to family members, friends, fans, and media. They remember all the good times—how he was a big part of the 1979–80 team that put together a professional sports record 35-game (25–0–10) unbeaten streak and took the Islanders to six games in the Stanley Cup Final, along with Final appearances against Edmonton in 1985 and 1987. How he would execute the fun-loving "guffaw" (taking off his glove and making a swooping gesture with his arm), much to the delight of sold-out crowds at the old Spectrum. And the way in which he made it look so easy, posting 849 points in just 790 games with a staggering plus-299.

POULIN: DOUBLE SHORTHANDED MEANS DOUBLE THE FUN

There have been some remarkable shorthanded goals in Flyers' history, but none can match the one that took place in Game 6 of the 1985 Stanley Cup Semifinal series against the Quebec Nordiques at the Spectrum.

With the Flyers up 1–0 but down two men early in the second period, it looked like a sure thing that the Nordiques' high-voltage power play would at least tie the score. After all, 1:23 of two-man advantage can seem like an eternity in a situation like this. Then came a moment that still gives every veteran Flyers fan goosebumps.

Poulin took a gamble, stepped into a blueline exchange between Mario Marois and Peter Stastny, then was off to the races.

The Flyers captain would later recall how he would have plenty of time to think about how to get a shot past Quebec goaltender Mario Gosselin. He remembered the scouting report, which said go high, preferably to the glove side, so that's exactly what he did, firing the puck high into the net.

That sent the Flyers' bench and a sold-out Spectrum crowd into a frenzy. The momentum was clearly on the Flyers' side at 2–0, and they went on to a 3–0 win, clinching the series and sending them to the Stanley Cup Final against the Edmonton Oilers.

"I had a breakaway for literally three-quarters of the ice, which is way too much time to think," Poulin would later recall. "All series we had been preaching to shoot high on Gosselin, shoot high. I got into the tops of the circles and then just beat him high to the glove side."

Through it all, he remained a modest sort, never calling attention to himself and always quietly making it known that his faith was his true inner strength.

No wonder then that late-'80s sidekicks like Ron Hextall and Craig Berube weren't all that surprised about the remarkable comeback Propp has staged.

"When you think of him as a player, he was the most driven player I've ever played with to score," said Hextall, former general manager and vice president of the Flyers.

"As a matter of fact, it used to drive me nuts because he would stand by the boards when the drill was going on, he would shoot pucks in the net [while] I'm trying to focus on what's coming at me. I didn't like pucks in the net. He would be shooting them, not to piss me off but just because he was driven to score.

"I appreciated him in practice because on every drill he wanted to score. I wanted guys to try to score. Because you want it to be as game-like as possible. Some guys come in and just kind of shoot the puck. He shot to score, every single shot."

That determination serves Propp well in his current battle.

"When you look at what he's been through and his drive to score, it's sort of been like that with his drive to recover," Hextall said. "That's extremely admirable to look at a guy that's been through what he's been through and come back as well as he has. It is certainly a testament to his desire."

Berube sat alongside Propp on the Flyers bench and now works behind one as coach of the St. Louis Blues. He saw firsthand the type of personality Propp brought to the team.

"Brian has always been a determined, focused guy," Berube said. "Look at his career—he scored a lot of goals, he was a good player. For a little guy back then, to be scoring goals like that was something.

"It was unfortunate to have a stroke at an early age like that. He's always been a positive, forward-looking guy. He doesn't dwell on the future or negativity so much. That was a big part of him just being able to pull through this and be where he's at right now."

Players from a generation back saw how Propp recovered from a devastating hit by Montreal's Chris Chelios in the 1989 Eastern

Conference Final, which sent him to the hospital. Despite the injury, he became an effective player the following season.

Berube figured nothing less—and the same with winning against the recent stroke.

"He could have just said, 'Okay, bad luck.' But he doesn't," Berube said. "He finds a way to do it, to live a normal life. To see him play golf, he's still pretty good. He looks ahead at what he has to do to live a good life. He does it. That's really what it boils down to."

To this day, the guffaw is Propp's trademark move. And something like a little old stroke isn't going to change that.

"Scott McKay and I went to see comedian Howie Mandel in concert at Atlantic City in 1986," Propp recalled. "Howie explained what a guffaw was, which is the left to right shorthand movement where you raise your arm toward the ceiling. I thought it was pretty cool, and I thought that I could use a little more personality after I scored a goal.

"I incorporated the guffaw as part of my celebration. I started the guffaw the following year after I scored my first goal of the season. I never intended it to be an 'in your face' type of celebration in front of the opponents. I would do it more toward center ice. The guffaw caught on, and I continued doing it ever since.

"I also do it when I am golfing at charity outings when I would make a great shot, perhaps a birdie. I will do it every once in a while when I am playing for the alumni, too. The guffaw is just a personality trait that has followed me around."

Only 87 players in NHL history have scored 1,000 points. Propp, who in 2019 was the winner of the Philadelphia Sports Writers Association's most courageous award, is one of them. He was something special in the game of hockey, and now he's showing he's something special in the game of life.

24

MARK HOWE: BORN TO BE GOOD

He was one of the fastest skaters in professional hockey, but on this night, in this moment, he could not move an inch.

In a game on December 27, 1980, Mark Howe slid hard into the pointed metal center of the net, leaving the Hartford Whaler player with a five-inch-deep gash in his lower back. Motionless, Howe thought his hockey career might be over.

For the son of Mr. Hockey, aka Gordie Howe, it was a horrific accident.

"I remember my dad came to the hospital," Mark recalled. "He looked at it, and he thought he was going to be sick. I knew I was in trouble."

Doctors told him that if the impaling metal had come one inch closer to his spine, he would have been paralyzed.

As bad as the outcome was—Mark would lose 21 pounds due to a forced liquid diet to prevent intestinal infections, and he would need months to fully recover—it turned out to be a fortuitous turn of events for the Flyers. Why? Because Hartford management lost faith in Howe, and they sent him packing to the Flyers in a four-player trade.

A healthy Howe played a decade for the Flyers, becoming the No. 1 defenseman in team history with three runner-up finishes for the Norris Trophy (best NHL defenseman), two Stanley Cup Final appearances, and induction into the Hockey Hall of Fame.

Oh, and he was plus-400 for his NHL career.

Howe had already established his hockey credentials by the age of 16 when he became the youngest player ever to compete on a U.S. Olympic men's hockey team, which took home a silver medal at the 1972 Winter Games in Sapporo, Japan.

Then it was off to the World Hockey Association (now defunct), where he won a pair of championships playing alongside his famous father and his brother, Marty. Mark was a left wing back in those days, but his smooth skating and brilliant hockey mind made it an easy transition to defense.

By the 1976–77 season, Howe was a full-time defenseman. Before the 1977–78 season, the Howes moved their family act to Hartford, Connecticut, to compete for the Whalers.

After the trade to the Flyers, Howe helped make his team a strong contender. When rookie coach Mike Keenan came on board in 1984–85, the Flyers finished with the most points in the NHL that season and made it all the way to Game 5 of the Stanley Cup Final before losing to Edmonton.

It was clear that anyone who partnered with Howe on defense would put up strong numbers. When Brad McCrimmon finished the 1985–86 season with a career-high plus-83 (his season closest to that number was plus-52), he was asked how he could account for such a lofty figure.

"Right over there," grinned McCrimmon, gesturing at Howe's locker. Howe had finished the year with an NHL-leading plus-85.

Paul Holmgren, now president of the Flyers, said he knew of only one player as driven as Howe—Hall of Famer Bobby Clarke.

"[Howe] was one of the most competitive guys I've ever played with," Holmgren said. "He was as competitive as Clarkie. People don't remember that because of his overall skill and talent."

The 1985–86 season was clearly Howe's best. Even though he was still bothered by back trouble, part of it stemming back to 1980, his numbers were spectacular. In addition to the plus-85, he scored seven shorthanded goals, which remains tied for the team record. His 24 goals and 82 points also remain in the Flyers' record books for a defenseman.

The following season would be the last in which Howe enjoyed the semblance of good health.

At 32, Howe led the Flyers back to the Stanley Cup Final, this time with rookie goalie Ron Hextall standing the game on its ear (he would win both the Vezina Trophy and the Conn Smythe Trophy for playoff MVP) and a front line of Rick Tocchet, Brian Propp, and Pelle Eklund.

If not for a debilitating shoulder injury that kept Tim Kerr out of the lineup, the Flyers might have made Game 7 against the Oilers a little more interesting. After that glorious performance, Howe's game began to decline, a victim of back and knee problems. Eventually he was reduced to part-time status.

"Mark had to overcome a lot," Holmgren said. "Besides the back, he was the son of one of the greatest players there ever was. Can you imagine what that must have been like?

"There are some players who look at the game like a chessboard. They anticipate and can see moves ahead. That was Mark."

DAIGNEAULT: THE GOAL THAT ECHOES AROUND THE WORLD

When the infamous wind storm blew the roof off the Spectrum on the afternoon of February 17, 1968, Philadelphia sports fans thought for sure they had seen and heard the last of such local sports arena craziness.

But it nearly happened again—at least in a figurative sense—the night of May 28, 1987. And this time it wasn't the weather's fault.

In Game 6 of the Flyers–Edmonton Oilers Stanley Cup Final battle, J.J. Daigneault scored with 5:32 to play, leading the Flyers to a 3–2 win and forcing a Game 7 back at Edmonton. Many say the roar of the crowd after that goal was the loudest they had heard in the 31-year history of the building.

"It felt like I was at a rock concert," goalie Ron Hextall said later.

The Flyers had been down 2–0 in this game, and with Edmonton stars Wayne Gretzky and Mark Messier patrolling the ice, it didn't look good for the home team. But Daigneault's long point shot, created by a Jari Kurri turnover, eluded goalie Grant Fuhr and completed the three-goal comeback.

"There's a lot of players over the years I talk to that were in that series that were with the Flyers or Oilers, and they all say it was the loudest they had ever heard a building," Daigneault said. "I can't disagree with them. I think it was a great moment, and one I'll cherish for the rest of my life."

The Flyers trailed 2–0 before Lindsay Carson scored at 7:12 of the second period, then Brian Propp tied it at 13:04 of the third. Daigneault's goal set up the first Stanley Cup Final Game 7 since 1971.

Following the 1991–92 season, Flyers general manager Russ Farwell granted Howe free agency. He returned to Detroit with hopes of winning an elusive Stanley Cup. It was a homecoming of sorts, because it was where his father had played for so many years. Howe helped a young defenseman by the name of Nicklas Lidström, who turned out to be a pretty good backliner in his own right.

Under coach Scotty Bowman, the Red Wings did make it to the Final in Howe's last season but were swept by the New Jersey Devils.

Upon retirement, Howe was inducted into the Flyers' Hall of Fame in 2001 and the U.S. Hockey Hall of Fame in 2003. He had to wait more than a decade past his eligible date to be inducted into the Hockey Hall of Fame in 2011. Shortly after, in 2012, the Flyers retired his No. 2, making him and his father only the second father-son combination to have their numbers retired by NHL franchises. (Detroit has retired Gordie's No. 9; the only other pair are Bobby and Brett Hull.)

Howe's plus-400 is a record for a U.S.-born defenseman, as is his plus-54 in the playoffs. Those seven shorthanded goals in 1985–86 are also the most ever by a U.S.-born defenseman.

Currently he's director of pro scouting for the Red Wings and uses his home in Jackson, New Jersey, as his base of operations.

Holmgren can relate to Howe because he went through a series of serious injuries of his own. In 1976, he nearly lost an eye when he went down to the ice and was hit by an errant skate. Then he almost died on a Boston hospital's operating table when doctors realized he had a terrible allergic reaction to the anesthesia they were using.

"I remember talking with Mark about [the back accident] a number of times," Holmgren said. "Horrifying. Horrifying to watch. It took him months just to get walking right again."

What compels athletes to come back from such terrifying events? Is it for the love of the game? A biological urge to compete?

"It's both," Holmgren said. "It's the love of the game, but it's also the need for the competitiveness that drives you."

Holmgren became good friends with Howe, maybe in part because they had been through so much together.

"Who knows what goes through your mind in that situation?" Holmgren said. "'Am I going to walk again, let alone play?' To bounce back from that, he didn't miss a beat. It was incredible.

"When you think about it, [the metal protrusion] just missed his spinal cord, his internal organs. To come back and play again at that level is pretty spectacular."

The Howe family filed a lawsuit against the league, which led to a change in the net design. Hopefully, that change spared a lot of young players a similar fate.

While Howe did spend time with Hartford and Detroit, he discloses the most memorable years of his career were with the Flyers. He said as much on March 6, 2012, when the Flyers retired his number, putting his name in the rafters along with Bernie Parent (1), Barry Ashbee (4), Bill Barber (7), Clarke (16), and Eric Lindros (88).

"It's the highest honor anyone can get from his individual team," Mark said. "I accept this honor with tremendous respect.

"When I got the call, I thought there was no better honor. The 10 years I played in Philadelphia were the best quality years of my career. Without those years, I never would have made it to the Hockey Hall of Fame. I'm grateful the Flyers think I'm worthy of that honor."

There never really was any doubt—not when someone gets off the deck to have the kind of career Mark Howe did.

25

TIM KERR:
BROAD SHOULDERS, BRAVE HEART

Tim Kerr was blessed with size (6′3″, 225 pounds) and talent, and not many showed more inner strength on the ice or faced down more personal tragedy.

And this we can be sure of—only one Flyer had the quickness and power to deliver four goals in an incredible span of 8 minutes and 16 seconds...and in one period of a playoff game no less.

Somehow, NHL scouts managed to miss all this potential in the late '70s when a broad-shouldered kid skated out of Windsor, Ontario, without so much as a mention at the NHL draft. At the time, little did they know that six years after signing with the Flyers, Kerr would do the unthinkable and light up Madison Square Garden in a Stanley Cup playoff game for those NHL-record four goals.

The only people who weren't surprised were his teammates. This was in the middle of Kerr's four-season stretch of 50-plus goals, and the Flyers knew that just about anything was possible.

"We always called him the Big Man for a reason," said Hall of Fame defenseman Mark Howe, a former teammate of Kerr's. "He was so big and strong. He was so important to our team. Normally when you get into a playoff series, you count on your goalie to win the game. [It's] very rare when you count on another player to win the game, but I always felt like having Timmy in our lineup—the goalie would win one and Timmy would win one.

"If we could find a way for the other 18 players to win two games, we would win the series. That's how important Timmy was."

Kerr had some of the best hands hockey has ever seen, and the only thing that may have kept him from becoming one of its all-time best players was getting dealt a bad hand or two from life. Kerr overcame countless injuries on the ice and personal tragedy off it to become the NHL's seventh-ranked goals-per-game scorer. And he did it all in a matter-of-fact, stoic fashion that made him one of the most popular players in Flyers history.

Kerr can look back with pride on a career that, at its peak, offered him the potential to become a future Hockey Hall of Fame resident.

But debilitating shoulder, knee, and groin injuries halted his spectacular mid-'80s run when both he and the Mike Keenan–led Flyers were at the height of their power.

Off the ice, Kerr was equally challenged by the death of his wife, Kathy, who passed away 10 days after childbirth in 1990.

Fans might wonder what Kerr could have done in those memorable Stanley Cup Final meetings with Edmonton in 1985 and 1987 if he had been healthy, but he doesn't.

"It's hockey. It's pretty much the luck of the draw," said Kerr, who now operates Tim Kerr Power Play Realty in southern New Jersey, is a minor league hockey team owner, and is actively involved in charity work.

"I had a lot of ups and downs through my time with injuries. But the great thing about our teams back then was that a lot of guys played injured. A lot of guys had ups and downs also.

"We battled together and we don't have any what-ifs. I did the best I could, fought as hard as I could to stay healthy, and unfortunately I missed a lot of games. We gave it a shot, we came up a little short, but the effort was there."

Even with all the broken body parts, Kerr's career numbers are staggering.

In 655 games, he finished with 674 points, including 370 goals, 150 of them on the power play. He led the NHL three times in power play goals, including an NHL record 34 in 1984–85. In the playoffs that year, Kerr registered that remarkable four-goal power play hat trick in one period (April 13 vs. the New York Rangers), a record which we may never see broken.

But the injuries began to conspire against him at this point. His shoulder was held together by surgical screws, and he couldn't dress for the '87 playoffs, including the monumental Game 7 at Edmonton.

Again, Kerr doesn't want to play the what-if game, but goaltender Ron Hextall, former general manager of the Flyers, says Kerr's presence in the lineup that night might have made a difference.

FOUR GOALS, EIGHT MINUTES: ALL IN A NIGHT'S WORK

Many NHL players are happy if they score four goals in a month.

Once upon a time, Tim Kerr must have been really joyous because he scored four goals in eight minutes. Make that 8:16 to be exact, but who's counting?

In a first-round Stanley Cup/Patrick Division playoff game against the New York Rangers on April 13, 1985, Kerr lit up Madison Square Garden with one red light after another, paving the way for a 6–5 win.

Eventually, the Flyers would sweep the series and go on to reach the Stanley Cup Final.

Kerr was in the midst of a four-season run in which he surpassed the 50-goal mark all four times. So his teammates weren't surprised when Kerr caught fire against the Rangers.

On the Flyers' bench, there were smiles all around.

"All we were thinking was, 'Get him back out on the ice,'" teammate Brian Propp said, "and keep shooting."

Three of the four goals came on the power play. Kerr still holds the record for most power play goals in a season at 34. Pittsburgh great Mario Lemieux would later go on to score four goals in a period in 1989. But he's considered one of the greatest goal scorers the game has ever known. Come to think of it, maybe Kerr should be mentioned with that elite company.

If not for serious injuries that cut short his career, who knows how many goals he would have scored?

"It was a huge factor," Hextall recalled. "He was our best goal scorer. Would he have made a difference? I believe he would have.

"Timmy had such a knack for scoring goals, and I think in a series as close as that was, to have a goal scorer like that in your lineup could have made a difference."

Kerr suffered three knee injuries and a broken leg in his first four seasons with the Flyers. But it was the shoulder that ultimately slowed him after seasons of 54, 54, 58, and 58 goals. The knee issues limited him to just eight games in 1987–88. But he battled back to score 48 goals the following year and was recognized with the Bill Masterton Trophy for perseverance.

Then came the family tragedy in 1990. Again, he stayed on course and showed his character.

"He was a really solid, stable guy," Hextall said. "You look at situations as a group, when the team was a little frazzled, you look at guys like Tim and he was always calm.

"Tim was a good example for the young players. Never got too excited, never got too down. I think that's why he was as consistent as he was."

Kerr never regained his prowess after that 48-goal campaign and, following 1989, would score only 41 goals over parts of four seasons, finishing up with the New York Rangers and Hartford before retiring at 32.

Some believe, if not for the injuries, he might have scored somewhere around 500 goals and been in the Hall of Fame.

"I certainly believe he would have had a shot at the Hall if he had been healthy and productive over a longer period of time," Hextall said. "On the power play, it wasn't just his size but his hands. He would jump in a hole and he would only have to be there for a tenth of a second. Bang!"

Kerr says just being in the Flyers' Hall of Fame will suffice.

"I'm not much of a public figure," he offered. "It's really not that important to me. What goes around, comes around. Do the best you can. I'm not in the NHL Hall of Fame, but it certainly doesn't change my thoughts about the game."

Today, Kerr stays active in the sport through his ownership of two teams in the Southern Professional League (Pensacola, Florida; Biloxi, Mississippi).

His realty business thrives, and his charities, overseen by his second wife, Midge, remain close to his heart. They have raised more than $2 million over two decades. Beneficiaries include the Wounded Warriors Project; a Splash and Dash kids event for a young cancer patient named Jay Devico; and a 7K run and 5K walk for the aid of the family of a fallen soldier, Johnny Kihm.

The Kerr family now has five children and life is good. In a sense, it's a nice payback for some of the tough luck on the road along the way.

"To lose Kathy, obviously it was a crazy period of my life," Kerr told hockey writer Jay Greenberg. "My kids know the story, but it's not a conversation in my house every day. I was blessed to meet another woman and wife and be able to grow my family.

"Everybody has periods in their life they look back upon as not an easy time, but I am certainly not one to dwell on what-if. I'm very fortunate with what I have today and look forward to tomorrow."

Howe remembers those days quite well.

"I got a chance to spend a little time with Timmy after his wife had passed," Howe said. "Actually, Homer [Paul Holmgren] was the coach and he brought Timmy and I out to Los Angeles with the team. The kind of person he was, Timmy was apologizing to me that he just hadn't been the same. He had come off his shoulder injury and everything else. I was like, 'Oh my God, Timmy, you're so strong.' I don't think he was ever the same after that as a player. And justifiably so.

"But for a number of years, Timmy was so vital to our team. When Timmy started breaking down, that's when our team began to decline. When you lose 50 goals a year, that's an absolute huge difference in an organization."

Like Hextall, Howe believes Kerr could have joined him in the Hall of Fame if not for the bad fortune of those injuries.

"Yeah, if not for the shoulder problems, he might have been in the Hall," Howe said. "If he was able to keep on scoring 50 goals a year like he was, I think that would have been a definite possibility."

Howe and Kerr had similar approaches to the game. The laughter stopped on the way out the locker room door. Then it was all business.

"The grumpier I was, the more ticked off I was, the better I would play," Howe said. "Timmy had the same demeanor all the time. Even when it came to guys getting together, a lot of functions, Timmy was a loner. But nobody minded that one bit. He's one of the nicest people I ever played with."

26

PELLE LINDBERGH: GONE TOO YOUNG

James Dean, Steve Prefontaine, and Paul Walker all died by going too quickly in cars. The thing is, they were accustomed to living life in the fast lane and accepted the risk.

Pelle Lindbergh knew that world, too, but he was a relative newcomer to such a culture and may not have known how to handle it. As a result, Flyers history was changed forever, both on and off the ice.

When the Flyers' young goaltender crashed his new Porsche 930 Turbo into a brick wall during the early morning hours of Sunday, November 10, 1985, news of the tragedy shocked the Philadelphia hockey community.

Teammates and coaches thought of the 26-year-old Swede as a fun-loving kid but certainly not a party animal. But on that fateful night he chose to take a different road and, just like the aforementioned trio, it cut short what was—and what could have been—a brilliant career.

Lindbergh seemed destined for greatness almost from the moment he stepped onto the international stage at the 1980 Winter Olympics in Lake Placid, New York. His performance there started innocently enough when Sweden managed an early 2–2 tie with the United States. Lindbergh obviously played well, but not much was made of the effort because the young American team was not considered a threat for the top two medals.

Imagine the retro-babble after the USA squad stunned the world by upsetting the mighty Russian team and then won gold in the Miracle on Ice classic. As it turns out, Lindbergh and his mates were the only ones to earn so much as a single point off the Yankee Doodle Dandies. At the time, Lindbergh was already property of the Flyers, who had just ended a professional sports record 35-game (25-0-10) unbeaten streak. The Flyers had selected Lindbergh in the second round (35th overall) of the 1979 NHL Entry Draft.

His rise to pro hockey stardom didn't take long.

After playing just a season and a half for the American Hockey League's Maine Mariners, Lindbergh joined the Flyers late in the 1981–82 campaign for a handful of games. The following year, a record of 23–13–3 earned him a spot on the NHL's All-Rookie team.

Then, in 1984–85, he reached his full potential, posting a league-leading 40 wins against only 17 losses and seven ties to win the Vezina Trophy. Bernie Parent and Ron Hextall are the only other Flyer goalies to win the coveted award.

He began the 1985–86 season in equally brilliant fashion, with a mark of 6–2–0 and a career-low 2.88 goals-against average.

And then, in an instant, it was over.

After a Flyers' 5–3 win over Boston (in which he did not play), Lindbergh chose this rare night to take in a team party. Then, after the festivities ended, he climbed into his car with two other passengers. At an estimated 80 miles per hour, he lost control of the vehicle as it smashed into a wall in front of an elementary school in Somerdale, New Jersey.

Officials later determined his blood alcohol level to be .24 percent, well above the New Jersey legal limit of .10. Medical experts declared the young player brain dead just hours later, but doctors waited until Lindbergh's father arrived from Sweden in order to get consent to take him off life support. Subsequently, a five-hour operation took place to harvest his heart and other organs for possible transplant to other needy recipients.

Late on that Sunday morning, players gathered at captain Dave Poulin's house at the behest of coach Mike Keenan. It was a chance to share the grieving process and somehow start to push through what everyone knew was going to be a difficult time.

"I knew a guy who worked at the school where the accident happened," said Mark Howe, who was one of the first to arrive at Poulin's house.. His daughter was our babysitter. "So it kind of touched home a little closer."

A young Flyers team had already made its mark just months before when it faced the Wayne Gretzky–Mark Messier juggernaut operating out of Edmonton and took the mighty Oilers to five games in the Stanley Cup Final. There was a sense that Lindbergh and the Flyers

ON THIS DATE

MARCH 22, 1984

The Flyers set a single-game record for goals, blasting the visiting Pittsburgh Penguins 13–4. Tim Kerr leads the way with six points (two goals, four assists) and a plus-7 rating. Dave Poulin and Ilkka Sinisalo each add three goals and an assist.

The Flyers equal the record in a 13–2 romp past visiting Vancouver on October 18, 1984.

were destined for even greater things just when the accident took all that away.

"When I got the call from Dave Poulin, Dave said there's been a bad accident," Howe said. "You get the news and your whole body just kind of goes numb. The only other time I can compare it to was when I got the call about Brad [McCrimmon, who died in a Russian jetliner crash]. It's just an absolute numb feeling.

"It was good to be at the house but the real sanctuary was skating. Once you got on the ice, that was my sanctuary. We had everybody out there and that's where you have closeness, your bond. Mike Keenan did an outstanding job keeping everybody together."

Needless to say, it took a considerable amount of time for the Flyers to get back on an even emotional keel.

"Next game, I scored a goal," Howe said. "I came to the bench and I think I cried three or four tears. Then I kind of kicked myself in the ass and said get going here."

All this perhaps could have been avoided if there had been some sort of curfew in place. But let's not forget, this took place not all that long after the rambunctious Broad Street Bullies had run roughshod over the NHL for two Stanley Cups and two other Cup Final appearances.

"We accepted [nightlife] as part of sports," said Bob Clarke, the Flyers' general manager at the time. "And it shouldn't have been.

"Pelle didn't do anything I didn't do. I probably didn't have a teammate who didn't do what he did."

Our destiny is determined by the decisions we make. For Lindbergh, this was a bad one.

"He wasn't even going to go out," said his fiancée, Kerstin Pietzsch, said days after the tragedy. "But he decided he should go out to meet the guys."

Indeed. The Flyers had just put together a 10-game winning streak to move them to the top of the Patrick Division standings. Why not celebrate with a few drinks at a bar in the Coliseum in Voorhees, New Jersey, where the Flyers practiced in those days?

Parent, who addressed a personal issue with alcohol over the years, was sort of an unofficial mentor to Lindbergh in those days and said he did not see a similar concern in his protégé.

"[Lindbergh] had a few beers after games," Parent said, "just like everybody else. But he never had a problem. I never had to talk to him about that."

Perhaps no one misses Lindbergh more than Parent.

"He had only scratched the surface of his potential," Parent told the *New York Times* shortly after Lindbergh's death. "As a goaltender, he had learned how to bounce back from a bad game, from a bad period. As a human being, he was like a son to me."

Goaltenders are known as somewhat fearless athletes who don't mind facing down 100-mile-per-hour slap shots, some directly off the front of their masks. In this case, that bravery bordered on recklessness.

"He had a fast car," Clarke said. "He enjoyed driving fast. He scared me."

Rick Tocchet, just starting his second season with the team, couldn't believe what had happened.

"We were a real close team," Tocchet said. "He was just an infectious guy on our team. Everybody loved him. He was easygoing. Usually, with some goalies, you were nervous to be around. With him, you could walk on his pads, you could touch his stick. Myself as a rookie, he made me feel welcomed."

The late Ed Snider, founder and owner of the team at the time, was caught up in the euphoria of the 10-game winning streak and believed his team could achieve great things with Lindbergh in its future.

"I will never forget walking out of the Spectrum that night," Snider said. "I was thinking that this was the best team we ever had. I was thinking they would be even better than the Broad Street Bullies. Pelle was the backbone of the team. The contrast between that night and the next morning was extreme."

Some believe the tragedy prevented the Flyers from going back to the Stanley Cup Final in 1986.

"It was very difficult," said Brian Propp. "We started off the season very well, but when you lose a friend and a rising star at the same time, it's on your mind."

Added Tocchet, "The world just stopped for us. Things were going good. It just stopped everything. Looking back, I was a walking zombie."

He wasn't alone. Thirty years later, people still shake their heads at the mention of the little Swede.

27

THE WILD GOALIE WHO BECAME A MILD GM

Alanis Morissette's 1996 hit "Ironic" describes the way Ron Hextall's career as a player and front-office executive has turned out.

Back in 1982, as he waited to be selected in the draft, the budding young goalie had particular disdain for one NHL team.

The Flyers.

Growing up and watching the Flyers try to intimidate his father and uncle—feisty NHL players during the Broad Street Bullies' heyday—Hextall did not have warm and fuzzy feelings about the Orange and Black.

"I absolutely hated them," he said in 2014, shortly after he was named the seventh general manager in the Flyers' history.

When he was 18 and working a summer job at an auto dealership, Hextall was changing the oil on a car when he received a phone call and learned the Flyers had drafted him in the sixth round. Little did he know that it would be a life-changing development.

"You think you hate a team—and I did at the time—but what I didn't realize [is that] I had a strong admiration for them as well," Hextall said, smiling at the memory. "And all of a sudden, when I got drafted by them, it was almost like an instant love affair with the Flyers. It was actually pretty ironic."

Maybe Morissette can work that story into "Ironic II."

When Hextall was named the Flyers' GM, he called it "my dream job." And with good reason. As a player, Hextall cut his teeth with the Flyers, and he had his best seasons with the team. So in a sense, the former standout goaltender was coming home.

"I've got a special feeling about this organization, and I am absolutely honored and thrilled to be sitting here," Hextall said when he replaced Paul "Homer" Holmgren, who was promoted to club president. "I'll do the best job I can, and I'll work hard to reach the ultimate goal of bringing the Stanley Cup back to Philadelphia."

It never happened. In a stunning move, Hextall was fired during his fifth season, getting dismissed on November 26, 2018. Holmgren did the firing. He and Dave Scott, the CEO of Comcast Spectacor, the Flyers' parent company, thought Hextall's rebuild was taking too long and that he wasn't aggressive enough in the trade market.

Hextall said he was "shocked" when Holmgren delivered him the news.

Both Holmgren and Scott lauded Hextall for improving the farm system, making shrewd draft picks, and getting the Flyers' cap situation in order. But they thought the Flyers should have made strides from the previous season, when they had 98 points and finished third in the Metropolitan Division. At the time Hextall was fired, the Flyers were seventh in the Metro and on pace for just 78 points.

"The good news is we're holding a good hand," Scott said after the firing was announced. "We have a lot to work with, more than when I came in five years ago, more than Ron had [when he became the GM in 2014]."

When he was hired, Hextall was dealt a difficult hand. Because of several questionable long-term signings, he inherited a team that had little cap space to maneuver—and it took him until the end of the 2017–18 season to dig out of the financial mess he was dealt.

Prior to the 2018–19 season, Hextall signed free-agent James van Riemsdyk, a left winger coming off a 36-goal season with Toronto, to a five-year, $35-million deal. It was, by far, the most significant signing since he took the job.

In his first four years after he replaced Holmgren, Hextall also rebuilt the farm system into one of the NHL's best when it had been near the bottom.

With Hextall calling the shots, the Flyers' lineup was filled with up-and-coming young players like Shayne Gostisbehere, Ivan Provorov, and Travis Konecny, along with veteran stars such as Claude Giroux and Jake Voracek. And with the farm system loaded and featuring goalie Carter Hart, it seemed to be a matter of time before the Flyers ended their long Stanley Cup drought.

Then came the slow start to 2018–19 and Hextall's shocking exit.

CHUCK FLETCHER IS LATEST GM TO TRY TO DELIVER A CUP

A week after Ron Hextall was stunningly fired on November 26, 2018, Chuck Fletcher became just the eighth different general manager in the Flyers' 50-plus-year history.

His mission? To deliver the Flyers' first Stanley Cup championship since 1975.

Of all the GMs, no one made a bigger impact than Keith "The Thief" Allen, whose shrewd trades helped the team win Stanley Cups in 1974 and 1975. Allen was the general manager from 1969 to 1983.

Bob Clarke, the franchise's most iconic player, is the only person in franchise history to have two different stints as a general manger, serving from 1984 to 1990, and again from 1994 to 2007.

Bud Poile was the first general manager, and he did a great job in the expansion draft, setting the Flyers on the right path. Poile and Allen are in the Hockey Hall of Fame. As a Flyers general manager, Poile was followed by Allen, Bob McCammon, Clarke, Russ Farwell, Clarke again, Paul Holmgren, Hextall, and Fletcher. Fletcher became the first GM hired by the Flyers who did not play for them since Farwell, who was there from 1990 to 1994.

Hextall was hired as the general manager in 2014, and by the start of the 2018–19 season, he had built up the farm system and done a commendable job digging out of the cap problems he inherited. No matter. The Flyers' brass thought his plan was taking too long, and they were unhappy he didn't make a signature trade to speed up the process.

Enter Fletcher, who formerly served as the general manager in Minnesota, helping the team to six playoff berths in his nine seasons.

"I'm extremely honored and humbled," Fletcher said after being hired by Holmgren, the club president, and Dave Scott, CEO and chairman of the Flyers' parent company, Comcast Spectacor. "I've been in the league for many years, and the Flyers have been one of the standard bearers for the National Hockey League. To have the opportunity to be general manager of the Flyers is a dream come true."

Hextall, who as an assistant general manager played a part in the Los Angeles Kings' 2012 Stanley Cup championship, has impressive NHL bloodlines. His grandfather, Bryan Hextall Sr., was a Hall of Fame right winger with the New York Rangers who twice led the league in goals. Hextall's father, Bryan Jr., a center, played for five NHL teams before his career ended in 1976; and his uncle, Dennis, a two-time All-Star left winger with the old Minnesota North Stars, had a penalty-filled, 12-year career that ended in 1980 with Washington.

"I wasn't born yet when my grandfather was playing, and I was pretty young when my dad played," Hextall said. "I was 12 years old when my dad retired. I would hear things about my grandfather and would certainly talk to him. I'd visit with him in the summertime." He paused.

"The nerve of him to actually be wearing a New York Rangers jersey!"

The Rangers, of course, are one of the Flyers' most hated rivals.

Hextall was 20 when his grandfather died in 1984 at age 70. "He was a quiet man who didn't say a lot, but when he spoke, you listened," Hextall said. "He didn't talk a lot about his playing days, but he would always tell my dad and uncle, 'You can't score from the penalty box.'"

That, apparently, was his not-too-subtle way of saying they needed to play with more discipline. As a player, Hextall didn't exactly take that advice. He was one of the league's most combative goaltenders.

Hextall said his father was his biggest influence in steering him toward hockey.

"He didn't put pressure on me to be a hockey player. There was no pushing or prodding," he said. "All he said was, 'If you want to play hockey, great. All I ask is you work hard.'"

Hextall, who helped the development of goalies Jonathan Quick and Jonathan Bernier when he was an assistant GM in Los Angeles, played 11 of his 13 NHL seasons with the Flyers.

"I wanted to be like my dad. And I had the exposure to it just from being around an NHL team as a kid and skating around with the guys," Hextall said, adding that he and his brother would watch practice, and skate before and after practice.

"The players would fool around with us on the ice. I think from a young age I knew what I wanted to do just because of the fact I was around the lifestyle and the excitement."

When Hextall was named Flyers GM, one of the first people he called was his father.

"He was excited for me, and so was my mom. My mom and dad are probably my biggest fans; they give me a lot of support," Hextall said shortly after he was hired. "They always have. Obviously, I've got my wife and kids as well, but going way back to childhood, [your parents] have to be your biggest supporters if you're going to be a hockey player. Someone said to me that minor-league hockey is a lifestyle, and it truly is for the parents. Pretty much your weekends are tied up for six or seven months, or nowadays maybe even more."

* * *

When he became the Flyers' GM in 2014, Hextall was left with little spending flexibility, and he inherited a weak farm system. In time, he dramatically improved both areas, and his team got younger and faster.

"There's always challenges, whether you have a lot of guys to sign or you're close to the cap or you need to get better," Hextall said after taking the job. "There are challenges every year. Quite honestly, when you're an ex-player, you love challenges. I look forward to seeing if we can move pieces for a better fit or whatever, and obviously get guys signed to fair deals that will fit under the cap. There's a little bit of manipulation in every area where we've got to look at everything."

Hextall was the Kings' assistant GM when they won the 2012 Stanley Cup with many ex-Flyers in their lineup. He played 11 years for the Flyers and is the franchise leader in games by a goaltender (498) and wins (240). After his playing days, he spent seven years in the Flyers' front office—three as a scout, four as director of pro player personnel—before joining the Kings in 2006.

With the Kings, Hextall aided in contract negotiations and oversaw their minor league operation, presiding over a Manchester AHL franchise that twice reached the Eastern Conference Final while he was there. Many of those minor leaguers later helped the Kings win the Stanley Cup.

Hextall returned to the Flyers in 2013 as an assistant GM and director of hockey operations. It was the Flyers' best move of the off-season, much better than signing past-his-prime Vinny Lecavalier.

"[Hextall's] probably the most highly thought-of guy who is not a general manager," Holmgren said at the time. "To add him to our staff is huge."

Hextall's family wanted to move back to the East Coast, and Philly is home to them, Holmgren said, adding that he and Hextall have been close over the years.

"The timing seemed right," Hextall said.

He added that he returned to the Flyers because of a "gut feeling," and claimed there were "no promises" that he would replace Holmgren at a certain point. "Did I think and hope this could happen at some point? Yes, I did...[but] there were no assurances from anybody."

One year later, Hextall replaced Holmgren.

"I wouldn't have taken this job if Paul Holmgren didn't want to move to the position he's moving to. I absolutely wouldn't. I would have refused. You can ask Homer. At one point when we talked about it, he said, 'Stop asking me that. I want to go where I'm going.... I'm very comfortable.'"

As a player, Hextall was perhaps the NHL's wildest goalie. His crease was his home. Enter at your own risk...and expect to get whacked by the goaltender's stick if you come close to him.

As a general manager, Hextall's demeanor was the complete opposite. Instead of making daring moves, he was patient in his decisions. He erred on the side of caution, for instance, before recalling a player from the minors or pulling the trigger on a deal.

Isn't it ironic.

28

MEET JOE KADLEC: THE FLYERS' FIXER

Joe Kadlec may not be recognized by many of today's Flyers fans, but he was one of the most influential people in franchise history.

As the Flyers' first public-relations director, he was there for their birth in 1967–68, for their two Stanley Cups, and as they became one of the NHL's winningest franchises in NHL history in the post-expansion era.

Thanks to the team's early success and Kadlec's tireless behind-the-scenes work, the Flyers' logo and brand have gone from unknown to iconic over the years.

According to his good friend Lou Nolan, the team's longtime public-address announcer, "Joe is a big reason for this franchise's success. In the early years, he was a pioneer in putting things together. He devised forms that kept the writers informed with different stats— forms that were then used by the entire league. He did lots of things that helped the team become known."

Before becoming the Flyers' PA announcer, Nolan worked alongside Kadlec in the public-relations department.

"Joe's famous words were, 'No problem,'" Nolan said. "If someone had a request, no matter how outlandish it was, he would find a way to get it done. And the players really relied on him for almost anything you can possibly think of. They'd be calling him for different things. Even in the off-season, he'd make travel plans for them, get a room for them, get a comp for them, air travel. He was their go-to guy."

Kadlec may be the only public-relations director to ever kick-start a trade.

The year was 1996, and former Flyers coach Mike Keenan was the coach and general manager of St. Louis. He was trying to deal one of his veteran players and he thought Flyers general manager Bob Clarke might have interest. Keenan couldn't get through to Clarke, so he decided to phone Kadlec.

"He called me and wanted to know if we'd be interested in Dale Hawerchuk," Kadlec said. "I finally got in to talk to Clarkie and gave him the message, and the next thing you know, Dale Hawerchuk was coming to Philadelphia. It was a fun day."

To get the 32-year-old center, the Flyers traded another center, Craig MacTavish, 37, to St. Louis, where he was reunited with Keenan, his coach when they won the Stanley Cup in 1994 with the New York Rangers.

A longtime resident of Cherry Hill, New Jersey, Kadlec has scads of amusing stories about his 40 years with the Flyers, including the time in 1975 he was keeping an eye on Reggie Leach's house while the star right winger was away, and he also had to "babysit" the Stanley Cup for him. The Flyers had just won their second Cup, and it was Leach's turn to spend time with it.

"My wife, Joan, was so scared that we would lose the Cup somehow or that it would get stolen, so we kept it up in the bedroom with us," Kadlec said. "We had all the people in the neighborhood come over and take pictures with the Cup."

Years earlier, Joe met his future wife while he worked for the Flyers and she worked for the 76ers, the NBA team located in the same building, the Spectrum. "She did some of the same things I did," Kadlec said. "She handled travelling arrangements for the Sixers, but she didn't travel like I did. I'd pass her office every day at the Spectrum on the way to the Flyers office."

They dated, fell in love, and got married on July 20, 1974—about two months after the Flyers won their first Stanley Cup. Rick MacLeish, who scored the winning goal in the Cup-clinching game that spring, was in the wedding party. So was assistant coach Mike Nykoluk and Nolan, among others.

* * *

Hockey was always an important part of Kadlec's life. His parents used to take him and his brother to Ramblers games in the old Eastern League. "We'd always go by the dressing-room door after the game for autographs," Kadlec said. Before the 1957–58 season, Ramblers trainer Frank Lewis—who later held the same position with the Flyers—asked

ON THIS DATE

SEPTEMBER 25, 1984

Bernie Parent becomes the first player who spent most of his career with the Flyers to be inducted into the Hall of Fame. In later years, many others (some players, some coaches, some executives) who spent significant time in Philadelphia would follow: Bobby Clarke (1987), Ed Snider (1988), Bill Barber (1990), Keith Allen (1992), Gene Hart (1997, Foster Hewitt Memorial Award), Mark Howe (2011), Fred Shero (2013), Eric Lindros (2016), Pat Quinn (2016), and Mark Recchi (2017).

him if he wanted to be a stick boy. Kadlec originally held that position for opposing teams and later for the Ramblers.

Years later, as a sports writer for the *Philadelphia Daily News*, Kadlec covered the Jersey Devils' minor-league team. While working as a sports clerk at the *Daily News*, one of Kadlec's jobs was picking winners in local horse races. They called him the "Kadlec Kid." He also went to all the news conference that dealt with the new NHL team that was rumored to be coming to Philadelphia. Before the Flyers' inaugural season in 1967–68, Kadlec wrote a series of stories for the *Daily News* that summer, advancing the club's arrival. He went to his paper's sports editor, Ben Callaway, and asked if he could be the Flyers' beat writer. He didn't have seniority, so he knew he wouldn't get the job. Two weeks later, he asked Calloway if he could put in a good word for him with the Flyers. Calloway complied. On August 1, 1967, Kadlec was hired by Flyers vice president Lou Scheinfeld as their first public-relations director. Nearly 300 people applied for the job.

"That made my year," Kadlec said of his new job.

There were adventures every day. Some not always wanted.

"Our first visit to Los Angeles that year, I'm in a cab going to the Forum," Kadlec said. "We go through a yellow light and, all of a sudden, these police cars converge on our cab—and a gun was sticking outside of each window. Four guns are staring at us."

Kadlec and Flyers trainers Dick Bielous and Lewis were asked to get out of the car. They were laughing because they knew they hadn't done anything wrong.

"Knock it off," one of the police officers said.

They quickly got quiet.

"They had us on the side of the road for 15 or 20 minutes and then they said, 'Sorry about that, guys.' It turned out that the cab had been used in a bank robbery the previous day. It had been cleared by the FBI, but I guess they had never told the local police," Kadlec said. "One of the police officers asked if there was anything he could do for us, and our trainer, Frank Lewis, a guy with great humor, told him, 'Find us the closest cleaners because we [s--t] our pants.'"

* * *

When the Flyers came into the NHL, it took them a while to draw fans.

"I remember coming back from our first training camp in Quebec City, and the first thing I did was go down to the Spectrum to see how it was coming along," Kadlec said of the building that was being erected. "And when I saw all those seats, I said, 'How the heck are we going to fill this building?' When I was with the old Philadelphia Ramblers, we would get less than 2,000 fans, so I didn't know how many [the Flyers] would be able to draw."

They sold just more than people 2,100 season tickets for their first year, and only 7,812 attended their home opener. But they had some success against the Original Six teams, and the fans started to get hooked. By the start of February, they had their first two back-to-back home sellouts for games against Chicago and Toronto, two Original Six teams. The Flyers won both games.

Kadlec remembers feeling pride when the Flyers got a prominent spot in the newspapers.

"The thing that got me," Kadlec said, "was a Monday morning when we had the top headline in the *Philadelphia Bulletin* sports page—we got that spot over the Eagles! That was pretty exciting. That's when we knew we were on our way.

"It was so important to get off to a great start that first season," he added.

Seven years later, more than two million people attended the Flyers' parade after they stunned the hockey world and won the Stanley Cup, defeating the favored Boston Bruins in the Final. They repeated as Cup champs in 1975, defeating Buffalo. Another parade followed.

Those two parades were definitely the highlight of his career with the Flyers, Kadlec said.

"Everybody was smiling, cheering for you. It was something special that I was not used to."

Another highlight was the out-of-nowhere unbeaten streak in 1979–80. The Flyers lost their second game of that season in Atlanta 9–2. On the plane ride home, Kadlec sat next to head coach Pat Quinn.

"He says to me, 'Joe, what a year this is going to be,'" Kadlec recalled.

Being a public-relations person, Kadlec stayed positive, telling the coach it was just one game and that better nights were ahead. The Flyers didn't lose in their next 35 games, going 25–0–10, the longest unbeaten streak in history for any of the four major sports.

"That's what you call a turnaround," Kadlec said.

* * *

From Kadlec to current award-winning public-relations director Zack Hill and everyone in between, the Flyers have become nationally known as one of the most media-friendly organizations in all sports. Kadlec is the one who built and nurtured that reputation.

"No matter what you needed, Joe was there for you," Nolan said.

In 2007, Kadlec retired after spending 40 seasons with the Flyers. Kadlec, who had been serving the team as director of fan services since 1997, remained a member of the organization as an ambassador.

During his four decades, "Joe has been an integral part of the team," Flyers chairman Ed Snider said at the time. "[We'll miss] all of Joe's charm, energy, enthusiasm and knowledge of our franchise," but he added it was comforting to know Kadlec would continue to spread the word about the hockey team as an ambassador.

During his 30 years of traveling with the Flyers, Kadlec had numerous duties. He was their traveling secretary at a time when teams flew commercial flights, making arrangements much more difficult than when they began taking charters. Kadlec kept impeccable stats, cranked out news releases, filled the media's needs, and was also the liaison between the Flyers and the Soviet Red Army when the teams met in that historic game at the Spectrum in 1976. The NHL also used him to handle PR duties with the Challenge Cup in New York in 1979, and for Rendez-vous '87 in Quebec City.

He handled his job with class, always going out of his way to accommodate people. Which is why, even today, 12 years after Kadlec retired, Flyers beat writers who travel to NHL cities all over North America are asked a familiar question: "How is Joe Kadlec doing?"

"The entire hockey world knows Joe Kadlec," Nolan said. "Whether someone is talking in French or English, in Montreal or Chicago or wherever, everyone knows Joe, everyone loves Joe. He always went out of the way for everybody. No matter what you needed, he would get it done. He was a little like Kerry Washington on that TV show *Scandal*. He was a fixer. And Lord knows, there were lots of incidents and things that happened with this pro team—as with any pro team—that had to be cleared up."

29

MIKE KEENAN: A LITTLE BIT OF HATE, A LOT OF RESPECT

It's one thing for a hockey coach to talk the talk. It's another to see if he can walk the walk.

The Flyers learned a lot from coach Mike Keenan in the mid-1980s. They also learned a lot about him, as well.

Keenan's first professional coaching gig came with the Flyers, and in his rookie season he took them all the way to the Stanley Cup Final. Only the Wayne Gretzky–Mark Messier juggernaut in Edmonton prevented Keenan's kids from raising the Cup for the third time in franchise history.

It didn't take long for Keenan to earn the nickname "Iron Mike" either. At 34 and not much older than his players, Keenan ran practices in stone-faced fashion, barking out orders like a drill sergeant and getting in the face of anyone who challenged his authority.

Some players harbored resentment at these sorts of tactics. Young Lindsay Carson was one of them. On a charter flight after a tough loss, Keenan, sitting in the traditional aisle seat in the first row, called Carson up from the back of the plane to join him. There he proceeded to give the kid a first-class chewing out, loud enough to be heard in the rear bathroom. Players put their heads down as Carson, red-faced with humiliation, returned to his seat.

Not too long after, the Flyers used a break in their schedule to visit Lake Placid for a few days to do some team bonding and informal scrimmaging. The players were getting dressed one morning when Coach Keenan stepped into the room in full uniform, fully intending to take part in the scrimmage.

"There were a lot of guys who really didn't like him," said Craig Berube with a sigh. "They were probably happy about it.

"But I remember that he walked right in the room in Lake Placid and had his gear on. I'm like, 'What is he doin'?' He's like, 'Well, boys, here's your chance!'"

"And he walked out and we had a scrimmage and he played."

Unfortunately for Iron Mike, Carson was playing on the opposing team. Eyewitness accounts state Carson spotted his coach along the boards from about 50 feet away, started skating full throttle, and created a crash that is still talked about some 30 years later.

But Keenan fancied himself a young Scotty Bowman, and sure enough, the next day, Keenan redesigned the scrimmage rosters and had Carson on *his* team. Then the whole team went out on the town to take in what little nightlife Lake Placid had to offer.

"He was different like that, being out that night at Lake Placid," Berube recalled. "He was out with the guys. He was kind of off the wall.

"He just coached differently than any coach I ever had. I think he just wanted to be unpredictable like Scotty. Mike really wasn't concerned about Xs and Os. He was just more concerned with how competitive you were, what was going on with your mind more than anything."

Keenan would go on to take the Flyers to a second Stanley Cup Final for the 1986–87 season. This time he had rookie goaltender Ron Hextall, a swashbuckling, stick-swinging whirling dervish who became the first netminder from a losing team to win the 23-year-old Conn Smythe Award for playoff MVP. (Since then, Anaheim's J.S. Giguere won the award in 2002–03.) The Flyers took the Gretzky-Messier well-Oiler-ed machine to a Game 7, only to fall short again.

The following season, there was mutiny in the air. Some of the veterans had had enough.

Philadelphia raced to a 3–1 lead in the best-of-seven first-round playoff series against Washington, only to have the Capitals rally with three straight victories, including an overtime crusher in Game 7. Soon after, Keenan was gone.

In perhaps a case of bad cop, good cop, the Flyers brought in Keenan's assistant, Paul Holmgren, as the next coach. As it turns out, it would take the Flyers a decade to get back to the Final.

Keenan went to the Final with Chicago in '92, then finally won it all with the New York Rangers in '94. Maybe if the Flyers had stuck with Keenan just a little longer.... After all, if you gave an honest effort, Keenan was likely to leave you alone.

ON THIS DATE

APRIL 13, 1985

Tim Kerr sets NHL playoff records for most goals in one period (four) and fastest four goals by one player (8:16) in the second period of the Flyers' 6–5 win over the New York Rangers at Madison Square Garden.

"He wasn't as much concerned with your positioning as he was about you competing hard, working hard," Berube said. "You had to bring something to the team. That's why he liked tough guys, because they brought something to him that he wanted."

Keenan sent writers running to their dictionaries (those old paper things, remember?) when he came in the door the first day in 1984 and started throwing around words like "synergy." By loose definition, he meant working together for a common goal or cause.

"We got beat real bad in a game and [Keenan] went around the room and pointed to about six of us—myself, [Dave] Brown, [Rick] Tocchet," Berube remembered. "He said to be at the rink at 8:00 tomorrow morning and be ready to go on the ice.

"So we got there and he just skated the s--t out of us for an hour. And he said, 'You know what? I just want to make sure you guys are ready for the playoffs.'"

File that one away under "R" for resentment.

One of the players who seemed to respond to Keenan's approach was Hextall. The goalie hailed from a hockey family. His grandfather, father, and uncle all played professionally. Maybe that old-school stuff worked on Hextall because of his appreciation for the fundamental side of the game.

"Mike was a smart guy," Hextall said. "He was really good to the core of the team—[Dave] Poulin, [Brian] Propp, [Mark] Howe, [Brad] McCrimmon. He was really good to those guys. And he was hard on some other guys. He kind of felt like he had to keep the big guys on his side to manage the rest."

In his final season, Keenan was having a tougher time getting players to take orders. One night in St. Louis, a young Scott Mellanby got taken to the woodshed by the Blues' Rob Ramage. Irate, Keenan walked over to Tocchet and instructed him to go out and settle the score. Legend has it Tocchet refused to go, perhaps signaling the beginning of the end.

When he replays this story, Hextall just grins.

"Mike actually liked it when players challenged him," Hextall said. "He felt like that was their character. If they were able to stand up to him, then they were going to go through the battle when it got really hard. So Mike liked stuff like that."

Which takes us back to Lake Placid. Hextall was there and shared a giggle or two himself when Keenan showed up in the locker room inviting trouble.

"Mike put the gear on," said Hextall, confirming Berube's version of the events. "He said, 'Boys, here's your time. Come and get me!'

"And Lindsay Carson ran him."

Grudgingly, players later admitted they respected what Keenan had done.

"Whether you liked him or not, Mike had courage," Hextall said. "He had success in that day. I don't know if that [style] would work today. But in that day and age, it worked.

"Guys might not have liked him but they respected him. I respected him. I didn't love everything he did. Didn't like it when he picked on Mellanby. Scotty was a worker, a gritty guy, and Mike was hard on him. I think he was hard on him just to piss off the rest of us. And it did."

Hextall does see some of the Bowman on-ice tactician and mind-game player in Keenan. Both coaches knew when to lean hard and when to back off, when to penalize poor play but reward good work even more.

"Mike didn't have to say much," Hextall said. "Just by his presence, walking around, you sort of knew what was going on.

"He could be a very personable guy. I like Mike the person but there were days when we would be in the room and it would be like,

'What the hell is going on today?' He would talk and joke around but when things weren't going well, you knew it.

"That's one of the reasons we were so successful. It wasn't acceptable to lose three out of four games. It just wasn't. And Mike made that very loud and clear."

Legend has it that one day during practice a veteran player known for pranks snuck into Keenan's office, took his car keys, and moved his car around the back of the building in South Jersey. Keenan came out, saw his car gone and, perhaps thinking it was stolen, started cursing, while several players cackled in the background.

The next day the Flyers were at a morning skate in Pittsburgh. Quietly, while the players were on the ice, Keenan instructed an equipment guy to grab a ladder, take the prankster's suit, and tape it to the locker room ceiling. The prankster walked in, saw his empty locker, and asked the guy next to him if he'd seen his suit. Without a word, the neighbor looked the guilty party straight in the eye and, while holding the stare, silently pointed one finger straight up.

Somewhere, Mike Keenan can still get a good laugh out of that one.

30

LINDROS CASE: THE TRADE THAT ALMOST WASN'T

When a bigger-than-life sports personality gets involved in a stranger-than-fiction legal case to decide his future, TV sets, radios, and newspapers almost burst into flames.

That's how hot the Eric Lindros trade/arbitration story was in June 1992. Even the most casual hockey fan had to sit up and take notice, especially in two of the largest cities in the U.S., Philadelphia and New York. For five days, team officials from the Flyers and Rangers practically held their breath waiting for a decision. Along with them rested the fate of nearly a dozen players, draft picks, cash, and maybe even a cheesesteak or corned beef on rye.

It all started when Lindros, the 6'4", 240-pound Goliath of a player, said he would not play for the Quebec Nordiques after they selected him first overall in the 1991 NHL Entry Draft. His reason was he preferred not to play in French-speaking Quebec, fearing it would restrain his endorsement possibilities. The Nordiques tried to get him to change his mind to no avail. Not even a rumored 10-year, $50-million contract could sway him.

So Lindros sat out a year (playing junior hockey for Oshawa and competing with the Canada Olympic Team at Lillehammer, Norway), forcing Quebec owner Marcel Aubut's hand. As the 1992 NHL Draft in Montreal approached, Aubut realized he couldn't hold on to Lindros much longer and began to entertain offers. The list of bidders reportedly included the Flyers, Rangers, Toronto Maple Leafs, Calgary Flames, and Detroit Red Wings.

There appeared to be some resolution to all the speculation when Aubut allegedly made a handshake agreement with Flyers president Jay Snider and general manager Russ Farwell on June 20. Things advanced to the point where Aubut gave Farwell permission to telephone Lindros and ask him if he would be willing to play in Philadelphia. Lindros' answer was yes.

So the Flyers scrambled to put their trade package together, initially including Rod Brind'Amour, Ron Hextall, Mark Recchi, Mike Ricci, Steve Duchesne, goaltender Dominic Roussel, multiple first-round draft picks, and $15 million in cash.

But hold everything.

Just hours after the Flyers thought they had a deal ready, Aubut got cold feet and reopened negotiations with the Rangers, who reportedly were ready to give up Alexei Kovalev, Tony Amonte, James Patrick, Sergei Nemchinov, and one of two goaltenders—either Mike Richter or John Vanbiesbrouck—plus $20 million in cash. Uh-oh.

Foul, cried the Flyers, who promptly filed a grievance with the National Hockey League. Acting quickly, the NHL appointed Toronto-based Larry Bertuzzi to settle the matter. Anyone who expected a quick verdict was sadly mistaken. Bertuzzi took his time, reviewing more than 400 documents (including handwritten notes), called 11 witnesses, and even spoke at length with Lindros. Finally, on June 30, he reached a decision. Lindros was a Flyer.

"Witnesses from more than one club clearly stated that Aubut would only permit the club to speak with Lindros once it had agreed on a deal with Quebec," Bertuzzi wrote in his ruling. "If Aubut intended the contact with the Lindros family to be something other than confirmation of the deal, he did not make that point clear to Philadelphia or Lindros' family."

So now it was official.

The price? Hextall, Peter Forsberg, Ricci, Steve Duchesne, Kerry Huffman, plus a first-round pick in the 1993 draft and $15 million. Because the '92 draft had already been completed, the Flyers added Chris Simon and a '94 draft pick as compensation.

"I really believed we were going to win," said Snider. "Going into it, I'd have to say we were the dark horse. There were two teams that said they had a deal. Knowing that in a court, which in essence was what this was, anything can happen."

The Rangers were mildly upset but realized the Flyers had the inside track.

Said Neil Smith, Ranger president and general manager, "I'm not mad. I can't be mad. I should learn from the experience. We dotted

The Flyers win a club-record 13th straight game, beating the visiting New York Islanders 5–4 on an overtime goal by Murray Craven.

every i and crossed every t. There was nothing more we could possibly have done."

As for Lindros, he was ecstatic about leaving Quebec and coming to Philadelphia.

"I'm just happy to get out of there," Lindros said at a Toronto news conference. "[The Nordiques] lacked a winning spirit. I didn't want any part of it."

Flyers owner Ed Snider sent his private jet to pick up Lindros, and when the aircraft arrived at Philadelphia International Airport, he was greeted with a hero's welcome. Soon after, Lindros signed a five-year contract worth an estimated $24 million. But it would take a while for Lindros to turn the Flyers into a contender again.

The Flyers had missed the playoffs three straight years before his arrival, and it would take another two years with Lindros on the roster before they would see postseason action again.

At the outset of his tenure, there was more controversy. Lindros did not accompany the team to Quebec for a preseason game due to concerns about the type of reception he might receive from fans at Le Colisée.

Meanwhile, the Nordiques benefited from all the players they received in the deal. After the team moved to Colorado and became the Avalanche, Forsberg and Ricci helped the new club win the Stanley Cup in 1996. Forsberg was an important player in the Avalanche's second Cup in 2001.

Lindros won the NHL's Hart Memorial Trophy for Most Valuable Player in 1995 and helped the Flyers make it to the Stanley Cup Final in 1997. However, the Flyers were swept in that series.

Bob Clarke, who in 1994 succeeded Farwell as the general manager of the Flyers, feuded with Lindros and his parents during his time with Philadelphia.

After suffering a series of devastating concussions, culminating with a knockout blow from New Jersey's Scott Stevens in the 2000 Eastern Conference Final, Lindros sat out for the entire 2000–01 NHL season after rejecting a one-year, $8.5 million offer as he demanded a trade from the Flyers. Ironically, Lindros wound up with the Rangers after a trade that sent Kim Johnsson, Pavel Brendl, and Jan Hlavac to the Flyers.

There are many who wonder what would have happened to the Flyers if they hadn't won the arbitration case.

Forsberg turned out to be one of the top playmakers in the NHL. Ricci and Hextall had a number of productive years. The Flyers did manage to keep Brind'Amour out of the deal, and he was an important player for the success the Flyers enjoyed in the late '90s.

Hextall, the team's former general manager, can look back at the whole time with a bit of humor. He lasted only a year with Quebec and another with the New York Islanders before returning to Philadelphia two years later. But it wasn't so funny on June 30, 1992.

"We were settled in Philly, I loved the Flyers, I could never imagine playing for another team," Hextall told hockey writer Pierre LeBrun a couple years ago. "Now all of a sudden you get a phone call to say you've been traded. It was difficult. It was hard for me emotionally. I had young kids [6, 4, 1]. It was tough. That was a little shot of reality for a naive Brandon boy."

Fences were mended when Hextall returned.

"I was mad as hell at Eric, until I got traded back two years later," said Hextall, laughing. "Then I thought, 'This wasn't so bad after all.' When I got back to Philly and [was] playing with Eric, then I thought he was more than okay."

31

ERIC LINDROS REVOLUTIONIZED THE GAME

Bobby Clarke was the best Flyer in franchise history. No one combined his talent, grit, and leadership.

But Eric Lindros was probably the most *distinctive* player to ever wear the Orange and Black. No Flyer before or since has combined such great skills with the imposing physicality that Lindros displayed. Quite simply, the 6′4″, 240-pound center revolutionized the game.

In one shift, he looked like a runaway freight train as he crashed into a player in the corner. In another shift, he played like a magician, deking past a player and displaying an artful finesse that someone his size is not supposed to have in his repertoire.

"He was a big, strong bull," said former Flyers right winger Wayne Simmonds, who is regarded as one of the NHL's premier power forwards. "He played the game both ways. He could out-skill you, but I think he took joy in going through you instead of trying to dangle you—and then he'd put the puck in the back of the net. He was always awesome to watch."

In 2016, Lindros was inducted into the Hockey Hall of Fame. In previous years, some voters penalized Lindros for not playing in as many games as other Hall of Famers. Primarily because of concussions, he played 70 games just four times in his 13-year career.

But on his seventh try, he was voted into the Hall.

"I haven't stopped smiling," Lindros said after learning the news.

The long wait didn't bother him, the one-time hulking center revealed.

"I'm in the Hall forever," he said.

"Eric had a shortened career," said Flyers president Paul Holmgren, mindful that Lindros suffered six concussions during his career in Philadelphia. "But the impact he had on the game was phenomenal."

Critics said Lindros didn't deserve to be in the Hall because he played in only 760 games in a career spent with the Flyers, Rangers,

RETIRED NUMBERS

In franchise history, the Flyers have had six numbers retired, including five players who have been inducted into the Hockey Hall of Fame: Bernie Parent (No. 1), Mark Howe (2), Bill Barber (7), Bobby Clarke (16), and Eric Lindros (88). Defenseman Barry Ashbee (4) is the only Flyer whose number has been retired who is not in the Hockey Hall of Fame.

Toronto, and Dallas. That translates into a little more than nine seasons' worth.

When he did play, however, he was dominating, with 865 points and 372 goals in 760 games. His points-per-game average (1.14) ranks 19th in NHL history. Lindros won one Hart Trophy as the league's MVP and finished in the top 10 in voting five times—one more than 2014 Hall of Fame inductee Peter Forsberg.

During his Hall of Fame acceptance speech, Lindros thanked John LeClair and Mikael Renberg, his Legion of Doom linemates who attended the ceremony, "for their intensity and joy. I was lucky to be your centerman."

At the end of his speech, an emotional Lindros called his brother, Brett, onto the stage. Brett's NHL career ended because of concussions. "I would like to close this chapter of my life with you by my side," he said.

Lindros cared more than most superstars. More than anything, he wanted to reward the fans for their loyalty. For proof, go to YouTube and watch Lindros, his voice cracking, his eyes filled with tears, in his emotional speech when he accepted the 1994–95 Hart Trophy as the league's MVP.

"In closing," he said toward the end of his 1995 speech, "I'd just like to say thank you to the Philadelphia fans who supported us when we weren't so good."

And here, Lindros became choked up with tears. After a long pause, he composed himself, barely, and said, "We're getting better, and we're going to do it."

They never did win the Stanley Cup with No. 88 in the lineup, but not because of Lindros, whose talent, drive, and physical presence made him stand above the rest.

"I was very fortunate to have coaches, teammates, billets, and parents who supported me throughout my career," Lindros said.

In 2018, the Flyers retired the big center's number in a ceremony prior to a game against Toronto at the Wells Fargo Center. He became the sixth Flyer to have his number retired, joining Bernie Parent (No. 1), Mark Howe (2), Barry Ashbee (4), Bill Barber (7), and Clarke (16). Simmonds said it was an honor to watch Lindros' number go to the rafters.

"[I] always used the Lindros curve on my Bauer stick; he was the prototypical power forward back in the day," said Simmonds of his younger playing days. "He was fun to watch. He could do it every way. He could score, he could out-skill anybody. He could go right through you. Whatever type of game you guys wanted to play, he would try to outclass you."

And he usually did.

* * *

Lindros ended a long feud with Flyers management—it centered on the medical treatment he received and on Clarke's belief that the player's parents interfered too much on their son's behalf—when he appeared in the 2011 Winter Classic alumni game at Citizens Bank Park. He patched things up with Clarke, his former general manager, who years earlier had been in a very public spat with the player known as "Big E."

The irony of Lindros' Hall of Fame selection was that he was inducted, in part, because of the support garnered by Clarke, a Hall committee member.

"When it's all said and done, everyone wanted to win, and that was the main focus," Lindros said of his battles with Clarke back in the day.

Lindros said there were "some times of friction" in his career, but he was grateful to Clarke for going to bat for him with the Hall of Fame committee.

"To have Bob's support, like so many, I have to thank them," said Lindros.

Entering 2018–19, Lindros was sixth in Flyers history in points (659), but he was first in points per game (1.36) during his time with the Orange and Black.

After receiving his Hall of Fame ring in Toronto, Lindros unknowingly simplified his journey to hockey immortality by talking about his deep admiration for the sport, one he still plays twice a week.

"I enjoy the action of it. I enjoy the rinks. I enjoy the ice and the sounds," he said. "I enjoy the clink of a post, the feeling of putting the puck past the goaltender and seeing the red light go on."

He voice was filled with passion, and the joy of a little kid who had just been asked to play in his first pickup game.

"It's quick, it's intense, it's graceful at times and really ungraceful at times," added Lindros, who used to have Mark Messier's poster hanging on his bedroom wall while growing up in Toronto. "It's the whole package."

So, of course, was Lindros.

32

LEGION OF DOOM: OPPONENTS DOOMED FROM THE START

When Flyers forward Jim Montgomery saw what havoc was wrought when his three star teammates were put together on one line, he realized a special nickname for the trio was in order.

What came to mind? Well, the way the terrific trio struck terror in the hearts of NHL opponents and the way the crowd became so over-the-top hysterical, only a comic book superhero moniker would suffice. Montgomery called it the "Legion of Doom," and a legend was born.

Shortly after John LeClair's arrival via a trade in February 1995, coach Terry Murray decided to put together a top line of Eric Lindros, the much-celebrated center who came to Philadelphia by way of a controversial 1992 trade with LeClair and Mikael Renberg, who had set a franchise rookie record with 82 points in 1993–94.

The threesome met with almost immediate success, making the Stanley Cup playoffs for the first time since 1989 and ending the longest postseason drought in team history.

The man perhaps best qualified to speak of the Legion's greatness is Keith Jones, who eventually succeeded Renberg on the line early in the 1998–99 season and currently serves as studio analyst on NBC's NHL coverage as well as commentator for the Flyers' TV broadcasts.

As a member of the Colorado Avalanche in the mid-'90s, Jones witnessed the power and charisma of these titans up close and personal as an opponent.

"They would have everything you would want in a perfect player," Jones said. "And it was combined into a line that had chemistry in all areas, including speed from Renberg, strength and power from both LeClair and Lindros, passing ability from Lindros, the ability to pass to either side."

Renberg, a smooth-skating Swede, followed up his brilliant freshman season with yearly goal totals of 26, 23, and 22 while playing with the Legion. Lindros performed some of his finest work with

LeClair and Renberg on his flanks. In fact, his 70 points in the labor-shortened 1994–95 season tied Pittsburgh's Jaromir Jagr for the league high and earned No. 88 the Hart Trophy for NHL most valuable player. (Jagr won the scoring title by having more goals.)

The following year, Lindros ran roughshod over the league and enjoyed the best season of his career with a personal high 47 goals and 68 assists for 115 points. For the three seasons with the Doom line, Lindros was a plus-84.

LeClair also reached astronomical heights, putting together seasons of 51 goals in 1995–96 and 50 in 1996–97, with a league-leading plus-44 in 1996–97.

No wonder the Legion of Doom was so imposing.

"It had Renberg, a left-handed shot, playing the right side, so he was always a threat to shoot, even though his shot wasn't the same as Lindros' or LeClair's," Jones stated. "[Renberg] played to his strengths, which was getting to loose pucks, loosening up plays on the rush, and forcing defenders to back up.

"When he did that, there was always a lot of room for Lindros and LeClair to operate. I have never seen a line or played against a line that was better down low in the offensive zone. So not only were they a threat to score on the rush, but [they were] also going to beat you into submission in your defensive end until you were crawling to the bench to get off the ice after they were done with you, whether they scored or not. And that would influence the shift after that."

Sellouts were the rule at the Wells Fargo Center. For several years, the Flyers were the hottest sports ticket in Philadelphia.

Lindros was all over commercials and advertisements on TV, newspapers, radio, and magazines in the City of Brotherly Love.

"The one thing I will always remember about that line is you didn't have to see them come on the ice," Jones said. "You heard the reaction from the crowd when they stepped over the boards."

LeClair was already somewhat of an accomplished player when he arrived in a trade from Montreal along with Eric Desjardins and Gilbert Dionne for Mark Recchi and a third-round draft pick. LeClair had scored a pair of overtime winners against Los Angeles in the 1993 Stanley Cup Final, the last time a Canada-based team has won the top prize.

"When I came to the Flyers I got the confidence in myself as a player," LeClair said. "Playing with Eric and Mikael, I had some success and built that confidence."

From the day of the trade through the 1996–97 season, LeClair scored 126 goals, third in the NHL behind Jaromir Jagr (134) and Peter Bondra (128), and his 243 points were seventh.

The sight of Lindros, LeClair, and Renberg hopping over the boards was eye-opening, to say the least. Lindros stood 6′4″, 240 pounds; LeClair at 6′3″, 233; and Renberg at 6′2″, 235. Even the Super Friends, the arch-enemies of the LOD, would have to blink once or twice at that specter.

"People talked so much about us that it feels like we played longer together than we really did," Renberg said. "We were together from pretty much the first day Johnny came here. It was great playing with them. We worked really well together."

Although considered a supplemental part of the line, Renberg was a valuable contributor, according to Lindros.

"Mikael was a fantastic player in his own right," Lindros said on the night when he and LeClair were inducted into the Flyers' Hall of Fame. "He did everything you could ask of a winger, of a player on your team.

"To have him consistently with us, on our line…. [I] can't say enough about him. One of the fiercest forecheckers you'd ever come across. Very fast, great hockey sense, and a terrific guy to be around."

The feeling was the Flyers would eventually ride the line's success to a Stanley Cup, and as the 1996–97 season wound down, it looked like that might happen. Most hockey people figured the Flyers should be favored over the Detroit Red Wings as Philadelphia reached the Stanley Cup Final for the first time since 1987. After all, Lindros and his pals had steamrolled the East.

Unfortunately for the Flyers, they were facing a Red Wings team led by the brilliant maestro Scotty Bowman, one that had survived a difficult journey to the last round. In almost the blink of an eye, the Flyers were ignominiously dispatched in four straight games. Of their eight all-time appearances in the Stanley Cup Final, it was only the second they have failed to win a game.

"The Western Conference was just that much better that year," Jones noted. "I was in Colorado then. Detroit beat us that year. Dallas was in that mix. Those were the three best teams in the league. You would be hard-pressed to find three deeper teams than that.

MURRAY: "CHOKING" COMMENT CAUSES COACHING CALAMITY

The word "choke" is about as strong a pejorative as a coach can use to describe both his team's performance and its psyche. And to have it uttered in the middle of a Stanley Cup Final series is enough to send shockwaves through the hockey world. Which is why Flyers coach Terry Murray's comments before Game 4 of the 1997 Stanley Cup best-of-seven title event caused such a stir.

During his press conference at Detroit's Joe Louis Arena on June 7, Murray chose to go after his team, which was down three games to none to the underdog Red Wings. Murray was asked if his team had lost its confidence.

"I wish I could find it," Murray said. "I wish I could find the answer for that. I don't know where it's gone. But many teams have been through this before. It's basically a choking situation, that I call it, for a team right now."

Players such as captain Eric Lindros took umbrage over Murray's evaluation and let his displeasure be known.

"It's tough to swallow when it's coming from your coach," Lindros said. "But I guess that's the way things are, and we just have to stick together as a team, and go out and win as a team."

If Murray was trying to inspire his team, the tactic didn't work. The Flyers lost Game 4 and were swept from a Final series for only the second time in their history.

Exactly one week later, Murray was fired.

The Flyers said the decision to can Murray went beyond that one infamous comment.

"The problems didn't just surface," said Bob Clarke, general manager at the time. "They've [occurred] basically over the last couple of years. We solved some and we haven't been able to solve others."

The coach speaking his mind was one of them.

"The Flyers weren't deep enough to beat Detroit. They had [Hall of Fame defenseman] Nicklas Lidström, who controlled the pace of play. Their back end was just that much better. That was the difference. They had one of the best defensemen ever to play the game backing them up in Lidström. I don't know if anyone at that time recognized how good he was."

In addition to that, Bowman paired Lidström with the mobile Larry Murphy. Their puck handling, skating, and ability to move the puck out of danger quickly overcame the Flyers' vaunted forechecking.

Ultimately, LeClair was limited in the series to the Flyers' only goal late in a 6–1 Game 3 shellacking, and Lindros experienced similar scoring woes, connecting only late in Game 4 of a series-clinching loss at Detroit.

Renberg, hampered by injuries connected to a sports hernia for much of the 1996–97 season, was traded to Tampa Bay the following season.

Not long after, Flyers coach Roger Neilson decided to put Jones with Lindros and LeClair. It was a good fit because Jones added an element of confrontational play, be it trash talk or chippiness in the corners. It was sort of like the Legion of Doom 2.0.

"When I arrived here, Roger said, 'We're going to try you on this Lindros-LeClair line. We'll see how it goes.' I said, 'You won't have to try; it will be perfect.' It wasn't because of me, because I wasn't that good. But I was a good enough player to read and react off of star players.

"Our line was dominant at times. I do believe there was chemistry. I'm a different player than Renberg—the speed was not there in my game—but the ability to play down low and distract the opposition, verbally or physically. There was that element that nobody wanted to play against us."

Actually, from a fan's standpoint, it really didn't matter that Renberg was no longer on the premises. The combination of Lindros-LeClair had always been the big draw, and those two would be partners for another three seasons. As the third wheel on that new but still impressive unit, Jones felt the Wells Fargo Center shake whenever 88 and 10 hit the ice.

"It was the same roar that I witnessed as an opponent that I got to experience playing with Lindros and LeClair whenever you went over the boards," Jones said.

"[In] the crowd there was just that buzz of anticipation. It was a great feeling. You just wanted to hit the guy, whoever the opponent was, through the end boards."

33

FIVE-OT GAME: NO END IN SIGHT

Ravaged pizza boxes and empty Pedialyte bottles.

Instead of sticks and skates, that's what filled the hallway outside the Flyers' locker room sometime around 2:00 AM on the morning of May 4, 2000. It looked like the remains of a five-year-old's birthday party.

This was between the fourth and fifth overtimes of the longest game in the modern era of the National Hockey League. Philadelphia and the Pittsburgh Penguins were locked in a 1–1 draw in Game 4 of their first-round Stanley Cup playoff series at the now-defunct Mellon Arena, affectionately known as the Igloo. Food and drink were at a premium.

"We were out of Power gels, Power bars, and Gatorade by the third overtime," game hero Keith Primeau would later recall. "We were literally looking for food to come into the locker room because you need to get something into your system."

Mercifully, a pizza delivery arrived, and the Flyers attacked the pies like they had not eaten in a week. Pedialyte is a drink often given to infants to replenish electrolytes, but the Flyers were in no mood to be picky.

Finally, in the fifth overtime, after a grueling 152:01 of hockey, Primeau made a dandy inside cut move on Pittsburgh defenseman Darius Kasparaitis and fired a shot over goaltender Ron Tugnutt's shoulder.

Primeau's move on Kasparaitis was a calculated one. He had tried different strategies in the game, and they failed to work.

"Two other times earlier in the game I had gone wide on Kasparaitis only to get cut off," Primeau said on the Flyers' 40th anniversary DVD. "So I faked like I was going to go outside and once he crossed his feet over I was able to pull the puck back on my forehand and get a shot off."

DECEMBER 8, 1987

Ron Hextall becomes the first goalie in NHL history to score a goal by shooting a puck into the net as the Flyers defeat Boston 5–2 at the Spectrum.

It was over. After falling behind in the series 2–0, with both losses at home in Philadelphia, the Flyers had squared things at 2–2. They would go on to win the next two games as well as win the series in six games.

The Flyers' reaction was more relief than joy. The arena clock read 2:35 AM. The players were almost too tired to jump off the bench when the winning goal hit the back of the net.

"Into the last period, whatever it was, I didn't say a single thing," Flyers interim coach Craig Ramsay said. "I just pointed to them when they came on the ice who would start. I was almost as exhausted as them."

Journeyman Keith Jones, he of the razor-sharp humor, was at his comic best. Jones was playing his last full season in the NHL, as a knee injury would force him to retire the following year. At one point in the later overtimes, Ramsay signaled Jones to hop over the boards and take a shift, which Jones did. Teammate Craig Berube, now head coach of the St. Louis Blues, takes it from there.

"The guy it wore on was Jonesy," Berube said with a chuckle. "It was late in the game, he jumps over the boards, then yells 'Change!' and [immediately] goes back over the boards back onto the bench. Then he turns around and tells the coach, 'Rammer, don't put me out there again. I'm done!' He'd had enough."

That sent a wave of laughter through the players within earshot.

Jones was known for keeping the Flyers' bench loose with his one-liners.

Berube said Jones was getting on Primeau throughout the game over missed opportunities. Maybe that spurred the Flyers' captain to his moment of greatness.

ON THIS DATE

MAY 4, 2000

Keith Primeau scores with 7:59 left in the fifth overtime, giving the Flyers an exhausting 2-1 win in Pittsburgh in Game 4 of the Eastern Conference Semifinals. It is the longest game (152:01) in modern NHL history.

"Yeah, he was getting on Keith about his hands," Berube said. "And then Keith scores the game-winner. Jonesy had been burying him from the bench, yelling, 'Look at this guy! What's he doing out there?' And he had to eat crow."

The only two longer games in NHL history took place back in the 1930s. Nothing has really come close since. While others were losing steam, Primeau apparently took advantage of the pizza and the Pedialyte.

"As the game went on, I started to feel a lot better," he said. "There was a lot more room in the neutral zone and I just wanted to capitalize."

Having come back from losing the first two games of the series on home ice, the Flyers looked like a team of destiny. They made it all the way to the Eastern Conference Final, but then fortune played a cruel trick.

Leading the New Jersey Devils in the ultimate best-of-seven series by a 3–1 margin, the Flyers couldn't find a way to get that magical fourth win. Instead, Devils defenseman Scott Stevens supplied a crushing hit on Eric Lindros, knocking the Flyers captain senseless, and the Devils went on to a win and continue to the Stanley Cup Final, where they easily handled the Dallas Stars for their second championship.

However, none of that took away from the Flyers' greatness that one night in Pittsburgh. On that night, it truly was a test of wills, one that hardly a soul could ever possibly think would happen. Hence the scrambling for sustenance.

"Usually on the road the team orders pizza for the locker room," Primeau said. "There's pizza for the guys, Power gels, Power bars were really popular. The trunk of those was gone, the pizza was gone. Trainers are going up to concession stands to see if there's anything there. [The] coaches' popcorn was eaten."

Up in the luxury suites, patrons were selling bottles of water for $5 (and up) to patrons of other boxes who had run out. Concessions had long run dry. Rather than when it would end, people started wondering if it would ever end.

Officials insist there was never a thought to calling things off even after the fifth—or possibly sixth overtime—and resuming play the following day for things like player safety. There would have been such an outcry and controversy that the NHL would still be explaining that one to this day. As the clock struck midnight, defenseman Chris Therien was wondering like everyone else when this historic night might end.

"There got to a point where I wasn't even sure a goal was going to be scored," Therien said, "because I didn't think that anybody had enough energy left."

Jones, now a national TV analyst for NBC when he isn't working local broadcasts for the Flyers, looks back on the occasion with a unique perspective.

"It became like the game was in slow motion because of the exhaustion level of the players," he said.

This was a baptism by fire for rookie goaltender Brian Boucher, who had seen his share of OT action in the American Hockey League with the then Philadelphia Phantoms.... But [that was] nothing like this.

"It was actually comical between periods because not a lot of us had played a game that long," Boucher said.

"We had gone through all the pizza, all the Power bars. I didn't know if there was any more liquid left in the locker room, for crying out loud. But we knew it was a game we had to win, so we just kept going."

Both goalies were exceptional. Tugnutt stopped 70-of-72 shots, while Boucher made 57 saves, including several spectacular stops in the overtimes.

"This was incredible," said Tugnutt. "Between periods you just tried to get a drink [because] you just started to feel yourself seizing up. People were starting to ask what period it was."

Alexei Kovalev drew first blood at 2:22 of the first on a long blast from just inside the blue line that caught Boucher by surprise. A fluke goal at 4:47 of the third tied the game.

On the power play, the Flyers' Daymond Langkow drew the puck back to Eric Desjardins, whose blast from the point looked like it was tipped by John LeClair past Tugnutt. However, with the Penguins howling that LeClair's stick was higher than the crossbar when it touched the puck, referee Rob Shick called upstairs for a video review to get more input. Officials called the replays inconclusive, and the goal was credited to LeClair, although it looked as if Penguins defenseman Bob Boughner was actually responsible for the tip.

There were several close calls in the third overtime, but play began to drag in the fourth extra session. By the fifth, with the crowd down to just several thousand, it was left to Primeau to provide the heroics. He took a pass from defenseman Dan McGillis, skated down the right side, and, in what seemed like a heartbeat, it was over at 12:01 of the fifth OT. The Flyers had hoped for this outcome as they prepared to hit the ice for the final overtime.

"I would say the mood in our room was light," Jones said. "We weren't overwhelmed by the situation. We had a feeling of, 'We have nothing to lose here,' and I think that worked in our favor."

34

WELLS FARGO CENTER: IF YOU BUILD IT, THEY WILL COME

From a historical standpoint, the location of the Flyers' new home made perfect sense. It was on the site where John F. Kennedy Stadium once stood, the place where the Flyers' victory parade for their second Stanley Cup culminated with a raucous party in May 1974.

Some 22 years later, a second-generation, multiuse, indoor arena initially called Spectrum II was built just across a parking lot from the original Spectrum, which had hosted the games of the Flyers' glory years.

Like the first structure, the second one was the brainchild of Flyers co-founder and chairman Ed Snider. Snider realized as early as 1989 that his original home for the team was becoming outdated. So he approached the city of Philadelphia with plans to put up a $215 million sports palace to serve as a playing spot for the Flyers, 76ers, and Wings (lacrosse); the new building would be privately funded but with the city and state helping to pay for the local infrastructure.

Original plans called for everything from a luxury hotel to a bowling alley, with an elevated glass walkway connecting the new and the old. Those plans were eventually scrapped, but after some financial wrangling, the new building came to pass.

Construction did not come about without some initial problems. For instance, Sixers owner Harold Katz, not crazy about the idea of paying exorbitant rent at the new building in Philadelphia, made some noise about moving his NBA team to a proposed edifice in Camden, New Jersey. Snider moved quickly to squelch those plans by grabbing up and signing much of the non-professional sports entertainment passing through Philadelphia. The list included Disney on Ice, Ringling Brothers–Barnum & Bailey Circus, and Sesame Street Live, along with the basketball exhibitionist Harlem Globetrotters. The Spectrum already had a lock on arena concert tours through Snider's strong ties

ON THIS DATE

OCTOBER 5, 1996

The Flyers play their first regular season game at the CoreStates Center, which is now known as the Wells Fargo Center. Florida wins the game 3-1. Dainius Zubrus scores a goal and becomes the youngest player in Flyers history: 18 years, three months, and 20 days.

to Electric Factory Concerts, Philadelphia's leading promoter of live music, which kept the arena thriving.

As a result of Spectacor signing those multiyear agreements and locking up all those touring events, the Sixers would have had a huge hole to fill at their new venue for dates beyond their roughly 45 home games. The club eventually dropped its arena plan.

To put a cherry on top of the confection, Snider struck a deal with Comcast cable television company to merge with his Spectacor company, then turned around and bought the Sixers away from Katz. Mayor Wilson Goode also factored into the final negotiations to get the city of Philadelphia on board.

"It seemed like a good opportunity to do something good for the city," Goode said at the time. "People don't realize how important sports teams are to the psyche of a city."

After some five years of planning and two years of construction, the newly named CoreStates Center was ready to host its first professional sports event, the 1996 World Cup of Hockey. On August 31, the U.S. team upset Canada, with the Flyers' John LeClair scoring the first goal of the game—and the new building.

While the new building hosted a number of events ranging from music to sports to political conventions, the schedule then was nowhere close to what it is now—namely 235 dates per year that the lights are on.

The Wells Fargo Center officially holds 19,537 for Flyers games, including 126 luxury suites, 1,880 club box seats, and a number of restaurants, both public and private. A record for attendance was set

With his flowing orange hair and wild eyes, Gritty has become a Flyers staple in a remarkably short amount of time, having made his debut at an exhibition game on September 24, 2018.

GRITTY TAKES PHILLY, AND THE NATION, BY STORM

Early in the 2018–19 season, the Flyers were getting lots of national publicity.

It wasn't because of Claude Giroux or Sean Couturier. It wasn't because of Wayne Simmonds or Jake Voracek, or even Shayne Gostisbehere or Travis Konecny. In fact, it wasn't about any of the players.

The national buzz was created by a fuzzy, seven-foot monster of a mascot named Gritty. He/she/it was called everything from creepy-looking to Muppet-like, among many other things.

Gritty, whose snarky tweets helped him amass nearly 200,000 Twitter followers in the season's first few months, became a topic (and, in some cases, a guest) on the late-night talk-show circuit. He was mocked in some circles, yet adored in others. Most kids seemed to fall in the latter category.

"We were looking for ways to introduce the Flyers in different ways to different areas," Joe Heller, the Flyers' marketing vice president, told the *Philadelphia Inquirer*. "We thought we were missing out on between 250 and 300 different appearances in any given season. So we made the commitment to add a mascot."

When he was introduced to Flyers fans at an exhibition game, Gritty slipped on the ice. The gaffe and the mascot's subsequent tweet—"Why didn't anybody tell me the ice is this slippery?"—seemed to enhance his popularity.

Gritty, created by David Raymond, the man who for 16 years was inside the Phanatic costume at Phillies games, was the Flyers' first mascot since Slapshot made a brief appearance in 1976. The furry creature with a wild orange beard and wilder eyes made his regular season debut in the home opener against San Jose, swinging down from the Wells Fargo Center ceiling on a rope as Miley Cyrus' hit song, "Wrecking Ball," blared through the speakers. The crowd loved it, but the Flyers weren't exactly inspired. They were hammered by the Sharks 8–2.

for Game 6 of the 2010 Stanley Cup Final when 20,327 fans crammed their way in on June 9 to watch Patrick Kane and the Chicago Blackhawks win in overtime for the championship.

In 2018–19, the WFC underwent a facelift estimated in excess of $200 million with hopes of keeping the place up to date for at least another 10 years.

"I think if you spend the money and keep it up and plan for the future, it can certainly go beyond what some of the older buildings were able to," John Page, president of the Wells Fargo Complex, told Frank Fitzpatrick of the *Philadelphia Inquirer*. "It's the right size. It's just a matter of what you do to update it. You look at the Spectrum, and the real reason we moved over here was amenities—premium seating and revenue opportunities that would make sure the teams could stay competitive."

Back at the start, the Wells Fargo Center was part of a huge wave of new arenas to rise up across North America between 1990 and 1996, many of them equipped to host hockey games, including Boston, Montreal, Chicago, and St. Louis.

"A lot of teams in major markets were playing in these old buildings," said Page. "Boston Garden. Chicago Stadium. With the escalation of salaries that was happening in sports, you needed other revenue sources to really compete. And those older buildings couldn't be easily updated because of their size and their very nature."

Originally named the CoreStates Center, the WFC has gone through several names like First Union Center and Wachovia Center thanks to merging corporations in the banking industry. The WFC's first big renovation came on its 10th anniversary in 2006, including flat-screen TVs in suites and improved Wi-Fi service. According to Page, it's important that buildings like the Wells Fargo Center keep up with the technological revolution.

"We're competing with the home, the couch," Page said. "There's so much that goes on with your TV now that we have to make sure that you not only have a great live experience but that you're able to keep up with all the social media and other interactivity that devices like your iPhone allow."

That said, it's hard to imagine a building in the world that's much busier than the WFC.

"Since opening in 1996, the Wells Fargo Center has been one of the busiest arenas in the world," said Page. "I don't think there's an arena anywhere that has done what we've done in a similar time span."

The Wells Fargo Center faithful have seen their share of spectacular games and players over the years. There was the 1997 Stanley Cup Final series with Detroit, which featured the Flyers' Legion of Doom line—Eric Lindros, LeClair, and Mikael Renberg. It would be the last chance to see the line play intact. The Red Wings won the series in a sweep, and Renberg was traded to Tampa Bay the following year.

And then, some 13 years later, the Flyers made the Final again, this time with a star-laden squad that featured Hall of Famer Chris Pronger along with Danny Briere, Simon Gagne, Mike Richards, Jeff Carter, Scott Hartnell, Claude Giroux, and Kimmo Timonen. Unlike the Detroit wipeout, the Flyers were much more competitive in this series but still wound up losing in six games on a Kane overtime goal.

In more recent times, the Flyers have introduced an even more exciting sensation to the venue: the 2018–19 season addition of Gritty, the overnight celebrity of a mascot who has already appeared on most of the late-night TV talk shows and gets the crowd going just by having his picture on the scoreboard.

On the ice, a new generation of aspiring stars—from Ivan Provorov and Shayne Gostisbehere on defense to Travis Konecny and Nolan Patrick up front—has made sure the Wells Fargo Center stays full.

Somewhere, Ed Snider is smiling.

35

MIKE RICHARDS: TALENT UNFULFILLED

To be compared in some fashion to Flyers legend Bobby Clarke is just about the highest praise you can bestow on a player.

Few have received that honor, and fewer still have done so and been out of the game of hockey barely past the age of 30. In fact, that club probably only has one member: Mike Richards. The talented center from Kenora, Ontario, is considered one of the most gifted forwards ever to wear an orange, black, and white uniform.

Richards was selected by the Flyers 24th overall in the 2003 NHL Draft, and from the get-go he seemed destined for greatness, first winning a Calder Cup with the Philadelphia Phantoms in 2005 and later serving as captain of a Flyers team that made it to the Stanley Cup Final in 2010. Everything seemed to be going his way. He established himself as one of the top penalty killers of his generation, scoring an NHL-record three times while the Flyers were skating three players against five.

But behind the scenes, club management and the coaching staff were alarmed by the lack of work Richards put in off the ice. Eventually, shortly after the 2010–11 season ended, Richards was traded to the Los Angeles Kings in a deal that saw Wayne Simmonds and Brayden Schenn come to the Flyers.

Richards would go on to win a pair of Stanley Cup championships with the Kings, but after a drug incident at the U.S.–Canada border in 2015, he had his contract terminated. He would play one more year with the Washington Capitals before he was out of the sport...presumably for good.

What happened?

Clarke, one of the hardest working players the game has ever produced, indicated that in some respects Richards didn't reach his full potential during his career.

"Mike was maybe the best young kid to come in as an 18-year-old after his draft," Clarke said. "His positioning on the ice, his checking.

Guys who tried to pass it by him, it was always hitting his foot. All those kinds of things. You have to be a pretty aware player to pick all that stuff up.

"I knew Mike didn't skate real well. I thought in my opinion this kid was going to be a real good second-line centerman if we ever have a really good first centerman in front of him. He'll develop, he'll kill penalties, he's really good on faceoffs. He was smart, and that's the way he started out.

"But what we found out afterwards was Mike only competed when he played. He didn't train in the offseason very good. He'd come to camp, get ready and, because of his skill, all of that stuff, he got away with it in junior. But at the NHL level, all of a sudden you're seeing Mike and saying to yourself, 'If he doesn't get going, he's going to be a third lineman center.' He didn't work at it. He didn't try to get better."

Some of Richards' shortcomings were able to be overlooked in Los Angeles because the team was such a strong contender.

"[The trade] was great for L.A. because they won the Stanley Cup," Clarke said. "And he was a big part of it, because he's so competitive. But he wasn't going to last long without the work ethic that he didn't have."

Richards was hampered by injuries throughout his career, and there has been widespread speculation that he needed painkillers to deal with the aftermath. Stomach surgery and operations on both shoulders dot the list.

Before the problems started to pile up, Richards was sensational in Philadelphia. In his rookie season, he opened with a bang. He scored a hat trick against the New York Islanders on February 8, 2006, two of the goals shorthanded. That was the first hat trick by a Flyer rookie since Mikael Renberg notched one on February 15, 1994.

In 2007–08, Richards led the Flyers in scoring with 75 points. Recognizing this, the Flyers awarded him with a 12-year contract worth $69 million. Not a media member covering the team thought it was a bad deal.

Richards would be named to his first NHL All-Star Game in Atlanta that season and later, during a playoff game against the Washington Capitals, scored his first NHL postseason goal on a penalty shot, becoming only the second player in NHL history to earn that distinction. By the following season, Richards had been named captain of a veteran squad.

During the 2008–09 season, he scored his third career three-on-five goal, the first NHL player to do so, then scored shorthanded goals in three straight games, the first player to do so since Colorado's Joe Sakic in 1998. In the offseason, Richards underwent the double shoulder operation, and it was later revealed he required anti-inflammatory medication throughout the following campaign.

The 2009–10 season was a highly eventful one for Richards, who, along with Jeff Carter, were the subjects of speculation in the media regarding partying lifestyles. This led to a media boycott by Richards, who felt such accusations were fabricated.

After a run to the Stanley Cup Final, Richards was back for his final season with the Flyers. Then came the trade to L.A.

"I was very shocked," Richards said at the time. "At first I was shocked and then excited—I'm excited to move out to L.A. and be a part of a team that has a ton of great players. I'm just looking forward to helping them out."

Paul Holmgren, general manager when the Flyers made the trade, agrees with Clarke that Richards could have achieved more if he had worked harder at his craft.

"He probably didn't train as hard as you would have liked," Holmgren said. "That's fair. But to flip that around, if you had to count on a guy in a game, he was up. You would say to yourself, if you were a manager or a coach, 'Gee, if Mike were only in better shape, how good he could be.' As great as Mike was in his career, it could have been better in my opinion."

The obvious question that begs to be asked is did the Flyers try hard enough to get Richards to work at his game? Several scouts said Richards would basically wait until he arrived at training camp to get himself into shape.

"We all talked to him about it," Holmgren said. "[Coach John] Stevens, Lavy [Coach Peter Laviolette], Clarkie, [Los Angeles general manager] Dean Lombardi did. We all tried to get him to train hard."

In retrospect, there are those who wonder if the captaincy of the Flyers weighed too heavily on Richards' shoulders. At times, he seemed reluctant to embrace that role. When he boycotted the media, it only made an uncomfortable situation even more awkward.

"It was always a torture for Mike to talk to the media," Holmgren said. "To me, it doesn't make him a bad guy. Mike was a good leader. I don't know how vocal he was in the room."

That said, Holmgren believes Richards' body of work stands up to the best in franchise history.

"Look at the shorthanded goals he scored or set up here," Holmgren said. Richards is tied with Brian Propp and Mark Howe for the franchise record for one season with seven. We haven't had a threat like that since he left."

Keith Jones says Richards couldn't just get by on his talent. He pointed to the 2010 Olympics in Vancouver as an example.

"I could see the year that he made the Canadian Olympic team when they won the gold, I was concerned that he wasn't going to make that team, because his skating wasn't there, Jones said. "He's not playing in the game today because he couldn't keep up. He couldn't skate as fast as the other guys. He had it but then the legs went quicker than most. So if I was analyzing what happened in his career, I would say the legs went a lot sooner than most. I don't know what the contributing factors were behind that but, that is why Mike Richards' career ended."

In his prime, though, Richards was a sight to behold.

"He was like the Chase Utley of hockey," Jones said. "Instant leader. Received the captaincy early on in his career. Made some outstanding plays at both ends of the ice. Fought, even though he wasn't a fighter. Did all the things you would expect a leader to do. It looked like he was going to be a 15-year Flyer."

Jones marveled at Richards' ability to be in the right place at the right time.

"He had a special knack, especially shorthanded," Jones said. "He would generate scoring chances. He would bury them. It just looked like his career was going to be incredible, almost like a Bobby Clarke influence on the Flyers."

As for the captaincy, that was a different story.

"Mike did not seem to embrace the spotlight," Jones said. "In this city, to be a captain, that's part of the deal. You are the spokesperson for the team. He was very modest, he came across as being almost shy at times. So that part of the role was not a strength of his as far as leadership went."

Holmgren and others can only wonder, 'What if?'

"For as great a player as he was," Holmgren says, "he could have been greater."

36

BEST TRADES IN FRANCHISE HISTORY: BERNIE AT THE TOP

Some of the trades by Flyers general managers have withstood the test of time. Here are their 10 best deals:

May 15, 1973: Flyers received the rights to Bernie Parent from Toronto, along with a second-round draft pick (Larry Goodenough) for a 1973 first-round selection (Bob Neely) and future considerations (Doug Favell).

This deal, more than any other, paved the way for the Flyers' Stanley Cup championships in 1974 and 1975.

Parent returned to the Flyers and was a much better goalie than in his first stint with the club. Many think the tutelage he received from his boyhood idol, Jacques Plante, made the difference. They were Toronto teammates for two seasons. In any event, Parent blossomed into a Hall of Famer and was a two-time Vezina Trophy winner. Neely played parts of five years with Toronto and, aside from a 17-goal season in 1976–77, had an undistinguished NHL career that ended when he was 24. Favell played three seasons with Toronto and struggled mightily toward the end of his tenure there.

February 9, 1995: Flyers acquired Eric Desjardins, John LeClair, and Gilbert Dionne from Montreal for Mark Recchi and a 1995 third-round pick.

This was the best deal made by Bob Clarke during his days as the Flyers' general manager. LeClair and Desjardins became two of the top players in franchise history at their respective positions.

LeClair became the left winger on the famed Legion of Doom line with Eric Lindros and Mikael Renberg. He had three straight seasons with 50 or more goals, followed by 43- and 40-goal campaigns. In 649 games with the Flyers, he had 643 points, including 333 goals.

Most longtime observers rank Desjardins as the second-best defenseman in franchise history, behind only Hall of Famer Mark Howe.

ON THIS DATE

MAY 15, 1973

In a trade that reshapes the franchise, the Flyers reacquire goalie Bernie Parent's NHL rights and Toronto's second-round 1973 draft pick (Larry Goodenough) for goalie Doug Favell and a first-rounder (Bob Neely) in 1973. ·

With the Flyers, Desjardins collected 93 goals and 396 points in 11 seasons, during which he had a plus-143 rating.

Recchi did help Montreal, collecting 322 points in 346 games with the Habs. But he returned to the Flyers in 1998–99 and had five-plus productive seasons for them.

January 31, 1971: The Flyers acquired Rick MacLeish and Danny Schock from Boston for Mike Walton.

The smooth-skating MacLeish helped lead the Flyers to a pair of Stanley Cups, and he became the youngest player (age 23 in 1972–73) to score 50 goals in a season in NHL history. In 12 years with the Flyers, MacLeish had 697 points in 741 games, including 328 goals. He was also a prolific scorer in the playoffs.

MacLeish was a 21-year-old prospect when he was acquired for Walton. The Flyers had acquired Walton and Bruce Gamble earlier in the day from Toronto as part of a trade that sent Parent to the Maple Leafs. The Flyers got Parent back two years later. Walton had two good full seasons with Boston (28 goals and 25 goals) before heading to the WHL.

June 23, 2011: The Flyers received forwards Wayne Simmonds and Brayden Schenn and a 2012 second-round pick from Los Angeles for Mike Richards and Rob Bordson.

This trade could climb the charts and, because it led to another promising deal, might still be benefitting the Flyers in the 2030s.

Simmonds has become one of the league's elite power forwards, scoring around 30 goals per season. Schenn had consecutive 25-goal seasons before GM Ron Hextall dealt him to St. Louis for a pair of first-round picks that turned into Morgan Frost and Joel Farabee. The latter two players were among the Flyers' top prospects entering 2019–20. Richards won two Stanley Cups in Los Angeles but scored just 46 goals in four seasons before the Kings bought out his contract. (Simmonds was traded to Nashville in 2019.)

June 18, 2007: The Flyers sent Nashville's first-round pick (previously acquired for Peter Forsberg) back to the Predators in exchange for Kimmo Timonen and Scott Hartnell.

The deal, made just before the 2007 draft, helped the Flyers make gigantic strides. They went from having the NHL's worst record in 2006–07 (22–48–12) to the conference finals the next season. And both players became a major part of the Flyers' nucleus for many years.

At the time of the deal, Timonen and Hartnell were upcoming unrestricted free agents, and the Predators didn't believe they could sign them. Immediately after the trade, however, the Flyers signed each player to a six-year contract. Timonen and Hartnell were also key players as the Flyers reached the Stanley Cup Final in 2010.

August 20, 1982: The Flyers acquired Mark Howe and a 1983 third-round draft choice (Derrick Smith) from Hartford for Ken Linseman, Greg Adams, a 1983 first-round draft choice (David Jensen), and a 1983 third-rounder (Leif Karlsson).

The Flyers ended up with the best defenseman in franchise history. Howe went into the Hockey Hall of Fame in 2011. To get him, the Flyers had to part ways with Linseman, who was coming off a 92-point season, a gritty prospect (Adams), and draft picks. It was worth it, however, because they got Howe as he was reaching his prime. As a footnote, Smith became a serviceable role player.

July 2, 2001: The Flyers sent Daymond Langkow to the Phoenix Coyotes in exchange for a first-round 2003 pick that turned out to be Jeff Carter. They also received a second-round pick (later traded again).

Carter became an All-Star, had a 46-goal season, and averaged 36 goals per season during his last four years with the Flyers before being dealt to Columbus in a deal that netted Jake Voracek and Sean Couturier.

Langkow scored 27, 20, and 21 goals, respectively, in three seasons with the Coyotes, and continued to be productive with Calgary. He returned to the Coyotes in 2011–12, his final season.

Still, this was a highly successful deal for the Flyers, one that is still yielding positive results.

July 1, 2011: The Flyers traded Kris Versteeg to Florida for a 2012 second-round pick, which was transferred to Tampa Bay, and a third-round pick that turned into Shayne Gostisbehere.

As it turned out, GM Paul Holmgren struck gold as he was able to get Gostisbehere—who became one of the NHL's most offensive defensemen—for Versteeg, a journeyman who played for seven teams in 11 years and was never an impact player. Gostisbehere, on the other hand, scored 17 goals as a rookie and 13 goals and 65 points in his third season.

May 24, 1974: The Flyers acquired Reggie Leach by sending Larry Wright, Al MacAdam, and a first-round draft pick in 1974 (Ron Chipperfield) to California.

In a 1974 trade made just five days after they won their first Stanley Cup, General Manager Keith Allen lived up to his nickname Keith the Thief.

Leach scored 45 goals in his first season with the Flyers and helped them to repeat as Cup champions. In his second season in Philadelphia, the right winger known as "The Rifle" erupted for 61 regular season goals before adding 19 in 16 playoff games. It was a record for most goals in a single playoff year. He won the Conn Smythe

Trophy as the best playoff performer that year, marking the first time in history the winner wasn't on the Stanley Cup–winning team.

September 22, 1991: The Flyers acquired Rod Brind'Amour and Dan Quinn from the St. Louis Blues for Ron Sutter and Murray Baron.

Brind'Amour became a Flyers fixture for the next eight-plus seasons, and he anchored the second line after Lindros was acquired, giving the team a dynamic one-two center combination. A workout fanatic, he rarely missed a game and was one of the franchise's best leaders. Brind'Amour finished with 601 points, including 235 goals, in 633 games with the Flyers.

Sutter had several good seasons with the Flyers, but he supposedly had grown disgruntled with the franchise's direction. He had a productive first season with the Blues before fading considerably.

Baron, a stay-at-home defenseman, had a long and solid career.

Quinn, a former first-round draft pick with Calgary who was high scorer early in his career, had two different one-year stints with the Flyers and was a serviceable forward.

Honorable Mention

January 28, 1972: The Flyers acquired Bill Flett, Ross Lonsberry, Ed Joyal, and Jean Potvin from Los Angeles for Serge Bernier, Jimmy Johnson, and Bill Lesuk.

Flett and Lonsberry played important roles when the Flyers won the '74 Stanley Cup.

37

EVERYONE NOW KNOWS CLAUDE GIROUX'S NAME

Back in 2006, when the Flyers selected shifty Claude Giroux with the 22nd overall draft pick in the first round, then general manager Bob Clarke walked up to the microphone and... momentarily forgot the player's name.

Now NHL fans all over North America know about Giroux. Quite simply, he was one of the best players the Flyers ever drafted. In any year.

Giroux blossomed into an All-Star and, in 2017–18, had a season for the ages. He finished fourth in the Hart Trophy voting as the league's MVP, but there was strong evidence that he should have been No. 1. The previous season, Giroux struggled mightily because he was coming off of hip and abdominal surgeries.

"When your mind wants to do something but your body doesn't do it, it's frustrating," Giroux said.

But he was fully healthy in 2017–18, and he led the Flyers to a playoff spot—finishing with a flourish by scoring 19 goals in the last 29 games—and had a career season. Oh, and he did it at a new position, shifting from center to left wing. As a result, center Sean Couturier took away a lot of the defensive responsibility from Giroux, who seemed rejuvenated.

Giroux's MVP-caliber season produced 34 goals, 68 assists, and 102 points—all personal bests. He was involved in a staggering 41 percent of the Flyers' goals, which was a higher rate than any of the other MVP candidates with their respective teams. (New Jersey's Taylor Hall won the award.)

"[Giroux] was the catalyst of this team all year long," said Mark Howe, a former Flyer who is the Detroit Red Wings' director of pro scouting. "In big times and big games, he came up big all year."

No one in the NHL had more assists, and Giroux finished second in the league in points and third in faceoff percentage (58.6). He became the 11th player in NHL history to reach the 100-point mark for the first time at age 30 or older.

And unlike Hall, Giroux had a big influence in the terrific seasons of his linemates. Couturier (31 goals, 76 points) and Travis Konecny (24 goals, 47 points) both had career years. Konecny scored 20 goals in the 41 games in which he was on Giroux's line. He had four goals in the 40 games he wasn't with Giroux.

The 5'11", 185-pound Giroux made a dramatic turnaround. Slowed by hip and abdominal surgery, the Hearst, Ontario, native produced just 14 goals, 58 points, and a minus-15 rating the previous season. The relentless, hell-bent style that had become his trademark was missing.

His second gear returned in 2017–18. Giroux credited the players who were most frequently his linemates during the season: Couturier, Konecny, and, for a time, Jake Voracek.

"They made me a better player," said Giroux, currently the longest-tenured Philly athlete among the city's four major sports teams. "It's not the other way around. I really feel lucky to play with some good players."

Giroux was being modest. To paraphrase baseball Hall of Famer Reggie Jackson, he was the straw that stirred the drink.

"I'm not surprised at anything G does," Dave Hakstol, the Flyers' coach at the time, said to reporters. "You guys know the hockey player and the person a little bit. But to know the person and know the competitiveness that burns inside of him—no, I'm not surprised."

* * *

Long before Giroux was drafted, many scouts thought his small stature would prevent him from playing in the NHL.

"We never expected him to be in the NHL at first," Raymond Giroux, Giroux's father, told the *Philadelphia Inquirer* in 2012. "According to lots of people, he was too small to be in the NHL. They put that in your head...and you have to forget about that and focus on one thing."

The scouts, of course, changed their opinion.

Raymond Giroux said his son was never obsessed with being a high draft pick.

After the 2018–19 season, Claude Giroux sat fourth on the Flyers' all-time scoring list with 762, behind only Bobby Clarke, Bill Barber, and Brian Propp.

ON THIS DATE

MAY 7, 2000

Andy Delmore becomes the first rookie defenseman in NHL history to notch a hat trick in a postseason game, keying a 6–3 win over Pittsburgh. Delmore played in 95 career games with the Flyers and managed seven goals.

"He wasn't thinking really about going higher and higher," he said. "He just loved the sport and continued to play and to work hard. It was fun for him to do."

Claude Giroux said he developed a lot of his creative moves while playing street hockey with his buddies in Hearst. When Giroux was 14, he and his family moved near Ottawa, and the future NHL star went to high school there.

In the 2006 draft in Vancouver, after Clarke momentarily forgot Giroux's name, the forward was selected following a 103-point season for Gatineau in the Quebec Major Junior Hockey League. Giroux spent two more years with Gatineau and was an emergency call-up in 2007–08, playing in two NHL games for the Flyers.

He spent the first half of the 2008–09 season with the AHL's Phantoms before being recalled by the Flyers and collecting nine goals and 18 points in 42 NHL games.

Giroux showed a hint of his future greatness in the Stanley Cup playoffs that year, leading the Flyers with five points in the six games against Pittsburgh.

His career was about to skyrocket, and NHL.com ranks him No. 22 in their list of best overall selections in the history of the draft.

Heading into the 2018–19 campaign, Giroux had 603 points in the previous eight seasons. That was the second-highest total in the NHL in that span, topped only by Sidney Crosby (610 points). Giroux's sensational 2017–18 season coincided with his move to a new position and his engagement to his longtime girlfriend, Ryanne Breton, on November 29, 2017. Shortly thereafter, Giroux went on a scoring binge.

"My little lucky charm!!" Giroux tweeted a few days after his engagement. He and Ryanne both grew up in the Ottawa area, and they were married in Allentown, New Jersey, in the summer of 2018.

After the wedding, Giroux gushed on Instagram, "The most amazing day of my life. Thankful for everyone who made it so special. Ryanne I can't wait to start this new chapter together, I love you [happy face emoji] #girouxpartyoftwo #weready."

It was a magical year for Giroux, who, in a span of about nine months, was engaged, got married, and had the best season of his career.

Philadelphia Phillies centerfielder Odubel Herrera (left) visited the Flyers' locker room late in the 2018-19 NHL season and exchanged fist bumps with goalie Carter Hart.

"When we came to camp, I was a little surprised to be put on the left wing," he said after the 2017–18 season ended with a six-game loss to Pittsburgh in the opening playoff round. "I wasn't against it; I was up to trying anything. I think it was a good thing that the first day of camp we did it right away. For me and Coots [Couturier] to play on the same line the whole year, usually you have a few games where it's not going so well, so you try a different combination. We had that chemistry early on, and we were able to keep building on it."

Giroux's superb season vaulted him to No. 5 on the all-time Flyers scoring list with 677 career points, enabling him to surpass Eric Lindros, Tim Kerr, John LeClair, Mark Recchi, and Rod Brind'Amour. He climbed to No. 4 the next season. Before his career is over, he could climb past Bill Barber (883 points) for No. 2 on the list, and he has an outside chance to replace Clarke (1,210 points) as the franchise's all-time leading scorer.

Even if he doesn't get to No. 1, one thing is certain—Clarke now knows his name. So does virtually everyone who follows the NHL.

38

CHRIS PRONGER:
IF ONLY HE DIDN'T GET INJURED

Because of injuries, towering defenseman Chris Pronger played just one full season with the Flyers. It is no coincidence that the Flyers reached the Stanley Cup Final in that season. Wherever Pronger played, you see, postseason success wasn't far behind. You can look it up.

"He brought a tremendous presence to the rink—both defensively and offensively," said Flyers president Paul Holmgren, who was the team's general manager in 2009 when he acquired Pronger in a blockbuster June deal with Anaheim. "He could defend. He could make plays like nobody. He was one of the best defensemen who ever played."

Which is why Pronger went into the Hockey Hall of Fame in 2015.

Pronger spent parts of three seasons with the Flyers but only played in 145 games with them, including all 82 in 2009–10. He played a key role in the seventh-seeded Flyers' surprising surge into the 2010 Stanley Cup Final. They lost to Chicago in a hard-fought, six-game championship series.

In 2006, during his only season in Edmonton, Pronger helped the Oilers become the first eighth seed to reach the Stanley Cup Final. A year later, he hoisted the Cup while playing for the Anaheim Ducks.

Right before Pronger went into the Hall of Fame, Holmgren called him a "combination of guys like Larry Robinson and Serge Savard—big guys who could defend and move the puck. They could play anyway you want. If you wanted to play physical, they could do that. If you wanted to play a finesse game, they could do that." Like Pronger, those defensemen are in the Hall of Fame.

The crease-clearing Pronger played the game on the edge—and sometimes beyond it—and was a five-time All-Star. He played 18 seasons with five teams, collecting 698 points, 157 goals, a plus-183 rating, and 1,590 penalty minutes in 1,167 games.

PHILADELPHIA FLYERS

At the NHL draft in 2009, Holmgren rolled the dice by acquiring Pronger in a stunning deal with Anaheim. It was a gamble because Pronger was almost 35 and no one knew if he had much left in the tank—and because he was in the final year of his contract, one season removed from becoming a potential free agent. Twelve days after the trade, the Flyers signed him to a seven-year, $34.9 million extension.

The Flyers hoped the 6'6", 220-pound Pronger was the missing piece who would steer them to their first Stanley Cup since 1975. He gave them a much-needed physical presence in front of the net. He also gave the Flyers someone who was an offensive threat from the back end—something that was missing from a defense that netted a league-low 20 goals the previous season.

The Flyers sent the Ducks' Joffrey Lupul, Luca Sbisa, and No. 1 draft picks in 2009 (John Moore) and 2010 (Emerson Etem), along with a conditional third rounder in 2010, for Pronger and AHL forward Ryan Dingle. The Ducks later traded the No. 1 pick they acquired in 2009 to Columbus.

"[Pronger] makes everybody around him better on our defense," Holmgren said after the deal was made. "It puts things in the proper pecking order. First of all, he's a winner. He's won a championship.... He's a tremendous character player who works hard and cares. Obviously he's a great defender. He's one of those guys who brings a presence in all zones on the ice, and in terms of what he's been through as a player in our league and his accomplishments. He'll be a guy who's looked highly upon by our younger players and a good role model for those guys."

Holmgren was asked if he had been searching for a physical defenseman.

"I made it sort of clear myself, would I like to get a hammer, a guy who makes life miserable for the other team? This is one of those guys," Holmgren said.

Pronger was known as one of the NHL's most physical players.

"I'm very excited. It's obviously a city that's very passionate for the sport of hockey," Pronger said after the trade was announced. "The style of play that the Flyers have been known to play certainly fits my game. They've got some great young talent, and I hope to help not

ON THIS DATE

OCTOBER 26, 2002

Justin Williams and Michal Handzus score goals in the first 31 seconds, the quickest two tallies at the start of a game in franchise history, to spark the Flyers to a 6-2 win over the host New York Islanders. At the time, they are the third-fastest two goals to start a game in NHL history.

only develop the team into being regarded as one of the top teams in the league, but also by winning a Stanley Cup."

The Flyers fell two games short in 2010, and Pronger was injury-riddled the rest of his career. Pronger's career ended when he suffered a concussion with the Flyers in 2011. He had two years left on his deal when the Flyers traded his contract and Nick Grossmann to Arizona as part of the Sam Gagner deal in 2015. Pronger's career was over, but the Flyers were able to clear some cap space.

Pronger, who had 55 points in his only full season with the Flyers, became the 18th captain in franchise history before the 2011–12 campaign. He played in just 13 games that year, his final season.

"Guys like that don't come around very often," said Holmgren, who coached Pronger during the defenseman's early years with the Hartford Whalers. "You take the top defenseman out of anybody's lineup, you're going to miss him. It's unfortunate for Chris that his career ended the way it did. He certainly didn't want it to end. I'm pretty sure he'd be a pretty good player today if he was still playing because of his ability to see the game and the way he could handle the puck."

Flyers captain Claude Giroux received his share of loud criticism from Pronger when they were teammates, but he said it benefited him.

"He knew how to win, and sometimes to win, you have to have tough love," Giroux said. "He wasn't scared of saying what he thought, and I don't think anybody didn't appreciate him."

Pronger, suspended eight times during his career, called it "very humbling" to be inducted into the Hockey Hall of Fame in 2015. "It's certainly something I didn't expect while playing," he said.

Pronger had his best season while with St. Louis in 1999–2000. He had career highs in points (62) and plus-minus rating (plus-52), and he became the second defenseman to win the Hart (MVP) and Norris (top defenseman) trophies in the same season. Bobby Orr did it three times.

The Hartford Whalers made him the No. 2 overall pick in the 1993 NHL draft. About four months later, he was a regular in the Whalers' lineup.

Pronger became the 11th person to be named to the Hall of Fame in the player category after spending a portion of his career with the Flyers. He also became the fourth former Flyers captain to receive the honor, joining Bobby Clarke, Bill Barber, and Peter Forsberg.

In 2017, Pronger was hired by the Florida Panthers as an advisor to General Manager Dale Tallon. At the time, Tallon told reporters he liked hiring people "smarter than myself, to make myself look smarter."

Pronger was a physical player with a high hockey IQ. Off the ice, he was a practical joker who never took himself seriously and enjoyed the give-and-take with the media. He liked having fun. For proof, take a look at the video of the 2017 celebrity All-Star event in Los Angeles, where Pronger checked pop superstar Justin Bieber into the boards. Pronger towered over the 5'9", 145-pound Bieber. Pronger, who worked for the NHL's player safety department at the time, joked that he fined himself $5 during a one-man hearing.

"A player of his caliber, you've got to take away his time and space," Pronger cracked to the *St. Louis Post-Dispatch*. "You don't want to have anybody who had those kinds of dance moves to have any space."

39

WAYNE SIMMONDS: "ULTIMATE FLYER" INSPIRED BY WILLIE O'REE

If you look up the definition of *warrior*, it's not true that it is accompanied by a mug shot of Wayne Simmonds. But it wouldn't be a bad idea.

Simmonds has been called the "ultimate Flyer" by then-head coach Dave Hakstol—and with good reason. The right winger plays with an edge, scores goals in bunches in the "dirty areas" around the net, and doesn't let injuries knock him out of the lineup. In other words, he's a warrior.

For proof, look at Simmonds' 2017–18 season. Most players would have been on the sidelines because of the injuries Simmonds sustained. But Simmonds, though limited in what he could do, still managed to score 24 goals. It was a season in which he broke an ankle from a blast fired by teammate Shayne Gostisbehere but stayed in the lineup because, in his words, "It wasn't weight-bearing on the bone, so you're still able to play with that."

There were more injuries. Several of them, in fact. He lost six teeth from getting hit with a stick, tore ligaments in his right thumb—causing him to be sidelined for seven games, the only ones he missed—and later played with a pin in his hand. Oh, and he played the entire season with a tear in his pelvis area, which caused him to overcompensate on the ice and suffer a pulled groin. Simmonds underwent surgery after the season to repair the pelvis tear and a torn abdominal muscle.

"He's a guy who lays it all out there every night and gives his all," center Sean Couturier said. "He'll do whatever he can for his teammates."

It's what makes Simmonds, who was traded to Nashville late in the 2018–19 season, so respected by his teammates, coaches, and fans.

Simmonds acknowledged he didn't play up to his expectations and didn't possess "the power I usually have" in 2017–18 and that it was frustrating. "Your brain's telling your body to do it, but your body's not doing it," he said. "But if I can play, I'm gonna play."

If he had surgery during the season, he probably would have missed six weeks, he said. "I don't regret playing through it," Simmonds said. "That's just my character."

A fan favorite known as "Simmer" and the "Wayne Train," Simmonds flourished since being acquired from Los Angeles in a megadeal before the 2011–12 season. The Flyers sent captain Mike Richards to the Kings for Simmonds and Brayden Schenn.

Advantage: Flyers.

In his first seven seasons with the Flyers, Simmonds blossomed into one of the NHL's most consistent right wingers, a power forward who usually scored around 28 to 30 goals a year. He was in the national spotlight in 2017 when he won the All-Star Game MVP Award, becoming the first Flyers winner since Reggie Leach in 1980. Simmonds was one of three finalists for the 2017–18 Mark Messier Leadership Award. The award, which was won by the Vegas Golden Knights' Deryk Engelland, is given to the NHL player who shows leadership on and off the ice.

"It was very humbling," Simmonds said of the nomination. "I was kind of surprised, but at the same time I think it's only right to be in a position that we're in to give back to the community and you want to be a leader on and off the ice. You don't want to talk about it; you want to actually do things. I've always been that type of guy who wears my heart on my sleeve. I kind of say what I want to say. I'm not gonna hold anything back. I think that's part of my leadership, but at the same time I like to set an example of playing the game the right way on the ice and still giving back to the community—especially the hockey community because they've given so much to me growing up and you've got a lot people to thank and it's just kind of paying it forward."

Simmonds said if it wasn't for Willie O'Ree, he may never have dreamed of reaching the NHL. O'Ree became the NHL's first black player in 1958. He made Simmonds believe at a young age that playing pro hockey was a possibility. In 2018, O'Ree went into the Hockey Hall of Fame.

"He had an effect on every single player of color coming into this league," Simmonds said. "Without him, we wouldn't even be in this

One of the Flyers' best tough guys, Wayne Simmonds was no stranger to the Gordie Howe hat trick (in which a player scores a goal, records an assist, and gets in a fight in the same game) in Philadelphia.

league...so there's a lot of respect I have for Mr. O'Ree. He's the reason I'm here."

In the United States, most people know the legacy of Jackie Robinson, who broke Major League Baseball's color barrier in 1947. In Canada, where hockey rules, O'Ree commands the same respect.

"He *is* my Jackie Robinson," Simmonds said.

He said he has been aware of O'Ree since he started playing hockey at the age of 6. He recalled doing projects in school about the trailblazer.

"I wanted to know as much as I could about him," Simmonds said. "I'm a black hockey player and you have to know your roots. You have to know where you came from before you go anywhere else."

O'Ree has inspired a countless number of black players to play hockey professionally. More than half a century later, Simmonds is doing the same.

Simmonds, who entered the 2018–19 season with 226 career goals, said he started skating when he was three years old. Every Saturday, his dad would take him to an outdoor rink behind the Scarborough Town Centre Mall in Toronto.

In a story he wrote for the *Players' Tribune*, Simmonds said his father had one rule: "I had to pick myself up when I fell. My dad would

CARNIVAL: FUN FOR ALL WHEN FANS MEET PLAYERS

It's been around 42 years, but it never gets old. The Flyers' Wives Carnival has been held in South Philadelphia since 1977 and continues to draw thousands of fans each year. It's a chance for Flyers players, coaches, and front office personnel to interact one-on-one with their admirers at the Wells Fargo Center.

In the past four decades, the carnival has raised more than $27 million for worthy causes.

New in 2018 for the carnival were outdoor activities, including an obstacle course. Inside, fans were treated to tours of the Flyers' locker room. But the star of the show was none other than new popular mascot Gritty, who was on hand for his first carnival. He hit all the popular spots at the event and kept folks in a festive mood.

All proceeds from the 2018 event were scheduled to benefit childhood cancer and leukemia research. Flyers Charities oversees distribution of funds raised to a multitude of worthy nonprofit organizations across the greater Philadelphia region. These charities provide educational and recreational resources to underserved youth, engage in important medical and healthcare research, and promote countless community investment initiatives to positively influence the community. These organizations include Michael's Way, the Center for Autism, Snider Hockey, Liberty USO, Living Beyond Breast Cancer, Mission Kids, PAWS, Ronald McDonald House of Philadelphia, and Simon's Heart.

"You meet a lot of fans, a lot of great people," Sean Couturier said. "It's always fun playing games. I remember one year playing one game for an hour. Playing games is more fun than just signing stuff—you actually get to interact with the fans."

That's why the grandfather of all carnivals continues to keep flying along.

never help me up. That was his version of tough love. By four or five years old, I was ripping around the rink like it was a NASCAR race. I had no brakes, man. Couldn't stop."

When he had to stop, Simmonds would crash into the boards.

He signed up to play hockey when he was six, and he and his parents would go to Play It Again Sports to buy used gear.

"All I could think about was waking up the next morning and becoming the next Sergei Fedorov," he said.

Simmonds' path to the NHL hasn't always been easy. He has heard racial slurs as a kid and as an adult. In 2011, while playing with the Flyers in an exhibition game in London, Ontario, someone threw a banana on the ice at Simmonds. A year later, while playing in the Czech Republic during the NHL lockout, some fans chanted racial slurs at him. Simmonds calls them a "small minority of idiots," and says O'Ree's quiet determination and class continue to be an inspiration for players of color today.

The same can be said for Wayne Simmonds.

40

A COMEBACK FOR THE AGES

This was the grim arithmetic facing the Flyers after opening Round 2 with three straight defeats to Boston in 2010. Only two of 161 NHL teams (1.2 percent) had won a Stanley Cup playoff series after losing the first three games. But somehow, the Flyers beat the odds. Not only that, but they became the first team in NHL history to overcome a 3–0 series deficit and a 3–0 deficit in Game 7.

They did it because Simon Gagne, a veteran winger who couldn't walk without crutches earlier in the series, snapped a 3–3 tie by scoring a power play goal with 7 minutes and 8 seconds left in regulation.

A gimpy Gagne still wasn't at full strength, but you wouldn't have known it by his play. It was his fourth goal in four games (all wins) since his heroic return from a broken bone in his right foot. Gagne downplayed the injury, saying his foot was "getting better and better" with each game.

"The Stanley Cup is all about sacrifice...like Simon did tonight," Flyers coach Peter Laviolette said after the momentous 4–3 victory before a stunned sellout crowd in Boston.

A shot by Mike Richards never reached the net, but it caromed to Gagne, who scored from the right circle to snap a 3–3 tie and silence the crowd at TD Garden.

Gagne's goal pushed Team Resilient into the Eastern Conference Final against the eighth-seeded Montreal Canadiens. Amazingly, the Flyers, who needed a shootout win on the last day of the regular season just to sneak into the playoffs, got the home-ice advantage as the seventh seed, the first time that has happened in NHL history.

They defeated Montreal in five games before falling to Chicago in the Stanley Cup Final, losing in a decisive Game 6 in overtime.

If they had won the Cup, the comeback over Boston would have meant even more. But it still has a special place in NHL lore. The Flyers joined the 1942 Toronto Maple Leafs and the 1975 New York Islanders as the only NHL teams to win a playoff round after being in a 3–0 series hole. (Los Angles became the fourth NHL team to accomplish the feat, doing it against San Jose in the 2014 Western Conference Quarterfinals en route to winning the Stanley Cup.) Heading into 2018, the 2004 Boston Red Sox were the only other team, in any sport, to make such a comeback from a 3–0 series deficit.

"We've been resilient all year, whether it was injuries or putting ourselves in a bad position in the standings," Richards said. "We have been through a lot together. Our mind-set was if you are going to go down, you are going to go down swinging."

Boston had been 16–0 in the series in which it had won the first three games. Trailing by 3–0 in the opening period, the Flyers—in a microcosm of this series—roared from behind to tie the score heading into the third period.

Milan Lucic's second goal of the night gave Boston a 3–0 first-period lead and prompted Flyers coach Peter Laviolette to call his time-out. The players huddled around their fuming coach.

"We just need one [bleeping] goal before the end of the period," Laviolette said, according to amateur lip-readers. "One goal and we're back in it."

What he said—it wasn't for a family newspaper, center Danny Briere reported—wasn't as important as how the players responded. The Flyers got to within 3–1 when James van Riemsdyk's soft shot deflected off Boston's Mark Stuart and past Tuukka Rask with 2:48 left in the first period. It was the first-year left winger's first career playoff score.

"That goal gave us momentum at the end of the first period," Richards said.

"When a young guy plays like he did you feed off his energy," defenseman Chris Pronger said.

Van Riemsdyk's goal started a streak in which the Flyers netted the game's final four scores and sent Bruins fans home in an angry mood— hundreds threw their rally towels onto the ice during the postgame handshake.

"It feels nice to finally get one after I don't know how many games it's been," said van Riemsdyk, who hadn't scored in 16 consecutive

HARTNELL: DOWN BUT NOT OUT

There are some bad things about social media, but once in a while there are some good things, too. For example, take the charity fund that former Flyer Scott Hartnell helped create during his stay in Philadelphia, specifically November 2011. It was called "Hartnell Down," and every time Hartnell went down to the ice, be it on a natural play, a fight, whatever, he would donate money to a worthy cause.

"It's still a shock to me," Hartnell said of the mini-craze at the time. "It's pretty surreal. I'm glad it gained popularity, but I'm even more excited that it's going to raise money for charity."

Hartnell was known as a locker room joker, and this endeavor fit his personality. But he actually took this one pretty seriously. As www.hartnelldown.com took off, the player had T-shirts made, which were sold for $15 each, with proceeds going to a charity of Hartnell's choice. The front read: #hartnelldown. The back read: "Down & Dirty 19—@Hartsy19"

Flyers fan Seth Hastings deserves credit for getting the project going. The site even featured a Hartnell "Down-O-Meter" to keep track of how many times he hit the ice. No word on the final tally, but it certainly was a lot of fun while it lasted.

games. "[Giroux] made a great play to get me the puck. I just threw it on net and the puck hit a stick and went in."

Van Riemsdyk's goal late in the first period calmed down the Flyers. "Maybe we were a little nervous at the beginning," Scott Hartnell said. Hartnell and Danny Briere used deft moves around the net to produce second-period goals and tie the game at 3-all.

"We didn't have that same jump and we kind of backed off," said Rask, the Bruins' rookie goalie, about their second-period performance.

The Flyers appeared to take a 4–3 lead with 5:14 left in the second period after a wild scramble in front, one in which Richards, van Riemsdyk, and Arron Asham had whacks at the puck. The Flyers threw up their arms to signal a goal as Rask went down in a pileup.

The video appeared to show the puck inching across the goal line and Boston defenseman Dennis Wideman gloving it and swiping it out of the net. The replay officials in Toronto disagreed, ruling that the puck did not cross the goal line.

It was no coincidence that the Flyers started their winning streak the next game after David Krejci, Boston's playmaking center, suffered a season-ending dislocated wrist when he received a heavy hit from Richards. And it's no coincidence that they didn't lose a game with Gagne in the lineup.

"He's a world-class player," Laviolette said.

Laviolette said the Flyers, in effect, played their fifth elimination game since the final contest of the regular season. They needed to win that game just to sneak into the playoffs, and they did as they outlasted the New York Rangers 2–1 in a shootout.

In the Eastern Conference Semifinals, the Flyers fell into a 3–0 series hole and staved off elimination with three straight wins, setting up the Game 7 showdown.

"The message hasn't changed from Day One since I've been here until where we are right now," Laviolette said before the series' final game. "Everything has stayed the same. The meetings are the same. The message is the same. What's expected is the same. I feel like we're ready for this."

He was right.

The Flyers' comeback against Boston created a legacy and left their fans inspired by their resilience, teamwork, and ability to overcome injuries to some of their core players. They didn't win the Cup, but they will be linked forever—in Philly and around the nation—to comebacks of the Nth degree.

41

THE GOAL THAT WILL LIVE IN INFAMY

It was a goal that will forever haunt the Flyers and their fans, a goal that ended an enchanted, unexpected run that fell two games short of a 2010 Stanley Cup championship. It was a goal scored from an extremely sharp angle that, to some, didn't appear to have gone into the net at first glance.

Patrick Kane felt differently.

"I just threw it on net, and I knew right away it was in," said Kane, the Chicago Blackhawks winger, as he exchanged hugs with friends and family members on the ice.

Kane raced past defenseman Kimmo Timonen and scored from deep inside the left circle, putting the shot under the pads and stick of Flyers goalie Michael Leighton. After his goal, the young winger made a mad sprint down to the other end of the ice to start celebrating his team's unforgettable Game 6 victory. Confusion sprouted, however, because the red light did not go on to signify a score, and many in the sellout crowd at the Flyers' arena, then known as the Wachovia Center, did not realize a goal had been scored until they saw Kane and his teammates jubilantly throw their sticks in the air.

The teams had to wait several moments until the officials confirmed the goal after reviewing the replay and searching for the puck in the padding at the back of the net. Kane said the review wasn't necessary.

"I saw it go right through the legs, sticking right under the pad in the net," he said. "I don't think anyone saw it in the net. I booked it to the other end. I knew it was in. I tried to sell the celebration a bit."

The goal, scored 4:06 into overtime, gave Chicago a 4–3 win and its first Stanley Cup since 1961, ending the NHL's longest drought at that time. The Blackhawks had lost their previous five Finals before the 21-year-old Kane scored his third goal of the series. Kane called it a "pretty surreal moment," especially since many of his teammates didn't realize it went into the net and there was a delay in the celebration.

"When it went in, I don't think too many people knew it," Chicago coach Joel Quenneville said at the time. "But it made a funny, strange sound. Like the back of the leather and the back of the net. And I asked Kaner, 'Where did it go in?' He said it went in long pad, five hole, in that area."

Added Quenneville, "When they lifted up the net, when they went searching for the puck, it was underneath in there deep. They lifted it up, it fell through. We knew that was the winner."

Flyers center Danny Briere thought play was stopped for a faceoff.

"All of a sudden I see a few guys jumping on the ice. I was confused," Briere said. "I thought, 'You can't win the Stanley Cup like that, not even knowing.' It doesn't change how much it hurts."

After 105 games—including a shootout win that earned a playoff berth on the last day of the regular season, and an epic comeback from a 3-0 series deficit in the conference semifinals—the Flyers' gritty, memorable season came to an unwanted end.

Afterward, the arena roared with "Let's go Flyers!" chants as the players lined up for the traditional handshake.

"They were with us the whole season and we wanted to win for them, too," said Claude Giroux, a third-line center who traded places with first-liner Jeff Carter in the second period. "This is not how we wanted to end it."

Kane's goal offset a frantic late rally by Team Resilient. With a record crowd watching at the reverberating Wachovia Center, a knocked-to-the-ice Scott Hartnell sent it into overtime with his second goal of the game, a rebound that he poked just inside the left post with 3:59 left in regulation. The Wachovia Center eruption rivaled the roar heard at the Spectrum in 1987, when J.J. Daigneault's late goal gave the Flyers a Game 6 Final win over Edmonton.

The Flyers, who were outshot by a 41–24 margin, were a step slower than the Blackhawks most of the night as they suffered their sixth straight series loss in the Final since they won the Stanley Cup in 1975.

The loss ended a remarkable run for the Flyers, who showed more resiliency than any team in the franchise's history. Despite a slew of injuries, they defeated New Jersey in the opening round. They then

MAY 14, 2010

The Flyers become the third team in NHL history to fall behind in a playoff series 3-0 and win the round. They overcome a 3-0 deficit in Game 7 and win in Boston 4-3 on Simon Gagne's goal with 7:08 left in regulation, sending the team into the Eastern Conference Final.

overcame a 3-0 series deficit to shock Boston in Round 2 and crushed Montreal in five games to reach the Finals.

"We just thought it was meant to be," said Briere, the diminutive center who set a franchise record with 30 playoff points that season. "We just thought we were going to find a way once again."

"It stings. It hurts," Hartnell said. "It'll give us more fuel in training camp next year." But the next season, the Flyers lost in the second round of the playoffs. Their long drought continued.

After Hartnell tied it at 3-3 late in Game 6 of the 2010 Final, the Flyers stormed the net. In the waning moments of regulation, they had their best chance when Chicago goalie Antti Niemi flopped to the ice, but Jeff Carter couldn't get enough lift on his shot from out front, and the goalie made the save.

"In the long run, we should be proud of what we've done this year," said Carter, who returned from his second broken foot that season to play in part of the playoffs. "With all the adversity we faced, the coaching changes.... We were basically last place in the conference and we battled our way back."

They battled but couldn't complete the job. They had seemed destined to win the Cup when they became the first team in NHL history to overcome a 3-0 series deficit *and* a 3-0 deficit in Game 7.

Leighton was brilliant in the conference finals, collecting three shutouts against Montreal. The waiver-wire pickup struggled mightily in the Final, but he played superbly in the first two periods of Game 6, keeping the outplayed Flyers close.

As for Kane's goal, Leighton knew he didn't get his stick down and that the puck had slid through his legs.

"Obviously, it's pretty tough to swallow," he said after one of the most painful and bizarre finishes in franchise history. "It's hard the way it ended. That's what they say. It's usually not a great goal. It's usually a fluky, stupid-type goal, and that's what happened."

Stupid and fluky are what the Flyers called the Goal That Not Many Saw.

The Blackhawks called it something else.

"It was crazy," Kane said. "At the moment it's just like, 'We won the Stanley Cup!' and that's all you're thinking about. To play this game, this is the only thing I want to do in the world and be a part of moments like this."

"I don't even know how to explain it," Chicago defenseman Duncan Keith said. "It gives me chills thinking about it."

Leighton was never the same after allowing the goal and was never again an NHL regular, playing primarily in the AHL. After surrendering the infamous goal, the Ontario native battled injuries and appeared in just two more games with the Flyers and then spent time in numerous organizations, including in Chicago (how's that for irony), Carolina, and Pittsburgh.

Heading into the 2018–19 season, Leighton had played in just seven NHL games since Kane's historic goal in 2010.

To Flyers fans, Leighton will always be a tragic figure, sort of like Ralph Branca to those who followed the old Brooklyn Dodgers. Branca allowed the Shot Heard 'Round the World to Bobby Thomson to give the New York Giants the 1951 National League pennant. Like Branca, Leighton did lots of good things for his team during what had been a magical year, including a 16–5–2 regular season record. And like Branca was to the Dodgers, the Flyers fans' lasting memory of Leighton is that goal by Kane that happened at the most critical time, when the magic turned to anguish.

42

DANNY BRIERE: LITTLE MAN, BIG-TIME PERFORMER

Danny Briere was one of the most clutch playoff performers in NHL history.

A little guy with a heart twice his size, Briere was deeply revered by Flyers fans because of his tenacity and because of the way he turned into Mr. Postseason.

Briere, whose terrific 17-year career ended in 2015, was one of the most notable free-agent signings made by former general manager Paul Holmgren.

Good signing. Great playoff performer. The epitome of class, on and off the ice. That will be how Briere will be remembered. With some help from goalie Michael Leighton, he could have been remembered as a Flyers icon. If Leighton had been better in the 2010 Final, Briere would have been forever idolized like those who played on the Flyers' 1974 and 1975 Stanley Cup champions.

Briere put together an epic playoff performance in 2010 as the Flyers stunningly reached the Stanley Cup Final. That was the Flyers team that needed a shootout victory over the Rangers on the final day of the regular season just to get into the playoffs. Briere had scored one of the team's shootout goals. That was the team that Briere carried on his diminutive shoulders to the brink of an improbable championship.

In 23 playoff games, Briere led the NHL with 30 points. That was more points than Bobby Clarke ever scored in one postseason. Or Rick MacLeish. Or Brian Propp. Or any player in Flyers history.

Briere was immune to playoff pressure.

"Is it pressure? To me, it's fun," Briere once said. "I grew up watching playoff hockey as a kid, and I always dreamed I would have a chance to play in those big games.... You try to enjoy it as much as possible. So it's not really pressure. It's a fun time, an exciting time."

If the Flyers had won the 2010 Stanley Cup, you could have made a case for putting Briere's face on the franchise's Mount Rushmore.

ON THIS DATE

MAY 18, 2015

The Flyers name Dave Hakstol as the 19th head coach in franchise history. He becomes the third coach in league history to go from the college ranks (North Dakota) to the NHL as a head coach.

But Leighton, who had three shutouts in the previous series and was a waiver-wire wonder that season, had a 3.96 goals-against average and .873 save percentage in the Final—yet allowed two soft goals in the decisive Game 6.

The Finals defeat took some of the luster off Briere's magical playoff run. Still, it was the high point of a career that produced 307 goals and 696 points in 973 games—and seven seasons with at least 25 goals.

"It was tough losing when you're two wins away from achieving the ultimate dream," Briere said. "But that two-month stretch—making the playoffs on a shootout the last day of the season against possibly the best shootout goalie [Henrik Lundqvist] in the league, and taking that all the way to two wins away from the Stanley Cup—was the best two months of my career."

In 2010, Briere had 12 goals in 23 playoff games. Four of his goals were game-winners as he led the Flyers to Game 6 of the Stanley Cup Final, when they lost 4–3 to the Chicago Blackhawks in overtime.

When he retired, Briere had 53 goals in the playoffs, tying him with Jeremy Roenick and Bill Barber for 45th on the NHL's all-time list. Briere had 116 points in 124 career playoff games.

"Some people rise to the big occasions," said Peter Laviolette, the Flyers' coach, about Briere's playoff heroics, conjuring memories of Reggie Jackson in the World Series. "It speaks to the player. I think through the course of the history of sports, there are people who answer the bell."

Signing Briere was one of the shrewdest moves made by Holmgren, spurring a turnaround for the team. The season before Briere arrived, the

Flyers went 22–48–12 and had an NHL-worst 56 points in 2006–07. The next season, with several additions on their roster, they went 42–29–11 for 95 points and reached the conference finals.

Two years later, they were in the Cup Final after a stirring run in which they overcame a 3–0 series deficit against Boston. In Game 7 of the Boston series, the Flyers also overcame a 3–0 first-period hole and won 4–3. Briere keyed the comeback with the tying goal, arguably the biggest of his career.

"That was amazing," said Briere of recovering from a 3–0 series deficit against the Bruins. "Within that two-month bubble that we were in, I think the comeback against Boston was probably the ultimate peak of that stretch.... That's a really cool thing to be a part of and to say my team did that and I was a part of it.

"It was a blast playing here," Briere added. "I loved how passionate this city got for the Flyers, especially in the spring when it was playoff time."

Briere announced his retirement in the summer of 2015, saying he wanted to spend more time with his three teenage sons—Caelan, Carson, and Cameron. Briere was 37 at the time.

"After taking a few weeks to think about it, it's time to hang them up and spend a little more time at home with the family," said Briere, who lives in Haddonfield, New Jersey. "The Flyers are where I played the bulk of my career. I've had a great time in Philadelphia and have been very, very fortunate to have the chance to play here."

Briere also played for the Phoenix Coyotes, Buffalo Sabres, Montreal Canadiens, and Colorado Avalanche. He spent six seasons with the Flyers, scoring 124 goals.

The toughest part about hanging up his skates?

"I know it's cliché, but it's being around the guys," he said. "You travel around with 25 guys, travel all over Canada and the U.S. I spent a lot of good times with all these guys. The bonds that you form [are immense]. I mean, we go out there protecting each other. So the bond is strong with your teammates; that's probably the toughest part of leaving."

The 5'8" Briere was MVP of the 2006 All-Star Game, the same year he helped lead the Sabres to the Eastern Conference Final.

A native of Gatineau, Quebec, Briere was a first-round selection (24th overall) by the Coyotes in the 1996 draft.

The Flyers signed Briere to an eight-year, $52 million contract in 2007. He played his final season with Colorado, scoring eight goals in 57 games.

Briere was one of the best team players in the Flyers' history. Not only was he a valuable center and a superb team spokesman, but he took two players (Claude Giroux and Sean Couturier) under his wing early in their careers, and they even lived with him at different times.

In 2015, Briere thought briefly about playing another year and even kicked around the idea of trying to finish his career as a fourth-liner with the Flyers. But in the end, he decided it was more important to spend quality time with his three sons before they headed to college in a few years.

His boys watched from the back of the room during Briere's emotional retirement news conference at the Flyers' training site in Voorhees, New Jersey.

"[The boys] have been my inspiration all those years, the reason I kept going, kept fighting, kept pushing, kept staying on the ice for more, going to the gym, to be able to keep playing," Briere said at the time. "Thank you, boys, for all of your patience and being there without me the last couple years."

Briere added he was a "big fan of the game, and in the future I hope to stay involved somehow in the hockey world."

He later became vice president of operations for the ECHL's Maine Mariners, owned by the Flyers' parent company, Comcast Spectacor. He hopes to be an NHL general manager down the road.

As for his playing career, Briere said he was jolted by comments made by NHL executives who watched him play junior hockey and said he was too small to make an impact. Briere kept those newspaper clippings in a box in his bedroom.

"That was kind of my motivation at the time to prove them wrong," he said.

Consider it done.

43

GOALIE SIGNING TURNS INTO A BRYZASTER

To the Flyers' brass, acquiring and then signing goaltender Ilya Bryzgalov to a nine-year, $51 million contract in 2011 seemed like a step in the right direction. Instead it turned into a Bryzaster, and the team eventually used a compliance buyout to send the colorful goalie packing in the summer of 2013.

Back in June 2011, the Flyers acquired the rights to Bryzgalov by sending minor-league left winger/enforcer Matt Clackson and a third-round pick in 2012 to Phoenix. The Coyotes also received a conditional pick because Bryzgalov, a potential unrestricted free agent at the time, later signed with the Flyers.

Some background on the Bryzgalov signing is needed to put the process in perspective. After the Flyers were eliminated by Boston in the second round of the 2012 playoffs, club chairman Ed Snider made it perfectly clear that the team's goalie carousel would stop. Now. Snider said the Flyers' recently completed season was a "major disappointment" and strongly implied that adding a goalie was atop his priority list.

After finishing second in the Eastern Conference and outlasting Buffalo in the opening round of the playoffs, the Flyers were swept by Boston in the conference semifinals. During the playoffs, the Flyers equaled a dubious NHL record by making seven in-game goalie switches—and they did it in just 11 games.

"It was strange, and something I never want to see again," Snider said.

The Flyers had a 3.46 playoff goals-against average, placing them 14th out of 16 teams.

When told that the fan base was crying for a No. 1 goalie for a few decades, Snider fired back, "I want one, too." He paused. "So either one of the goalies we have has to step up in training camp, or we have to make improvements to make sure it happens. But we are *never* going to go through the goalie issues we've gone through in the last couple of years again."

Snider made it a point to say that rookie Sergei Bobrovsky was viewed as the Flyers' "goalie of the future." But those words became hollow after Bryzgalov was signed, and Bobrovsky—who had a strong rookie season—was unhappy with his diminished role and eventually told the Flyers he wanted to go someplace where he could play regularly.

Bobrovsky was granted his wish and dealt to Columbus before the 2012–13 season. He won the Vezina Trophy, awarded to the NHL's top goaltender, that season and again in 2016–17. The Flyers haven't had a Vezina winner since Ron Hextall in 1986–87.

From the start, Bryzgalov was shaky with the Flyers. In his first season with his new team, Bryzgalov had a 3.01 goals-against average and .890 save percentage as the Winter Classic approached. Both stats were career worsts.

As the Flyers prepared to play the New York Rangers in the Winter Classic at Citizens Bank Park, Bryzgalov held an impromptu news conference in the locker room that seemed more like a comedy routine. Bryzgalov revealed that Bobrovsky, his backup, would be the team's starting goalie in the hyped matchup.

"I have great news and even better news," Bryzgalov said. "Great news: I'm not playing [in the Winter Classic]. And good news: We have a chance to win the game."

He was mocking himself for his poor play. In his last four games, he had a 4.58 GAA and .816 save percentage.

"It's not the end of the universe," Bryzgalov, 31, said of being benched.

While saying they still had confidence in Bryzgalov, virtually everyone in the Flyers' locker room seemed pleased Bobrovsky was getting the nod.

"Bryz has maybe had a tough couple games, but Bob has been pretty steady the whole year," winger Scott Hartnell said. "I think it might be good for Bryz to get a wake-up call and work on some things and get back to the goalie he can be and that we all know."

"Obviously, Bob deserves it," Claude Giroux said. "He's been playing well, and since the start of the season he's been working hard. I think guys see how hard he works."

No one outworks Bobrovsky, defenseman Braydon Coburn said. "This guy probably is the last guy to leave from the practice rink every day. I know, because I'm usually the second-to-last," Coburn said. "He's

AFTER LONG WAIT, GOALIE ZEPP MAKES HIS MARK

Goalie Rob Zepp's time with the Flyers was short but memorable. Originally drafted in the fourth round by the old Atlanta Thrashers in 1999, Zepp had spent most of his career in Europe before breaking in to the NHL with the Flyers in 2014–15—at age 33.

The Newmarket, Ontario, native played in 10 games that season, finishing with a 5–2 record, a 2.92 goals-against average, and an .888 save percentage. He also made some history. In his first game, a 4–3 overtime victory in Winnipeg on December 21, 2014, Zepp became the oldest goalie since Hugh Lehman in 1926 to win his NHL debut.

"I've really been reflecting on the journey since I got called up," said Zepp after that game, referring to his promotion from the American Hockey League's Lehigh Valley Phantoms—and his other stops in the OHL, ECHL, and AHL. "There were so many moments that had to happen for this to come together.... I've been playing hockey for 26 years and to be able to get here and play—you know, the game wasn't perfect—but to get the win like that at the end was just incredible. I appreciate this more than anyone knows."

Later in the season, in his third stint of the campaign and his career, Zepp won a duel against one of the NHL's superstar goalies, Nashville's Pekka Rinne. Zepp and the Flyers scored a 3–2 shootout win over Rinne and the Predators. When he sealed the win by making a glove save on Craig Smith, Zepp celebrated with an exaggerated fist pump with his goalie stick in hand.

"I might have overdone it," Zepp said with a smile. "I got caught up in the moment."

Zepp would not spend another season in the NHL, but he had more magical moments than most youngsters who only dream of playing professional hockey.

kind of a little bit of an opposite to Bryz. He's easygoing, and Bryz is a personality."

Bryzgalov, whose announcement that he was benched infuriated Flyers coaches, was asked about his mind-set for the Winter Classic.

"Make sure I don't forget early in the morning my thermos. Put some nice tea in and enjoy the bench," he deadpanned.

Bryzgalov went 33–16–7 with a 2.48 goals-against average and .909 save percentage in his first season with the Flyers, and 19–17–3 with a 2.79 GAA and .900 save percentage in his second and final year with the club.

He filled reporters' notebooks with his, as he would say, "humongous big" way of looking at things. Before the 2012 playoffs against Pittsburgh, for instance, he said in charmingly broken English: "You know, I'm not afraid of anything. I'm afraid of bear, but bear in the forest." The comment prompted some Penguins fans to dress up as bears in the first two games of the series.

But he became a locker-room distraction, and in the summer of 2013, the Flyers bought out Bryzgalov and, in essence, gave the job to Steve Mason, who excelled in a seven-game stint with the Flyers late that season.

Bryzgalov had an up-and-down two seasons with the team and had a sometimes contentious relationship with Coach Peter Laviolette.

The Flyers paid Bryz $23 million (two-thirds of the $34 million left) over 14 years, or $1.6 million per year.

"It's obviously a costly mistake," then general manager Paul Holmgren said. He called it a "very difficult" decision, but that it was done for cap flexibility. At the time, it was the largest buyout in NHL history.

Bryzgalov, who was 33 at the time, oozed sarcasm when a reporter told him that the buyout decision had been made public. "Congratulations to you guys," he said.

Sources say Bryzgalov and Laviolette had many verbal spars during the season.

When asked to comment on his feelings on the buyout, Bryzgalov said, "I don't want to talk to you guys."

After the goalie's first season in Philadelphia, Holmgren made it clear he wanted Bryzgalov to focus more on hockey and less on his bizarre comments.

"His job is to stop pucks and help us win games," Holmgren said at the time in a good-natured tone. "It's not Comedy Central."

In his first season with the Flyers, Bryzgalov said he was "lost in the woods" and that the goal cage behind him seemed as big as a soccer net. He was the zany star in HBO's documentary series *24/7,* which led up to the Winter Classic. Bryzgalov seemed to be imploring the Flyers to buy him out by continuing to be a distraction after his second season in Philadelphia.

In an interview with the Russian sports site Championat, he was quoted as saying he disliked the city of Philadelphia and that he admired Joseph Stalin, who ruled the Soviet Union for more than two decades. It is not known whether those comments were lost in translation into English.

"He's said some off-the-wall things," said Peter Luukko, who was then the club's president, "but this was strictly a business decision. Claude Giroux's [contract extension] is coming up and we want to be able to look at players in free agency and in the trade market."

"I think Ilya's a colorful guy," Holmgren said. "Does he make dumb comments sometimes and get off on tangents sometimes? Yeah, but I think deep down he's a good guy and I know he's a good goalie. That's what makes this [buyout] so difficult."

When asked if Bryzgalov had become a distraction in the locker room, Flyers forward Brayden Schenn said, "I don't know. Everyone knows Bryz is Bryz. Some people may think he's a little different, but I'm not going to say one way or another. I'm sure you guys know how Bryz was."

After the Flyers bought out his contract, Philly.com cartoonist Rob Tornoe drew a picture of Bryzgalov wiping away tears with $100 bills and the words "I'm going to miss you guys!!" Tornoe drew Holmgren to Bryzgalov's right, handing the goalie a box of money with "$23 million" on it.

Bryzgalov played briefly with three more NHL teams—Edmonton and Minnesota in 2013–14, and Anaheim in 2014–15. He later did some entertaining TV work for *The Players' Tribune*, and on April 11, 2017, he informed the Flyers—who were still paying him—he was available to return.

As goalie Brian Elliott struggled mightily in a 7–0 loss to Pittsburgh in Game 1 of the first round of the playoffs, Bryzgalov went on Twitter. Above a photo that showed "Elliott's Restaurant," Bryzgalov tweeted, "I'm ready whenever you are @NHLFlyers."

Not surprisingly, the Flyers did not respond.

44

SEAN COUTURIER:
ROOKIE 3, MALKIN 0

On the biggest stage against the biggest stars, you want to come up with your biggest performance, right? But what if you're only 19 and barely have a season under your belt in the National Hockey League? No matter—at least not for Sean Couturier back on April 14, 2012.

Playing in front of a raucous Consol Energy Center crowd in downtown Pittsburgh during the first round of the Stanley Cup playoffs, Couturier put on a show for the ages. Speaking of ages, Claude Giroux had this observation after Couturier scored his first career hat trick in Game 2 to lead the Flyers to an 8–5 win: "He's 19, but he plays like he's 28."

To make it even sweeter, Couturier put the clamps on Pittsburgh's Evgeni Malkin, frustrating the Russian superstar to the point where he took a stick swing at Couturier and earned himself a trip to the penalty box. When it was all said and done, Couturier had registered the Flyers' first hat trick by a rookie since Andy Delmore way back in 2000.

Perhaps the only downside to this effort was the way it raised the expectations among the fans in Flyer Nation. Many thought Couturier would be capable not only of Selke Trophy–type defense but regularly post 25 to 30 goals a year. Turns out it was an almost impossible level to attain, mainly because coaches like Peter Laviolette, Craig Berube, and Dave Hakstol chose to use him in more defensive roles.

It took until the 2017–18 season and a pairing with Giroux on the first line that Couturier was able to show his true two-way ability. His 31 goals more than doubled his previous high of 15. Likewise his 76 points easily surpassed his best career standard of 39.

Jake Voracek, who came over from Columbus along with a 2011 first-round draft pick (No. 8 overall, which was used to select

Since his selection in the 2011 NHL Entry Draft, Sean Couturier has become an integral Flyer, earning the honor of being named alternate captain and scoring his 100th goal in 2018.

Couturier) in a trade for Jeff Carter, says he knew Couturier had the right stuff straight from the get-go.

"He's that kind of player, impactful, every time he steps on the ice," Voracek said. "To step in at 19 and perform like that, we knew we had something special."

Coincidentally, Couturier scored his second playoff hat trick in 2018—against the same team, no less—in Game 6 of a first-round playoff series against the Penguins. In a bizarre almost repeat of history, the score was the same at 8–5. But this time the Penguins won, despite five points from Couturier, who was practically skating on one knee after suffering ligament damage in his other leg during an earlier game.

As impressive as the hat trick was in 2012, the defensive effort against Malkin might have been even more noteworthy. Malkin was held to just three goals for the series, the second-lowest total of his 11-year playoff career. And it might have been a harbinger of things to come. In 2018, Couturier was a finalist for the Frank Selke Trophy as the NHL's best defensive forward. That put him in the same boat as winner Anze Kopitar of Los Angeles and Patrice Bergeron of Boston.

"Yes, it was impressive," Voracek noted. "At 19, not everyone can do what he did to Malkin in that series."

Former general manager Ron Hextall was still a year away from returning from Los Angeles to Philadelphia when Couturier put together that first great display of scoring against the Penguins, but Hextall saw enough of it on video to understand what it meant to the future of the Flyers.

"He's an interesting guy because if you don't show patience with someone like that, he's playing somewhere else," Hextall said. "He has such strong value with his checking game.... Those guys are hard to find. He has every asset you need in terms of checking; he's got size, he's got hockey sense, he's got a great defensive stick.

"Two or three years ago, we talked about having him step up the 'north' [offensive] side of his game. It's great to see. He's an honest player, he plays for the team. Sometimes it takes a little longer for players to figure things out at this level."

While it happened more than six years ago, Couturier still has vivid memories of that night in Pittsburgh. It was a hostile crowd, and the Penguins were already down 1–0 in the series. The Flyers knew they had a battle on their hands.

As it turned out, Couturier wasn't even the top Flyers player on the ice that night. That distinction belonged to Giroux, who registered a franchise-record six points (three goals, three assists). That said, Couturier scored what might have been the most crucial goal, tying the score at 4–4, just when it looked like the Penguins had the momentum and might pull away. On the flip side, keeping Malkin off the board was just as crucial.

"I feel like I was put in a situation where I had to play a defensive role," Couturier said. "We had so much talent, so much skill, there really wasn't much room in the top six, the top nine. So if I wanted to have an impact on the team, the role I had to play was a shutdown guy. I took pride in it. That hat trick just kind of showed that I could step it up offensively, had the ability to do it. But that kind of put a sticker on me that he's a shutdown guy because he did it one year."

Indeed. Each ensuing training camp, there was talk of elevating Couturier to a more offensive role. Then, when the season began, he would find himself once against centering a "checking" line.

"I didn't really see myself that way but it was just the position I was put in," he said. "It seemed like I did so good that first year, it was kind of like, 'We'll just keep him there. He has a big impact on our team on that side of the game, so we'll just let him do it.' But I always knew I could help the team more. And finally last year I got the chance to show it."

With a chuckle, Couturier acknowledges it was fun frustrating Malkin, who, by the way, owns three Stanley Cup rings.

"I remember all series I was sort of in his pants," Couturier said. "I was just following him all around, trying to get him off his game. It was the role I had, so I tried to take pride in it. I tried to get him off his game as much as I could. I think it worked at times in that series."

Couturier always calls his parents after games, but on this night, there was an unusual amount of whooping over the phone line. Welcome to NHL stardom.

FEBRUARY 20, 2016

Shayne Gostisbehere scores the game-winner in overtime against Toronto, giving him a point in 15 straight games—the longest streak in Flyers history for a rookie or a defenseman, and the longest in NHL history by a rookie defenseman.

"Everyone was pretty proud of me," he recalled. "For me, at the time, you're just in the moment. You're living it. It's playoffs. So it was nice to get the hat trick and have a big game. But like everyone else, you forget it quick and focus for Game 3."

The Flyers would go on to win the series in what was considered a bit of an upset. For Couturier, it was a stepping stone to a solid pro career.

"I knew I had a big game," he said. "I enjoyed it but it's afterward when people remind you about it that it becomes something special."

The Selke consideration for 2017–18 shows just how far Couturier has come. His team-leading plus-34 demonstrates that.

"It's become an award for producing at both ends of the ice," he said. "Having an impact all over the ice. It's not going to change my game. I try to be reliable as much as possible defensively, and the offense kind of takes over from there."

Hakstol said the progression of Couturier is just a natural evolution of a solid player who now has more freedom to create at both ends of the ice.

"I think it's a combination of two things," Hakstol said. "Him wanting more and being ready to do more—that combined with the opportunity [on the top line]. It's a case of, 'Hey, I'm ready for more I want to do more, and I can do more.' Then going out and backing it up."

Now Couturier, who had a career-best 33 goals in 2018–19, is a linchpin in all phases of the Flyers' game.

"There's a real mental toughness there in terms of being able to focus on the job at hand." Hakstol said. "I think he had to change the way he went about his job a little bit, but he found a way to do the same job and for me that speaks a lot to physical toughness. But that also really speaks for me to [a player's] mental ability and mental presence to be able to go out and do a job even if you have to alter the way you do it."

No one knew it on that fateful night of April 14, 2012, but the wheels were about to be set in motion. They're still turning quite nicely to this day.

45

"GHOST" STORY

There are many NHL players who weren't selected early in the draft who became stars, including Pavel Datsyuk (selected 171st overall), Jamie Benn (129th), Brett Hull (117th), Henrik Lundqvist (205th), Doug Gilmour (134th), Henrik Zetterberg (210th), and Theo Fleury (166th). The list also features Pekka Rinne (258th), Luc Robitaille (171st), Daniel Alfredsson (133rd), and Joe Pavelski (205th).

Defenseman Shayne Gostisbehere wasn't taken quite as late as those standouts, but he *has* made a lot of scouting staffs look bad.

All except the Flyers.

The Flyers selected Gostisbehere in the third round (78th overall) in the 2012 draft, and he has made them look like geniuses, emerging as one of the league's premier offensive defensemen.

As a rookie in 2015–16, Gostisbehere was recalled from the AHL's Lehigh Valley Phantoms in mid-November because of an injury to veteran defenseman Mark Streit. Gostisbehere made an immediate impact, exceeding General Manager Ron Hextall's expectations and captivating the NHL with his speed and scoring prowess.

"The day before we called him up, we saw him up there and he played a pretty good game," Hextall said at the time, referring to Gostisbehere's play with the Phantoms. "I don't think at that point you could say he was ready to take charge like he has. It's been a little bit unique, which has been great for us. He's done a great job."

In his first season, Gostisbehere burst onto the scene, collecting 17 goals (a franchise record for a rookie defenseman) and 46 points in 64 games, sparking the Flyers to a playoff berth. He highlighted his season with a 15-game point streak, an NHL record for a rookie defenseman.

Gostisbehere finished second in the Calder Trophy voting as the NHL's rookie of the year. Left winger Artemi Panarin, then with Chicago, won the award. Edmonton's Connor McDavid, who played in just 45 games because of an injury, and Buffalo's Jack Eichel finished third and fourth, respectively.

No Flyer has ever won the Rookie of the Year award, but Gostisbehere came close.

"I didn't think I was going to come in and make the impact I did," admitted Gostisbehere, who missed most of his previous season with the Phantoms after undergoing knee surgery. "But I came in wanting to contribute to the team and help the team along the way. That's what stuck with me all the way—just put the individual stuff to the side and keep your teammates always with you."

Gostisbehere, perhaps slowed by off-season hip and abdominal surgery, had just seven goals and 39 points in his second season. He followed that with 65 points (13 goals, 52 assists) in 2017–18, placing him fourth among NHL defensemen. It was also the fourth-highest total in franchise history for a defenseman.

* * *

Nicknamed "Ghost," the Florida native became interested in hockey as a kid because he used to tag along to figure-skating practices attended by his big sister, Felicia Gostisbehere.

Years later, that same sister—a one-time Olympic hopeful whose promising skating career was cut short because of hip surgery—was a major reason her brother made such a smooth recovery from surgery to repair a torn anterior cruciate ligament in his left knee.

"Her dreams were cut short," Gostisbehere said during his rookie season, "but she helped push me toward mine. She's got a great heart."

The year before his rookie season, Gostisbehere went through a grueling rehab. During that time, he was constantly in touch with his sister, who is a nurse. She stayed with him for a week when he had his surgery, and after she left, she was on the phone with him at all hours. She became his unofficial attitude coach, not allowing doubts to creep in as he worked at his recovery.

The next year, Gostisbehere burst onto the NHL scene after a November call-up from the AHL's Phantoms, becoming just the eighth Florida-born player to ever reach the NHL.

His journey was an intriguing one. Growing up in South Florida, he didn't see a lot of ice rinks, and there wasn't a lot of nearby competition for figure skaters or young hockey players. In their teenage years, Shayne and his sister moved to other parts of the country to train and enhance their talents. At 15, about six months before her hip surgery, Felicia moved to Colorado Springs to train at the World Arena with Olympic coaches and Olympic skaters. Shayne left Florida and attended South Kent Prep in Connecticut during his junior and senior years of high school.

Shayne Gostisbehere gets his work ethic from his sister. Her competitive nature during her early teenage years, he said, left an impression.

"It was inspiring just to see how motivated she was," he said. "To see her get up every morning at 4:30 with my dad and go train, and then go to school and be a straight A student—I wish I could have been like that, too—and then go right back to [skate] after school. It was amazing to see a young girl doing that and to show her maturity."

Felicia Gostisbehere was a big reason Shayne wanted to go to the rink at a young age. So was his grandfather, Denis Brodeur. Brodeur, a Quebec native who moved to South Florida, put Shayne on skates when he was three years old and later coached him in a youth league. When the Florida Panthers were unveiled in 1993—the year Shayne was born—Brodeur became a season ticket holder. As soon as Shayne was old enough, he accompanied his grandfather to the games. The sport mesmerized him. He even got caught up in the team's tradition of throwing plastic rats on the ice to celebrate Panthers wins.

As a youngster, Gostisbehere was always at the rink with his sister. At around the age of 6, he gravitated toward hockey.

"My mom would say, 'Don't get into too much trouble. Here's a stick. Go be a rink rat somewhere,'" Gostisbehere said.

Soon he began taking skating lessons with his sister's coach. Before long, the siblings' parents were driving to out-of-state hockey games and figure-skating competitions on most weekends.

Gostisbehere is considered the first player born and raised in South Florida to reach the NHL. He doesn't look at himself as a pioneer.

"I'm just a kid who loves hockey," he said during his rookie season.

Early in the 2017–18 season, Gostisbehere reached 100 career points at the start of his career quicker than Mark Howe, Eric Desjardins, Bob Dailey—quicker, in fact, than any defenseman in Flyers history.

THANKS TO JAGR'S INFLUENCE, VORACEK BECOMES A STAR

The Flyers' Jake Voracek has emerged as one of the NHL's most consistent point producers, and he credits the season he spent with his boyhood idol, future Hall of Famer Jaromir Jagr, as a key to his development.

Both wingers grew up in Kladno in the Czech Republic. Voracek said one of his earliest hockey memories was when he was a young child—maybe three or four years old—and would watch NHL games on TV. Specifically, he would watch Jagr. Seeing a guy from his hometown become an NHL superstar, Voracek said, "motivated me and gave me a push."

Nearly 20 years later, Voracek got to learn from Jagr when they were Flyers teammates in 2011–12. They also played together on several national teams.

When Jagr played for the Flyers, the team gave him the keys to its practice rink in Voorhees, New Jersey, and there were numerous times when he went on the ice around midnight for his second workout of the day. Those work habits influenced Voracek.

"He was practically my idol since I was a kid, and to be around him all year long and to watch what he does before the games, after games, and during practice was something priceless," Voracek said.

Voracek, who cherishes a photo he had taken when he was four years old and was with Jagr at a Kladno hockey rink during the 1994–95 NHL lockout, is a speedy player who is strong along the boards and a slick playmaker.

Jagr had a different style.

"He was never the fastest skater, but I think he was one of the best players to ever play the game," Voracek said. "Such strong legs, such a strong player on the puck. Great vision, quick hands, and one of the top five shots in the game."

He reached 100 points in his 155th game. The old franchise record for a defenseman to start his career was set by Behn Wilson, who got to 100 points in his first 163 games with the Flyers.

"It means my teammates are getting me the puck a lot," Gostisbehere said after breaking the record.

"Ghost is an unbelievable player. I don't think there's one player he resembles the most," right winger Wayne Simmonds said. "I just think he's a very unique player and what he brings to the game is really hard for other people to emulate."

With Gostisbehere leading the way, the Flyers had one of the NHL's highest-scoring defensive corps in 2017–18.

"We were a five-man unit and not just forwards and defensemen," Gostisbehere said.

The NHL used to have numerous stay-at-home defenders such as former Flyer Ed Van Impe. That trend has changed. Now most defensemen have great skating ability and become part of the attack.

"It's huge for us," Gostisbehere said. "I mean, as a D corps, we're preached to get up in the play—and not just us offensive guys, but anyone. You can see it in the way we play."

Gostisbehere combines speed and skating creativity with a quick, hard shot that makes him especially dangerous on the power play. The smooth-skating defenseman was minus-21 in 2016–17, a year in which he was coming off hip and abdominal surgery and didn't look as fluid as he was in the previous season. He was plus-10 in 2017–18 and made lots of improvements on the defensive end, which then-coach Dave Hakstol attributed to his off-season workouts.

Moving forward, Gostisbehere has a good chance to become the highest-scoring defenseman in Flyers history. He entered 2019–20 with 187 career points. The franchise record for career points by a defenseman is 480 by Mark Howe.

If Gostisbehere stays healthy and has a lengthy career in Philadelphia, he figures to be at the top of the charts. Not bad for a player from the Sunshine State.

46

THE WORST TRADES IN FRANCHISE HISTORY

The Flyers have made their share of poor trades over the years. Here are the 10 worst:

June 22, 2012: The Flyers traded Sergei Bobrovsky to Columbus for 2012 second- and fourth-round draft picks (Anthony Stolarz and Taylor Leier, respectively), and a 2013 fourth-rounder, which was later dealt to the Kings.

The franchise's goaltender woes are well-documented. That's what makes this trade extra painful. Bobrovsky became a footnote with the Flyers after they acquired Ilya Bryzgalov and then signed him to a nine-year, $51 million deal. A year later, a disgruntled Bobrovsky was sent to Columbus. After he was dealt to the Blue Jackets, the player known as "Bob" blossomed into one of the NHL's elite goalies, twice winning the Vezina Trophy as the league's top goaltender.

August 26, 1987: The Flyers dealt Brad McCrimmon to Calgary for a 1989 first-round choice (later transferred to Toronto; Steve Bancroft) and 1988 third-round selection (Dominic Roussel). McCrimmon, known as "The Beast," combined with Mark Howe to give the Flyers the league's best defensive pairing during the Mike Keenan era.

In hindsight, the deal is even more head scratching because it would not have taken much for the Flyers to re-sign McCrimmon. Reportedly, McCrimmon wanted $250,000 per season for four years, and GM Bob Clarke initially offered $225,000 per season and then reduced the offer. McCrimmon then asked to be dealt.

The deal crippled the Flyers' defense, and McCrimmon played 10 more seasons and went on to win a Stanley Cup in Calgary, recording a plus-43 rating for Terry Crisp's championship team in 1988–89.

December 5, 2005: Flyers traded Patrick Sharp and Eric Meloche to Chicago for Matt Ellison and a 2006 third-round pick, which they later dealt to Montreal.

Sharp became an NHL star and won three Stanley Cups. Ellison played seven games with the Flyers. Enough said.

In 11 seasons in Chicago, Sharp collected 249 goals and 532 points.

January 20, 2004: Flyers traded Justin Williams to Carolina for Danny Markov.

Selected 28th overall in 2000, Williams displayed potential at an early age, scoring 12 goals and collecting 25 points as a 19-year-old. However, Williams also struggled playing under different systems with three different head coaches in his first four years, while also dealing with a myriad of injuries. Once Williams got his career on track, it was too late for the Flyers, who traded him to Carolina for the tough guy Markov, whose career in Philadelphia lasted just one season.

With a new salary cap in place, the Flyers had to shed salary and shipped Markov to Nashville in 2005. Williams reached the 20-goal mark six times in his career, earned the label "Mr. Game 7" for his performance in the clutch, and has won three Stanley Cup championships.

June 23, 2012: The Flyers traded James van Riemsdyk to Toronto for Luke Schenn. This trade, made when Paul Holmgren was the GM, left a void in the Flyers' offense for several years.

Van Riemsdyk, the No. 2 overall pick in the 2007 draft, became one of the most dependable left wingers in the NHL. Schenn, the No. 5 overall selection in the 2008 draft, became a liability and was traded during his fourth season in Philadelphia.

With Toronto, van Riemsdyk surpassed the 25-goal mark four times, including a career-high 36 in 2017–18. He signed as a free agent with the Flyers before the 2018–19 season.

June 20, 2008: The Flyers traded a 2008 first-round pick (John Carlson) to Washington for Steve Eminger and a 2008 third-round selection (Jacob DeSerres).

FROM FRANCE TO PHILLY, BELLEMARE LEAVES LASTING IMPRESSION

At 29 years old, after a long and unusual journey that culminated with him signing a free-agent deal with the Flyers in June 2014, center Pierre-Edouard Bellemare reached the NHL.

Raised in Paris, Bellemare became the ninth France-born player to reach the NHL, according to Hockey-Reference.com. Bellemare called it "an honor for our whole country to have a French guy here."

Because of his hustle and his charismatic personality, Bellemare became one of the most popular Flyers among fans and teammates. Late in the 2016–17 season, Bellemare was emotional as he talked about being named an alternate captain.

"Obviously, I'm proud," he said. "Super happy to be able to represent the team this way and to be able to help the guys more in the locker room."

"Belly," then-coach Dave Hakstol said, "embodies all the characteristics and traits of a Flyer."

Bellemare replaced Mark Streit, who was traded to Tampa Bay (and then Pittsburgh). Bellemare and Wayne Simmonds were the alternates behind captain Claude Giroux.

Fast-forward to the 2017–18 season. After three years in Philadelphia, the Flyers lost the happy-go-lucky Frenchman to Vegas in the expansion draft.

"It was bittersweet for me," he said. "I've never been a guy who scores 70 points. I was working with the tools I had to help Philly as much as I could. Because of the way I play, I had some decent success in Philly. Just worked hard...on a team with a lot of stars, and when I got an 'A' on my jersey, I got rewarded big-time and my confidence got boosted up. So I bought a house, I have an 'A' on my jersey, and then here comes Vegas and I got picked. I was excited because you know the possibilities there."

As it turned out, Bellemare became a key part of Vegas' stunningly successful inaugural season, helping the Golden Knights reach the Stanley Cup Final.

"Life," he said, "could not be better."

With each stellar season by Carlson, this trade could climb the charts among the worst deals in franchise history. Eminger played just 12 games as a Flyer and totaled two assists and eight penalty minutes. Carlson became a premier NHL defenseman who had 15 goals and 68 points in 2017–18 and helped lead the Capitals to their first Stanley Cup. Carlson averaged nearly 25 minutes per game of ice time in 2017–18 and finished fifth in the voting for the Norris Trophy, awarded to the league's best defenseman.

January 16, 1990: The Flyers traded Dave Poulin to Boston for Ken Linseman.

Dealing Poulin, one of the best captains in franchise history, for the aging Linseman was a move the Flyers would regret. A superb penalty killer, defender, and faceoff specialist, Poulin made an immediate impact with the Bruins. Linseman, then 32, did not rekindle the magic he displayed in an earlier stint with the Flyers. He played just 29 more games with the Flyers, who missed the playoffs, and then had a cup of coffee with Edmonton and Toronto.

Poulin, meanwhile, had 25 points in 32 regular season games with Boston and helped the Bruins reach the Stanley Cup Final. He had eight goals and 13 points in 18 playoff games that year. Poulin ended up playing parts of five more seasons.

June 20, 1992: The Flyers acquired Lindros by sending Ron Hextall, Steve Duchesne, Mike Ricci, Kerry Huffman, Peter Forsberg, Chris Simon, first-round picks in the 1993 and 1994 drafts, and $15 million to Quebec.

It's difficult to put a trade on the "worst" list when it enabled the Flyers to get the right to one of the best centers in franchise history. That said, hindsight tells us the Flyers clearly overpaid to get the Big E.

A year after being drafted by the Nordiques, Lindros was still refusing to play in Quebec, and the deal was made. Actually, the Rangers also had a deal in place for Lindros, but an arbitrator ruled in the Flyers' favor.

While Lindros was a dominant player, injuries slowed his Hall of Fame career. The Nordiques, who later moved to Colorado, used the deal to build a Stanley Cup champion.

Lindros helped the Flyers reach the Stanley Cup Final in 1997, won the Hart Trophy as the league's MVP in 1995, and had four seasons of at least 40 goals. But Forsberg won a pair of Stanley Cups with the Avalanche and also won a Hart Trophy in 2003 when he led the league in points. Like Lindros, he is in the Hall of Fame.

Ricci won a Stanley Cup with Colorado in 1996 and went on to play 1,099 NHL games in a quality career. Duchesne played in three NHL All-Star Games, while Simon became one of the league's most respected enforcers and once scored 29 goals in a season. Twice he played on teams that reached the Stanley Cup Final.

Hextall spent a year in Quebec and one with the Islanders before returning to the Flyers and playing five more seasons with them.

June 7, 2011: The Flyers acquired rights to goalie Ilya Bryzgalov, who was about to become a free agent, from the Coyotes for Matt Clackson and third-round draft picks in 2011 and 2012.

The worst part of this deal—which you could argue deserves to be higher on this list—is that, in retrospect, it caused the Flyers to bench Bobrovsky and eventually trade him.

Holmgren, getting pressured by club chairman Ed Snider to end the team's goalie carousel, acquired the rights to Bryzgalov 24 days before he was scheduled to hit the unrestricted free-agent market. The Flyers quickly signed him to a nine-year, $51 million contract.

After two inconsistent and bizarre seasons, the Flyers were so desperate to get rid of Bryzgalov that they used a compliance buyout on him. They were spared his cap hit but forced to pay him $1.64 million for 14 seasons from 2013–14 through 2026–27.

March 2, 1990: The Flyers traded Brian Propp to Boston for a 1990 second-round pick (Terran Sandwith).

By that point of the 1989–90 season, the Flyers knew they weren't making the playoffs. At the time, Propp had been limited to 40 games and slumped to 13 goals and 28 points. GM Clarke believed the 31-year-old Propp—whose contract was going to expire at the end of the year—was nearing the end of his career.

But Propp, a five-time All-Star, collected 12 points in the final 14 games that season and then added 13 points in 20 playoff games to help the Bruins reach the Final. The next season, he joined the Minnesota North Stars and returned to the Final again, compiling 73 points in 79 games and 23 points in 23 playoff contests.

As for Sandwith, he spent two-plus seasons with the Flyers' AHL affiliate in Hershey. He never played a game with the Flyers and later appeared in eight games with Edmonton before returning to the minors.

PROVOROV AND KONECNY: FLYERS' ODD COUPLE WILL ALWAYS BE CONNECTED

For Flyers fans, defenseman Ivan Provorov and his close friend, winger Travis Konecny, will always be connected—even if they do have vastly different personalities.

Both were selected by the Flyers in the first round of the 2016 draft, both made it to the NHL in 2016–17, and both appear headed to becoming stars. Both also had excellent sophomore seasons in 2017–18, helping the Flyers make the playoffs and finish with a 42–26–14 record.

Provorov made a great improvement from his first to second season. He had six goals, 30 points, and a minus-7 rating in his first year. In his second season, he scored 17 goals—tied for the most in the NHL among defensemen—and had 41 points and a plus-17 rating.

As a rookie, "I was probably a little more cautious, didn't join the rush as much as I could have, and played a little more safe," Provorov said.

By his second season, "[I] felt a little more comfortable joining the rush more, creating plays." There were times, he conceded, he overdid things. "I tried to do too much in some games and that turned into turnovers, but that's part of playing and learning."

He got off to a slow start in his third season as he tried to find more consistency in his game.

Like Provorov, Konecny made significant strides in his second season, improving in goals (11 to 24), assists (17 to 23), and his plus-minus rating (minus-2 to plus-17).

"I thought I came in a little uptight, thinking about the sophomore slump," Konecny said. "I was concerned about that."

His game began to flourish, however, when he was put on a line with left winger Claude Giroux and center Sean Couturier.

"I learned a lot. I was able to build my game defensively a lot better," he said. "Being able to go through those games with G and Coots was a good opportunity to grow as a player, as well."

In 41 games with Giroux and Couturier, the speedy 5'10", 175-pound Konecny had 20 goals. He had just four goals in 40 games with different linemates.

Konecny and Provorov have come a long way since they were 19-year-old rookies and summoned to meet with General Manager Ron Hextall late in training camp.

"Me and Provy were pretty nervous walking over there," Konecny said at the time.

Provorov was outstanding in the preseason. Ditto Konecny.

"They earned it," Hextall said after Provorov and Konecny gave the Flyers two 19-year-old rookie regulars in their lineup for the first time in more than three decades.

Konecny said his father was "really proud" when he gave him the news and that his mother was "crying joyously."

Provorov, who was paired with veteran Mark Streit at the start of his career, said his dad "couldn't fall asleep" after he was told his son had won an NHL spot. "It was really exciting. This is what you work for in the summer, the whole 14 years of playing hockey. It's kind of the end of one road and starting a new one."

Provorov was selected No. 7 overall in the 2015 draft, while Konecny was chosen 24th. The Flyers acquired the 24th selection in a trade with Toronto, sending the Maple Leafs the 29th pick (acquired from Tampa Bay in a trade for Braydon Coburn) and a second-round pick (acquired from Toronto as part of the Kimmo Timonen trade).

It didn't take long for Provorov and Konecny to make an impact.

As a rookie in 2016–17, Provorov was the Flyers' best all-around defenseman by the end of the season. He played in all situations, and his ice time rose dramatically as the season progressed.

Konecny's first season was a little bumpier than Provorov's, but he still managed 11 goals and 28 points in 70 games.

"There were a lot of ups and downs," Konecny said. "There's obviously going to be mistakes in a rookie season and things you learn from. And there are also highs, when you feel like you have your game."

There was also a handful of games in which Konecny was a healthy scratch.

"It's a humbling league," Konecny said of his rookie season. "As soon as you feel you have a grasp on it, it's definitely going to knock you down a few steps. It's just all about learning."

He learned he could be creative at the NHL level.

"You start to realize there's more room than you think there is," Konecny said. "A lot of times you get the puck and think a guy's going to be right on you. But the NHL is all about gaps, and sometimes the guy might be pressuring you and he backs off. If you have patience and allow yourself to slow down the game a little bit, it starts to open up."

Provorov, however, gave opposing forwards little room, especially during his sophomore season. The Russian native said he had a "pretty good year," but he can improve.

"There were three, four, five games where I didn't play like myself," he said. "It's not because I wasn't mentally prepared or did anything like that; it's just sometimes it happens to all of us. You just have to try to limit those games. Every game I came out, I tried to do everything to help the team win and gave everything I had every single game. I've improved. I'm a better player than I was a year ago.... I'm going to continue to grow and continue to get better. There are no limits."

There also is no limit to how much Provorov cares about winning—and his play. Never was that more evident than when he tearfully blamed himself for their 8–5 loss to Pittsburgh in the clinching game of the 2018 first-round playoffs.

Provorov was being too hard on himself. Much too hard. He struggled in Game 6 (minus-4, two turnovers that led to goals) because the Flyers allowed him to play 20:31 despite a separated left shoulder he suffered in the previous game.

"He's a warrior," defenseman Andrew MacDonald said. "Everyone in here knows it and respects the hell out of him."

Provorov plays with a demeanor of someone who has been in the league for 15 years.

"I think he's like 35, really," cracked teammate Shayne Gostisbehere after the 2017–18 season.

Like Provorov, Konecny is a student of the game who is always looking to improve. He said he wants to reduce the scoring chances he allows when he gambles in the offensive end.

ON THIS DATE

APRIL 11, 2016

Flyers cofounder and club chairman Ed Snider dies after a two-year battle with bladder cancer. The Flyers wear "EMS" (Edward Malcolm Snider) patches on their jerseys during their first-round playoff series with Washington, and on April 21, a celebration of Snider's life takes place at the Wells Fargo Center between Games 4 and 5 of the series.

"I've got to limit my mistakes," he said.

Konecny said there's a fine line in knowing when to make a high-risk play—which could lead to a rush the other way if it's not done correctly—and when to play conservatively.

You have to learn "when and where is the right time," he said. "I think that's something I need to take pride in learning, and the other thing is just making sure the 200-foot game is always there."

Added Konecny, "Nobody's ever lied when they say good defense leads to good offense. I'm slowly learning that. It's tough, because when you're young and just coming out of junior, you expect to make a play every shift. You want to be a difference-maker on the ice, and there's nothing wrong with that. It's just taken me two years to finally realize if guys like [Giroux and Jake Voracek] are dumping the puck, anybody can."

Playing on a line with Giroux and Couturier "gave me that confidence to make plays and not be afraid to try and step up and maybe make a big play or be a difference-maker in a game," Konecny said. "I just felt once I played with those guys it kind of gave me that extra step to not be afraid to try something that I hadn't tried before; make that extra risky pass that maybe I wouldn't have made before."

Konecny and Provorov both starred in the junior ranks before being selected by the Flyers. The 6'1", 201-pound Provorov left Russia at age 14 to get used to the North American culture and the smaller rinks. He combines speed, physicality, and intelligence, and he figures to be a candidate for the Norris Trophy, which is awarded to the league's top defenseman, for many years.

"To me, there's a lot of different challenges in the game for defensemen," said Craig Button, the former Calgary general manager who now works for TSN in Canada, to the *Philadelphia Inquirer*. "There are defensive challenges, offensive challenges, and he meets them all and exceeds them because he's so smart. He understands how to play in different situations; he understands what's coming at him. That's a hockey sense thing to me. His hockey intelligence is outstanding."

Provorov, who speaks perfect English, is a quiet, soft-spoken sort. Konecny is a talkative prankster. But they have a lot in common. They were taken by the Flyers in the first round of the same draft, and they reached the NHL at the same time.

But from the Flyers' perspective, the most important qualities they share are their talent, their burning desire to improve, and their unusually high hockey IQs—traits that should make them franchise cornerstones for a long time to come.

48

THE FLYERS AND POP CULTURE: SPREADING THE ICONIC LOGO

The Goldbergs, a popular ABC sitcom, has a distinct Philadelphia flavor, and its characters frequently wear T-shirts or jerseys that celebrate one of the city's sports teams, especially the Flyers.

The Flyers have become a big part of pop culture. Actor David Boreanaz's characters have displayed the Flyers' logo while starring in *Bones* and *SEAL Team*. And in the miniseries *Manhunt: Unabomber*, the main character, Jim Fitzgerald, played by Sam Worthington, is shown wearing a Flyers T-shirt in some scenes. The Flyers have also been featured in *It's Always Sunny in Philadelphia*, and their new mascot, Gritty, became a national phenomenon when he/she/it was introduced in 2018.

Those are just a handful examples of how the franchise's iconic logo has been spread around the nation.

The Goldbergs is based on executive producer Adam F. Goldberg's experience of growing up in Jenkintown, a Philadelphia suburb, in the 1980s. In a 2018 episode, young Adam Goldberg (played by Sean Giambrone) attended his first Flyers game at the Spectrum, and his dad was by his side. Tim Kerr and Dave Brown, who were Flyers at that time, received mentions in the segment, and high-scoring forward Brian Propp crushed a Winnipeg player into the boards.

In the episode, Adam tried to introduce theater to his dad and used hockey tickets as a way to connect with him. After he was offered the tickets, the dad, Murray Goldberg (played by Jeff Garlin), told his son, "Once you discover the magic of hockey, then you'll see what I see and you'll become a puck head."

The real Goldberg said it was art imitating life. He said the episode is a real-life re-creation of how he and his father actually reconnected.

"When I was 12, my dad got season tickets, and when he brought me to my first game, it was instant love," Goldberg said. "I finally learned how the game worked, and it was such a rush seeing it live.

My best memories are going to the Spectrum with my dad. He was a grumpy guy who parented from his TV chair. Those games brought him to life in an amazing way and it was where we did our best bonding."

In a 2016 episode that was dedicated to the club's late cofounder, Ed Snider, Barry Goldberg (played by Troy Gentile) came to say good-bye to a close-knit "friend," the tattered remains of his cherished Flyers T-shirt, which he named "Big Orange." Viewers learn that Barry's treasured piece of apparel was destroyed in an act of "shirt murder" by his mother.

"All my greatest memories were in that shirt," Goldberg said. "Dad, I was wearing it when we went to our first Flyers game."

"It's a shirt!" his father yelled from across the room.

Not to Barry.

According to Goldberg, the show's creator, "Whenever I can put Flyers stuff in a show, I love doing it."

It makes him feel connected to his roots. His family shared Flyers season tickets from 1985 to 1994. Watching players like Kerr, Rick Tocchet, and Ron Hextall play "got my dad out of his chair and on his feet screaming," Goldberg told the *Philadelphia Inquirer*, adding that going to games at the Spectrum was the one place they would stop yelling at each other and come together.

Boreanaz, whose character on *Bones* had a framed Bobby Clarke jersey hanging from his office, was also a diehard Flyers fan growing up, and he still is. Born in Buffalo, Boreanaz moved to the Philadelphia area at age 7 when his father, Dave Roberts, became a television weatherman for Channel 6, the ABC affiliate.

Boreanaz soon became a devoted Flyers fan. Years later, he shared his love for the hockey team by having his *Bones* character, FBI special agent Seeley Booth, wear Flyers T-shirts or jerseys in numerous episodes.

In a story he wrote for the 2012 Winter Classic program, Boreanaz's passion for the Flyers could be felt. In part, he wrote, "There's no team that so completely reflects its city the way the Flyers do. Philadelphia is a blue-collar, hard-working city with a flair for excitement. Sure, it can be a little rough and tumble on the outside, but on the inside it's just about the love for the game. All games. It's just a great sports town. The fans treat the players like they're family. So when guys like Clarke and Barber gave way to the Legion of Doom and on up to the skilled players we have today like Claude Giroux and James van Riemsdyk, the fans never let go of that old Broad Street Bullies legend."

Added Boreanaz, "When you play for Philadelphia, it's not about the name on the back. Tt's about the crest on the front. You play your

TIMONEN: HIS CUP RUNNETH OVER

On the ice, Kimmo Timonen is considered one of the greatest defensemen in Flyers' history, right alongside Mark Howe, Eric Desjardins, and Jimmy Watson.

Off the ice, his battling through career-threatening blood clots at the start of his final NHL season (2014–15) also puts him among the best when it comes to courage.

Timonen was placed on medication and told he couldn't play for months. When he neared his return to the game, he told the Flyers of his desire to try to win a Stanley Cup for the first time in his career before retiring. The Flyers gave him his wish, sent him to the Chicago Blackhawks, and in his last NHL game, he finally got his wish.

During the celebration, Timonen was the first player to receive the Stanley Cup following captain Jonathan Toews.

Timonen reflected on his career stating, "I was dreaming about this moment for a long time, and it's right here. This game has given me so much, and I'm relieved, happy, ready to leave this game, and I'm leaving this game as a Stanley Cup champion."

The following year, President Barack Obama received the winning Blackhawks team in the White House. During his speech, the president unexpectedly gave Timonen kudos for his persistence and bravery.

"This was absolutely a total surprise," Timonen said later, "and he really made a funny speech, and even to get a mention from him was such an honor for me, and then, of course, when he took a stand on my problems with blood clots, and when you think of what kind of a program I had to go through before I could put my skates on again, it really stirs some powerful feelings in an old man like me, I must admit. I'll certainly remember this for the rest of my life."

THE BIG 50

heart out for the organization, and no matter what happens with trades or whatever, you are a Philadelphia Flyer. You embrace it."

* * *

It's Always Sunny in Philadelphia also loves the Flyers. A 2010 episode, for instance, opened with Mac and Charlie calling a Philadelphia radio show to answer a Flyers-related trivia question. Mac stumbles upon the correct answer—right winger Reggie Leach—and earns the chance to take a shot from center ice at a Flyers game for a weekend at the station's beach house.

Later in the episode, some filmed footage from a Flyers game is shown, and Mac nails his shot, completely destroying the cutout figure of a goalie in front of the goal. The crowd is on its feet and chants his name as the announcer calls him a "Philly sports legend." But Mac was dreaming about the shot. The "Mac, Mac, Mac" chant he thought was coming from the crowd was actually Charlie trying to wake him up. It turned out Mac fell flat on his face on the ice and knocked himself out, and Charlie ended up taking his shot and missing badly. Charlie found a bright side. He told Mac he would become a sports legend because the video of him falling will end up as a staple on ESPN.

TV isn't the only medium where the Flyers reached wide-ranging audiences from around the world. Their logo also was spread thanks to the work of Ike Richman, the vice president of public relations for Comcast Spectacor, who used to get many musical groups or solo artists to wear the team's jersey in concerts or other appearances. Among them were Metallica, Phish, the Dave Matthews Band, Van Halen, Barenaked Ladies, Ozzy Osbourne, Mötley Crüe, Garth Brooks, Shania Twain, and Alice Cooper. Richman also presented jerseys to Billy Joel, Taylor Swift, and Justin Bieber.

"The driving force was knowing that here were internationally known superstars who could help carry the brand when they wear your jersey on stage, or share a photo of themselves wearing the jersey," said Richman, who now owns his own public-relations firm, Ike Richman Communications. "Knowing there was the potential for an international audience when filming a video in the building, such as they did for Barenaked Ladies or the Dave Matthews Band, we jumped at the opportunity."

Richman said the late Ed Snider, the franchise's cofounder and longtime chairman, loved when he went into an opposing arena and saw some fans wearing Flyers jerseys. "It didn't matter if they were fans who had moved to that location, people who were born and raised there, or fans from Philadelphia who traveled there," Richman said. "It gave him great pride."

The Flyers, Richman said, are a "well-loved team that goes beyond Philadelphia. That's a testament to Ed, who built such a successful franchise—and a testament to the men who wore the orange and black."

Along the way, Richman encountered some amusing developments. There was the time the New York Rangers' Sean Avery asked Trey Anastasio from the rock band Phish to wear his jersey for a concert. Anastasio, who grew up attending Flyers games at the Spectrum and idolized the Broad Street Bullies in the 1970s, told him he had to stay loyal to his roots and that he only wore Flyers jerseys.

"Trey is a huge Flyers fan," Richman said. "No matter where in the country they perform, there is always somebody wearing a Flyers jersey or T-shirt, and usually that person isn't from Philadelphia but just wants to connect with Trey in a special way at the show."

On another occasion, Richman handed Ozzy Osbourne a No. 88 Eric Lindros jersey before a 1994 concert at the Spectrum.

"If you wear this on stage, the crowd will go crazy," Richman told him.

Osbourne gave Richman a quizzical look.

"The crowd *always* goes f-----g crazy when I'm on stage," he shot back. "I'm Ozzy Osbourne."

In 1997, Richman gave James Hetfield of Metallica a black Flyers jersey during an encore break at a Philly concert. They returned to the stage and Hetfield riffed the famous ESPN *SportsCenter* theme song on his guitar. That night, ESPN opened *SportsCenter* with Hetfield wearing his Flyers jersey and performing the theme song.

The free publicity was a great "get" for Metallica...and the Flyers.

49

HAKSTOL'S HIRING: A GUTSY MOVE THAT DIDN'T END WELL

When Flyers general manager Ron Hextall stunningly hired a college coach in 2015, he had the support of upper management, including club chairman Ed Snider, the franchise's cofounder.

"A gutsy move," Snider said on the day Dave Hakstol was named the 19th coach in the franchise's history. At the time of the hiring, the Flyers had just missed the playoffs for the second time in three years. Out went coach Craig Berube. In came Hakstol, who had an inordinate amount of success at his alma mater, the University of North Dakota.

"We needed a fresh approach," Snider said. "We aren't hopeless. I think we have a lot of young guys coming. We have a damn good nucleus, and we know that we have to sort out our defense and we think that's coming very well. Our defense is going to be totally different over the next few years. It's going to be fast, mobile, young."

Fast-forward to the start of the 2018–19 season, Hakstol's fourth year with the Flyers. The young defenseman started to blossom, and the team had a nice blend of veterans and up-and-coming young players on their top three lines. But the season started poorly, Hextall was fired as the GM on November 26, and Hakstol's job was in jeopardy. Hakstol was fired 22 days later and replaced by interim coach Scott Gordon, who was promoted from the AHL's Phantoms. At the time Hakstol was dismissed, the Flyers had a 12–15–4 record and were in last place in the 16-team Eastern Conference.

"To my eyes, there was a disconnect to what he was preaching and how the players were playing," General Manager Chuck Fletcher said. "As the leader of the team, that responsibility falls on him."

Fletcher said the team needed a "new voice."

In the previous season, the Flyers also got off to a slow start, which included a 10-game losing streak, and fans chanted for the coach to be fired. But Hakstol got the team to regroup, and the Flyers had the league's fifth-most points from December 4 until the end of the regular season. They finished third in the Metropolitan Division and reached the playoffs, where they were eliminated in six games by the hated Pittsburgh Penguins in the opening round.

* * *

When the Flyers hired Hakstol in the spring of 2015, there were lots of big-name coaches available, including Mike Babcock, Dan Bylsma, and Todd McLellan.

Instead, Hextall thought outside the box. Hextall was familiar with Hakstol because his son, Brett, a winger, played for him at North Dakota from 2008 to 2011, scoring 12, 14, and 13 goals in each of his respective seasons. He later played for the Phantoms, the Flyers' AHL farm team.

While watching his son play at North Dakota, Hextall said, "I grew an appreciation for Dave and the way he coached. I thought about him long before this as a head coach in the National Hockey League. I believe he was destined for it. He's got a lot of pro qualities. He's got a lot of experience as a head coach. So I started going through the process here, and the guy that I needed to get to know the most was Dave."

At first, Hakstol, an Alberta native, didn't want to leave North Dakota. But he was eventually convinced it was time to move ahead to the next challenge and time to move away from the college ranks.

"I had a list of things that I wanted from a head coach and went down the checklist in my mind, and every box was checked except for the NHL experience," Hextall said at the time of the hiring. "Quite frankly, for me, that was one that was least important."

Hextall liked the fact that Hakstol preferred a fast-paced style and getting the defensemen involved in the attack. He spent 11 seasons at North Dakota, compiling a 289–143–43 record, a .643 percentage. In his last season at North Dakota, Hakstol directed the team to a 29–10–3 record and a spot in the NCAA Frozen Four.

North Dakota earned a tournament berth in all 11 of Hakstol's seasons and reached the Frozen Four seven times. He was an eight-time finalist for national Coach of the Year honors and spent four years as an assistant at North Dakota before becoming its head coach.

Alain Vigneault (left) is introduced as the 21st head coach in the Flyers' history on April 18, 2019. At right is general manager Chuck Fletcher. (Courtesy of Sam Carchidi)

Hakstol became the third person to go directly from the college ranks to the NHL as a head coach.

"He's a proven winner," Hextall said. "I think one of the strongest points that he has is his ability to push people…. He gets the most out of his players."

A stay-at-home minor-league defenseman who never played in the NHL, Hakstol said he was excited and proud to be named the new coach.

"Through the process here with Ron, and everybody in the Flyers organization, I have gained even more of an understanding of the history and tradition of the organization," he said.

While at North Dakota, Hakstol's program produced 20 NHL players, including Jonathan Toews, T.J. Oshie, Travis Zajac, Drew Stafford, and Chris VandeVelde, who had a stint with the Flyers. His teams produced 42 NHL draft picks, including eight first-round selections.

Two of Hakstol's first three Flyers teams made the playoffs but failed to win a postseason series. And the year they didn't earn a playoff berth, the Flyers became the first team in NHL history to fail to reach postseason play during a season in which they won 10 in a row.

That and his stoic nature behind the bench made Hakstol a lightning rod for fans' criticism in his three-plus seasons with the Flyers. After the Flyers lost their 10th straight game in 2017–18, they had won 28 and lost 48.

But Hextall strongly defended his coach.

"Dave Hakstol is our coach and he will remain our coach. Period," Hextall said forcefully before a game in Calgary. "I've said it over and over, and I'm not going to say it again."

After winning five of their first eight games, the Flyers had fallen to the bottom of the Metropolitan Division. "I think he's done a good job," Hextall said. "We're in a rut. They happen throughout a year. You can't value and judge your team on 10 games or 15 games or 20 games. It's a long season, and you're going to have your ups and downs."

The Flyers turned around their season on that western Canada trip. Hakstol's job was saved, and the Flyers finished third in the Metro with 98 points.

OCTOBER 9, 2018

In the Flyers' home opener, Gritty—a seven-foot fuzzy creature with a wild orange beard—makes his debut as the team's mascot. The Flyers allow the most goals in a home opener in their history as they lose to San Jose 8–2. Ouch.

"Ninety-eight points is respectable. Being a playoff team is respectable," Hakstol said at his season-ending news conference a few days after the Flyers were eliminated from the playoffs by the Penguins. "We're not here to be respectable. We're here to be better than that."

The Flyers' goaltending and defensive play were shoddy, and their special teams were outplayed during the series against Pittsburgh. They were outscored 28–15. In five-on-five play—which was a Flyers strength and a Penguins weakness in the regular season—the Flyers were outscored 21–10.

Hakstol called the Pittsburgh series winnable and said, "We have to recognize the failure of the playoffs. We have to find a way to learn from it. There's a lot of lessons in there. The fact we went to six games, for me, covers up a lot of things we didn't do well. We weren't good enough. We'll take the failures out of the playoff series and those are some things that are going to spur us on to be a lot better."

Despite the playoff shortcomings, the bar was set much higher for the 2018–19 season. For one, the Flyers' promising young players—guys like Nolan Patrick, Shayne Gostisbehere, Ivan Provorov, Travis Sanheim, Travis Konecny, Oskar Lindblom, and Robert Hagg figured to take another step forward. For another, high-scoring left winger James van Riemsdyk was signed as a free-agent in the off-season, adding to a gifted group of veterans that included Claude Giroux, Jake Voracek, Wayne Simmonds, and Sean Couturier.

But a lot of the young players regressed in the first part of the 2018–19 season, and Hakstol was soon replaced by Gordon. After the season, Gordon was replaced by Alain Vigneault, the 12th-winningest coach in NHL history.

* * *

In the summer of 2018, Hakstol opened up about himself to Mike Sielski of the *Philadelphia Inquirer* and *Daily News*. He talked about his defensive nature with the Philadelphia media in his first three seasons on the job.

"Early on, you're guarded a little bit," said Hakstol, 50. "Especially in Philadelphia, guarded is not the way to go. We all have rough edges. What I'm finding out in Philly is that rough edges are part of who we are. You know what I mean? When you try to keep those out of the media, out of the spotlight, out of the public eye, you almost become a little bit… phony? I don't know if that's the right word."

Entering the fourth season of Hakstol's five-year deal, the Flyers had not won a playoff series since 2012. Expectations were high in 2018–19. That seemed to make it almost mandatory that the Flyers advanced a playoff round or two to avoid putting Hakstol on the hot seat.

"You don't start anything with 'I've got to,'" Hakstol told the *Inquirer* and *Daily News*. "That's not a good way to go about business. The organization has a really strong, clear plan in place. It is moving forward. We've made a lot of progress. I know where the expectations are and where we want to go."

Heading into the 2018–2019 season, the Flyers had not won a Stanley Cup since 1975, back when Bernie Parent, Bobby Clarke, Bill Barber, Reggie Leach, and Rick MacLeish were the team's stars. As for the Flyers' high hopes, Hakstol said, "You can choose to look at it whichever way you want. The way I look at it is as an opportunity. The players have done a lot of heavy lifting over the last few years. The organization has, too. That continues. With that comes expectation, which is fine. Where would you rather be?"

For the fans, the answer was easy. They want to be at a Stanley Cup parade on Broad Street. Unfortunately for the hardworking Hakstol, if another parade was ever held, he would not be a part of it.

CARTER HART: THE ANSWER TO THE FLYERS' LONG GOALIE SEARCH?

The Flyers' future, entering the 2018–19 season, revolved around the development of one player more than any other.

Say hello to Carter Hart, the goalie with the impeccable stats in the Western Hockey League. The Flyers hope those numbers will translate into success in the NHL.

Hart began the 2018–19 season, his first as a pro, with the Lehigh Valley Phantoms in the AHL. And though he was going through typical growing pains early in the season, the NHL was just one stop away.

He got there quicker than most expected. When Ron Hextall was the general manager, he was cautious with Hart's development, figuring it would help him in the long run if he spent more time in the AHL. But after Hextall was replaced by Chuck Fletcher early in the 2018–19 season, the new general manager made a bold move—he quickly promoted the 20-year-old Hart to the Flyers.

Hart stopped 20-of-22 shots in his NHL debut as the Flyers outlasted visiting Detroit 3–2 on December 18. The fans cheered loudly on his saves, even the easy ones.

"I had a blast tonight," Hart said after becoming the youngest goalie in Flyers history to win his NHL debut—and the youngest in the league to win his debut since Carey Price in 2007. "It was a night I'll never forget."

"He's got ice in his veins," left winger James van Riemsdyk said. "He's very poised and tracks the game real well."

Two nights later, Hart outdueled the great Pekka Rinne—the Vezina Trophy winner as the league's best goalie in 2017–18—as he led the Flyers to a tense 2–1 victory over Nashville at the percolating Wells Fargo Center. According to the NHL, Hart became the 23rd goaltender in league history to win each of his first two career starts before celebrating his 21st birthday. (He was 20 years, 129 days old.) Hart was tied for the seventh-youngest at the time of his second win.

His career was off to a promising start.

Hart finished his rookie season with a 16–13–1 record, a 2.83 goals-against average, and a .917 save percentage. He tied an NHL record for goalies under 21 by winning eight straight decisions.

In the preseason, Hart had the best stats—a 1.87 goals-against average and a .922 save percentage—of any Flyers goaltender, but general manager Hextall wanted Hart to get some minor-league seasoning.

"Carter had a real good camp and played enough games obviously for us to get a feel for him," Hextall said during training camp, a few

Flyers executive Bob Clarke (left) chats with goalie Carter Hart, who had an impressive rookie season in 2018–19. (Courtesy of Sam Carchidi)

months before he was fired. "These are all tough decisions toward the end."

Someday, Hart may be regarded as one of the NHL's best goaltenders and could be the Flyers' cornerstone—and perhaps the guy most responsible for ending their long Stanley Cup drought.

Hart is expected to be the Flyers' No. 1 goalie in 2019–20.

"He's a very confident guy back there," defenseman Shayne Gostisbehere said. "He's going to be a great goalie. He's got a good head on his shoulders, and that's the most important thing."

Hart said there were things he could have done better during training camp before the 2018–19 season.

"I'm going to learn from this experience and apply it to practices," he said. "I'm just gathering these learning experiences and learning from them and then putting them behind me.

"It was good to play with some of the older guys and experience that pace and speed of the game—and adjust to the differences from junior to pro," Hart added. "It's definitely faster and guys shoot harder, and the execution level is definitely a lot higher. At the junior levels, you have one or two guys on a team who can execute at that pace and speed, but up here, everyone does."

Hart is mentally strong, and that should help him have a long career playing his sport's most scrutinized position. The mental part of his approach has been nurtured from working with sports psychologist John Stevenson since he was in grammar school in Alberta. Hart stops shots partly because of his great reflexes and athletic ability, but he thinks a sports psychologist has made him more focused and more calm in the nets.

"I'd probably say about 90 percent of it is mental," Hart said. "Confidence is everything. Everything is between your ears."

Hart was named the Canadian Hockey League's top goaltender during his final two junior seasons for the Everett Silvertips. His statistics were jaw-dropping. In 2016–17, he had a 35–23–4 record with a 1.99 goals-against average and .927 save percentage. The next season, he was even better with a 31–6–3 record, a 1.60 GAA, and a .947 save percentage.

He attributes a lot of his success to Stevenson, who has worked with many pro athletes, including Braden Holtby, the gifted goaltender who helped Washington win its first Stanley Cup in 2018. When Hart was 10, Stevenson was his first goalie coach.

"He doesn't do that part of the game anymore," Hart said. "He just does work with the mental side. He's a psychologist, and I've worked with him for a number of years. He's helped me a ton, and I wouldn't be where I am without his help."

"He has helped me not only through hockey, but life, as well," Hart added. "I've learned a lot from him. He's not only just my sports psychologist, but he's a good friend of mine, so I can talk to him about pretty much anything, which is really nice to have. You can talk to your parents pretty much about anything, but there are some things you can't tell your parents."

Stevenson, who used to be the goalie coach for the Edmonton Oilers and Ottawa Senators and now does work with military and medical professionals, said Hart was intent on making the Flyers in 2017–18—even though he just turned 19. "He just overdid it and wore himself down," Stevenson said.

That, Stevenson believes, is what led to Hart missing about five weeks early in the 2017–18 WHL season because of mononucleosis. The next summer, Hart worked "hard but smart" and didn't overdo it, Stevenson said.

"He really knows himself and understands himself and knows what makes him tick," Stevenson said before the 2018–19 season. "As a young guy, he used to really worry about what other people thought about him, and now that would not faze him at all.

"He's surrounded himself with really good people. He's very open to criticism, whether it's from myself or [Edmonton goalie coach] Dustin Schwartz or Braden Holtby or Cam Talbot. [Ed. note: Talbot was traded to the Flyers in 2019.] He listens to them and takes the feedback. That's one thing he did so well at Team Canada's camp with all these different goalie coaches. He's able to take different ideas and incorporate them into his game and grow from them."

Every day, Hart goes to someplace Stevenson calls "his mental gym. Whether it's five minutes or 45 minutes, he goes there. It

Carter Hart (left) and Connor Parkilla exchange hugs in the Flyers' locker room. Parkilla watched Hart's home games when he played in the Western Hockey League for the Everett (Washington) Silvertips, and he and his family traveled across the country to watch him play in Philadelphia.
(Courtesy of Sam Carchidi)

could be five minutes of breathing. It could be 10 minutes of mental imagery" in which he recalls past successes. "It could be 10 minutes of concentration grids. It could be ball drills. It could be juggling or meditation. What I've done over the years is give him a whole bunch of [mental] exercises, and he has a smorgasbord to choose from. He doesn't consider the mental part of the game as an adjunct. It *is* part of his training. So just as much as he goes to the gym to work on his core, he'll spend time every day working on the mental part of the game."

Hart also does yoga. "It incorporates a lot of the mind and body work together," Stevenson said. "You're breathing; you're focused.... We talk a lot about having that quiet mind and being more in the moment."

Before each game, Hart gives himself a mental image of that opponent's strengths and how he will respond to the shooters. It's something, he hopes, that will give him an advantage in the NHL.

The Flyers have not had a dominating goalie since Hextall in the 1980s and '90s. Hart knows all about the Flyers' history and that they have been on the Great Goalie Search for many decades.

"Everybody brings that up to me," he said. "I don't think it really matters for someone coming into that situation or coming into the organization. That's the past. I mean, coming in, it's a new opportunity; it's a fresh start, coming up from juniors to pros. I know when I came into junior at 16 years old, I was at the bottom of the chain, one of the younger guys. I was just kind of feeling things out because I wasn't familiar with everything. Now it's kind of restarting all over again as I go up to the pro level. I'm going to be one of the younger guys and learning new experiences. It's a pretty cool opportunity."

Shane Clifford, Hart's goalie coach at Everett, told the *Philadelphia Inquirer* he has high expectations for his former pupil. During his career, which included a stint as Penguins goalie coach, Clifford has worked with several goalies who have made it to the NHL, including Marc-Andre Fleury and John Gibson.

"[Hart] reminds me, in bits and pieces, of Carey Price," Clifford said of the Montreal standout. "And in other parts, he reminds me of Fleury. His own physical attributes are pretty special. His mobility reminds me of Carey Price because there's no goalie-specific movement that he can't do. He has amazing speed, and he can change directions to combat a situation. As far as Fleury goes, Carter likes being around the rink and being around the guys. Fleury loves being on the ice, and Carter is the same way."

If Hart turns out to be a combination of Fleury and Price, the Flyers' long search for a dominating goalie will be over. So, too, might be their quest of 40-plus years for another Stanley Cup.